When Art Became Fashion

KOSODE

[Japanese ko (small), sode (sleeves)]:

> *the principal outer garment of all classes in Edo-period Japan;*

the predecessor of the modern kimono

First she [the courtesan Kaoru]

commissioned the renowned artist Kano Yukinobu

to paint a picture of flaming autumn on plain white satin.

Eight court nobles

were next asked to inscribe vignettes

in verse, in black decorative calligraphy,

on this gorgeous design.

The result was a picture of breath-taking beauty,

admirably suitable for a hanging scroll.

But Kaoru had no idea

of putting it to such trifling use.

She had it made

into a robe for herself.

—Ihara Saikaku,

Kōshoku ichidai otoko

(The life of an amorous man), 1682

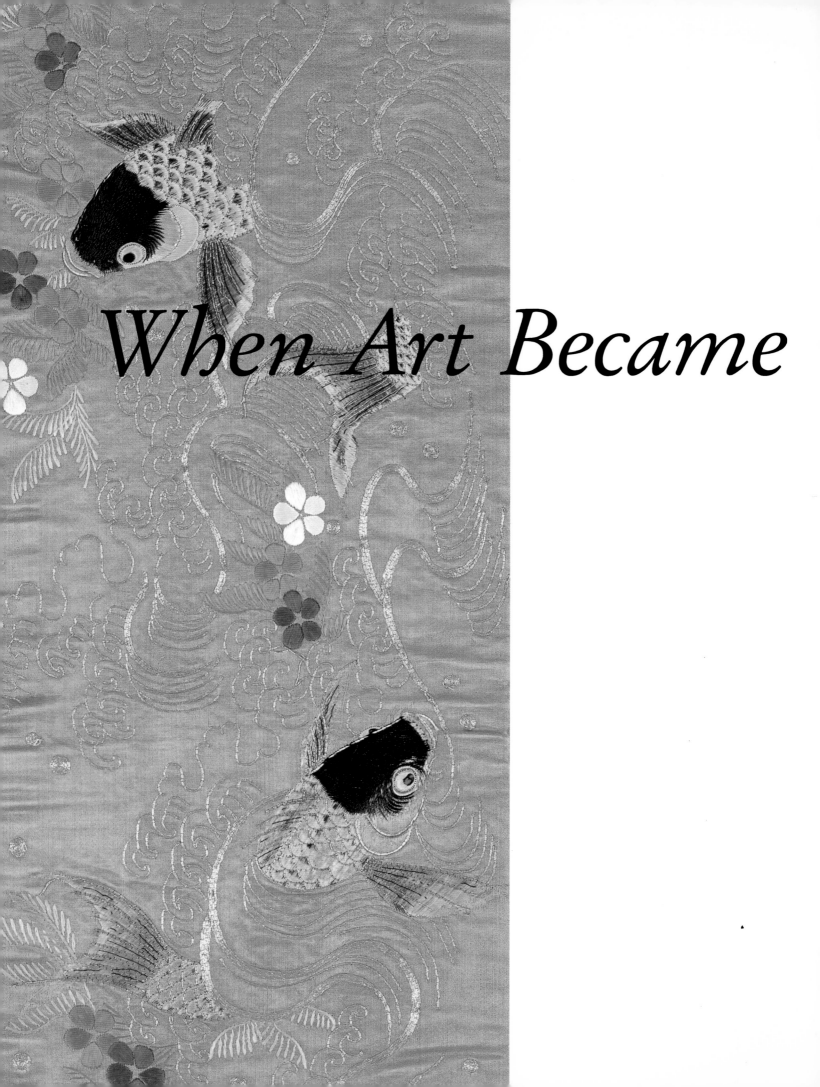

When Art Became

Fashion

KOSODE IN EDO-PERIOD JAPAN

DALE CAROLYN GLUCKMAN & SHARON SADAKO TAKEDA

WITH CONTRIBUTIONS BY

MONICA BETHE

HOLLIS GOODALL-CRISTANTE

WILLIAM B. HAUSER

KIRIHATA KEN

MARUYAMA NOBUHIKO

NAGASAKI IWAO

ROBERT T. SINGER

Los Angeles County Museum of Art

First edition, 1992

Published by the Los Angeles County Museum of Art, 5905 Wilshire Boulevard, Los Angeles, California 90036. The trade hardback edition is copublished with Weatherhill, Inc., 420 Madison Avenue, 15th Floor, New York, New York 10017.

Published in conjunction with the exhibition *When Art Became Fashion: Kosode in Edo-Period Japan,* held at the Los Angeles County Museum of Art from November 15, 1992, to February 7, 1993.

This exhibition was organized by the Los Angeles County Museum of Art in cooperation with the Tokyo National Museum and the National Museum of Japanese History.

It was made possible through the generosity of the Japan Foundation.

Additional support was provided by the National Endowment for the Arts, All Nippon Airways, Toppan Printing Co., Ltd., the Glen Holden Foundation, the Costume Council of the Los Angeles County Museum of Art, and the Asian Cultural Council.

EDITOR: Gregory A. Dobie
DESIGNER: Amy McFarland
ILLUSTRATOR: Amy McFarland
PHOTOGRAPHERS: Iida Isao, Barbara J. Lyter
TYPESETTER: Andresen Graphic Services, Tucson, Arizona
PRINTER: Toppan Printing Co., Ltd., Tokyo, Japan

FRONT COVER:
Catalogue no. 121
Kosode with Plank Bridges (Yatsuhashi), *Irises, and Butterflies*

ENDSHEETS:
Catalogue no. 163
Kosode Fragment with Fan Roundels, Flowering Vines, and Wild Ginger Leaves (detail)

HALF-TITLE PAGE:
Calligraphy by Arafune Kiyohiko

FRONTISPIECE:
Catalogue no. 34
Kosode with Scene of Horse Racing (detail)

TITLE PAGE:
Catalogue no. 155
Obi with Carp, Duckweed, and Waves (detail)

COPYRIGHT PAGE:
Catalogue no. 93
Kosode on Screen (detail)

PHOTOGRAPHS COURTESY OF:

Ishimoto Yasuhiro, photographer; p. 144

Metropolitan Museum of Art; p. 187 (Copyright © 1975 by the Metropolitan Museum of Art)

Takagi Tarō, President, New Color Photographic Printing Co., Ltd.; pp. 85, 125, 129, 173, 176, 267, 269, 274 (cat. no. 87)

Yoshioka Yukio, Shikōsha; pp. 164, 256 (cat. no. 45)

LIBRARY OF CONGRESS CATALOGING-IN-PUBLICATION DATA

Gluckman, Dale Carolyn.
    When art became fashion : kosode in Edo-period Japan / Dale Carolyn Gluckman & Sharon Sadako Takeda : with contributions by Monica Bethe . . . [et al.].
        p.   cm.
    "Los Angeles County Museum of Art, November 15, 1992–February 7, 1993; this exhibition was organized by the Los Angeles County Museum of Art in cooperation with the Tokyo National Museum and the National Museum of Japanese History."
    Includes bibliographical references and index.
    ISBN 0-87587-163-1 (LACMA). — ISBN 0-87587-164-x (soft : LACMA). — ISBN 0-8348-0266-x (Weatherhill)
    1. Kimonos—Exhibitions. 2. Costume—Japan—History—Edo period, 1600-1868—Exhibitions. 3. Textile design—Japan—History—Edo period, 1600-1868—Exhibitions. I. Takeda, Sharon Sadako. II. Los Angeles County Museum of Art. III. Tōkyō Kokuritsu Hakubutsukan. IV. Kokuritsu Rekishi Minzoku Hakubutsukan. V. Title.
    NK4784.A1G68   1992
    746.9' 2 ' 095207479494—dc20   92-17606
                                                                                    CIP
                                                                                    r92

Contents

CATALOGUE NO. 66
*Kosode with Flowering Plants of the
Four Seasons and Decorated Papers*
First half nineteenth century
Kanebo, Ltd.

Foreword

When Art Became Fashion: Kosode in Edo-Period Japan is the most comprehensive exhibition of Japanese kosode to be shown in the United States. The kosode, similar in cut and proportion to the modern kimono, was originally a simple robe worn by commoners. By the Edo period, however, it had become the elegant attire of all classes. Many of the garments in this exhibition have never before left Japan. The Los Angeles County Museum of Art is proud to offer this exclusive presentation to the public not only because of the sheer beauty of the objects but also because it further demonstrates the museum's commitment to the art of Japan.

The exhibition catalogue, under the skillful supervision of Dale Carolyn Gluckman and Sharon Sadako Takeda, associate and assistant curators of costumes and textiles, respectively, functions on two levels. The eight essays, written by Ms. Gluckman, Ms. Takeda, and six other Japanese and American scholars, provide different perspectives on kosode. It is as if eight viewers were looking at the same garment but seeing different aspects of it, one, the patterning, another, the color, and so on. The catalogue also serves as a guide to the exhibition, with the checklist being structured to reflect the presentation of objects in the show. There will be a rotation of artworks halfway through the exhibition owing to their fragility.

I am very grateful to Mr. Keijirō Inai, director general of the Tokyo National Museum, and Mr. Naoshige Tsuchida, director of the National Museum of Japanese History, for their assistance in the organization of the exhibition. In the early planning stages the support of Mr. Yūsuke Watanabe, former executive director of the Japan Foundation, was crucial. Initial funding from the National Endowment for the Arts, All Nippon Airways, Toppan Printing Co., Ltd., and the Costume Council of the Los Angeles County Museum of Art allowed the exhibition to proceed. I also wish to extend my sincerest gratitude to the Japan Foundation for its generosity and to the Agency for Cultural Affairs for its guidance. My gratitude is extended as well to Supervisors Michael D. Antonovich, Deane Dana, Edmund D. Edelman, Kenneth Hahn, and Gloria Molina; Mayor Tom Bradley; Ambassador Michael H. Armacost and the American embassy in Japan; and Steven C. Clemons and the Japan America Society of Southern California for their enthusiastic response to this project in its formative stages. The unselfishness of the lenders, who have allowed their treasures to be shared with the people of Los Angeles, is worthy of our greatest admiration and deepest appreciation.

The kosode is a magnificent expression of the best of Japan; the exhibition and catalogue are concrete examples of the spirit of cooperation that exists between Japan and the United States.

EARL A. POWELL III
Director
Los Angeles County Museum of Art

Preface

The kimono, almost emblematic in its association with Japan, has all but disappeared from the daily life of the population. For "once-in-a-lifetime" events, however, such as weddings, coming-of-age ceremonies, and graduations, the kimono is still worn, bringing a host of nostalgic feelings to both participants and observers. Capturing the essence of Japanese female beauty, it is the embodiment of traditional cultural values. The word *kimono* replaced, in the late 1800s, the term used for centuries to describe the garment: *kosode*.

This exhibition draws together approximately 150 examples of kosode from the Edo period, the high point in the flowering of this most exquisite of arts. It was during this time that fashion became a highly developed industry in Japan, one that affected all levels of society. The popular literature of the period abounds with minute descriptions of dress.

When Art Became Fashion: Kosode in Edo-Period Japan features many outstanding examples from Japanese and American collections and focuses on the different forces that influenced their designs. Whether through color, dyeing technique, or decoration, they reveal a continuum in Japanese textile artistry that extends to the kimono of today. Like the kimono, the kosode is Japan.

YAMANOBE TOMOYUKI
Director Emeritus
Tōyama Memorial Museum

Acknowledgments

This project began as a descriptive catalogue of the seventy-one kosode fragments in the collection of the Department of Costumes and Textiles of the Los Angeles County Museum of Art. During a research trip to Japan in 1986, Nagasaki Iwao, curator of textiles at the Tokyo National Museum, suggested an exhibition of Edo-period kosode combining works from American and Japanese collections. His encouragement, guidance, enthusiasm, patience, and good humor have helped to sustain us over the six years this project has taken to reach fulfillment. Our debt of gratitude to him can never be adequately repaid.

Professor Yamanobe Tomoyuki, director emeritus of the Tōyama Memorial Museum, has been a guiding light since the first days of this undertaking. His generosity of spirit and sharing of his vast knowledge have been exemplary. We are honored that he agreed to write the preface to this volume.

The other authors of this catalogue bring to it a remarkable breadth and depth of scholarship in the fields of Edo-period history, culture, textiles, and art. They are: Monica Bethe, Japan Stanford Center, Kyoto; Hollis Goodall-Cristante, assistant curator of Japanese art, Los Angeles County Museum of Art; William B. Hauser, professor of history, University of Rochester; Kirihata Ken, professor of textile history, Ōtemae College, Osaka, and curator emeritus of textiles, Kyoto National Museum; Maruyama Nobuhiko, research associate, museum science department, National Museum of Japanese History, Chiba Prefecture; Mr. Nagasaki; and Robert T. Singer, curator of Japanese art, Los Angeles County Museum of Art. In addition to their duties as authors, each has contributed professional advice and encouragement on numerous occasions over the years. Professor Hauser's warm response to a telephone query from a stranger asking if he would be an advisor to a project still in its infancy will forever be appreciated. Monica Bethe freely offered hours from her busy life to discuss the project with us. Professor Kirihata allowed us to closely examine kosode at the Kyoto National Museum. Mr. Maruyama gave us unfettered access to his museum's collection, patiently discussed details of each object, and shared his perceptive thinking with us on countless occasions. Hollis Goodall-Cristante promptly responded to our requests for information. Special thanks should also go to Amanda Mayer Stinchecum, who brought her considerable expertise in Japanese textiles to bear on excellent annotated translations of the Japanese essays, and to Thomas Blenman Hare, associate professor of Asian languages and comparative literature at Stanford University, who masterfully translated much of the classical poetry and graciously fielded numerous phone queries.

Rob Singer proved to be a good friend and colleague. Both in Los Angeles and Japan he worked tirelessly on our behalf. Drawing on his years of residence in Japan and his extensive contacts on both sides of the Pacific, he was instrumental in promoting our endeavors. His efforts are deeply appreciated.

In addition to Professor Yamanobe and Dr. Hauser, five others were advisors to this project in its formative stages: Dr. John Rosenfield, curator of Asian art, Arthur M. Sackler Museum, Harvard University; Professor Imanaga Seiji, curator emeritus of textiles, Tokyo National Museum; Japanese textile historians Mary V. Hays and Ralph E. Hays, Los Gatos, California; and John Vollmer, curatorial consultant, Toronto. They were all extremely generous with their time and advice, for which we wish to express our sincerest appreciation.

In Japan, Watanabe Yūsuke, former executive director of the Japan Foundation, was a staunch supporter of this project. Watanabe Akiyoshi, director of the fine arts division, Agency for Cultural Affairs, gave sound advice. Tokugawa Yoshinobu, executive director of the Tokugawa Reimeikai Foundation, kindly arranged for the prompt delivery of photographs to meet a pressing deadline. Edward Conyngham, cultural attaché, his successor, Robin Berrington, and Ishibashi Fusako, senior advisor in the cultural affairs office, American embassy in Tokyo, were very helpful.

No project of this scale could be accomplished without the goodwill of museum professionals and private individuals both in Japan and the United States. We want to extend our gratitude to the staff of both the Tokyo National Museum and the National Museum of Japanese History. At the former we would especially like to thank Okumura Hideo, director, curatorial board; Washizuka Hiromitsu, head curator, programming department; Arakawa Hirokazu and Katori Tadahiko, former head curators of the Japanese applied arts department; and Kōno Tetsurō and

Terashima Yōko, international relations department, for their kindness on innumerable visits to their institution. At the latter museum Kimura Nobuo, collections manager, Nishikawa Hirotaka, and Ishiwata Yoshiki have assisted in every way possible.

At the Tōyama Memorial Museum, Tomobe Naoshi, Ikeda Kazuko, and Mizukami Kayoko were very accommodating. At the Bunka Gakuen Costume Museum, Dōmyō Mihoko and Ueki Toshiko received us warmly on several occasions. At the Suntory Museum of Art, Sakakibara Satoru and Ogikubo Kiyoko kindly allowed us to examine and photograph their collection. The Azabu Museum of Arts and Crafts graciously lent twenty-four paintings to the exhibition. We particularly want to thank Umehara Monoru, Okamoto Hiromi, and Kawamura Akiyo. Murai Ryōichi and Muramatsu Hiroshi, Tokyo National University of Fine Art and Music, were instrumental in securing a loan of printed pattern books from that institution.

At the Sendai City Museum, Katō Miyoko was extremely generous with her time. Yanagida Kunisuke, Miyazaki Takashi, and Sugai Masafumi, Nara Prefectural Museum of Art, permitted us to review their collection. Sano Masao, Kanebo Textile Museum, Ariyoshi Sōichi, Kanebo Fashion Research, Ltd., and Karasawa Kimio, Kanebo, Ltd., provided access to the Kanebo Collection on several occasions and gave freely of their time and knowledge.

Kanazawa Hiroshi, Kawahara Masahiko, and Kawakami Shigeki, Kyoto National Museum, made special arrangements for us. The Kyoto offices of Marubeni Corporation and Matsuzakaya Co., Ltd., were both very cooperative. At the former, Inokuchi Hideo, Ueba Kōzō, and Kawamura Yukinori were particularly helpful; at the latter, Hiragane Yūichi, Nishizawa Yoshio, and Ijiri Masao were of great assistance. Miura Saburo and Kōya Masashi, Kawashima Textile Museum, were most hospitable.

Tabata Kihachi VII generously showed us his family's treasures. Ōya Shūji, Kuriyama Kōbō Co., Ltd.; Okajima Jūsuke and Okajima Shigeo, Okajima Collection/Okajū Co., Ltd.; and Ueda Sadao, Kyoto Senshoku Kaikan, took time from their demanding schedules to meet with us.

Our appreciation also goes to colleagues Fujimoto Keiko, The Museum of Kyoto, and Satō Rie, Tokugawa Museum of Art, Nagoya. Takeda Kōzō, K. Takeda and Co., Ltd., in Arimatsu, supplied us with slides and videotapes of tie-dyeing processes; Shirai Mamoru, Shirai Garahakushō, kindly led us through his studios, where gold thread is produced. We also wish to thank Professor Kawamura Machiko, Kyōritsu Women's University, for conserving some of the kosode lent by the Tokyo National Museum.

Numerous individuals in Japan made our task easier. We would like to thank Takagi Tarō, New Color Photographic Printing Co., Ltd., Kyoto, who donated research books and helped in ways too numerous to mention; Yoshioka Yukio, Shikōsha, also contributed books and lent photographs; Iida Isao and his assistants, Ogawa Takumi and Imasaka Kazuko, made photographing the objects in Japan an artistic adventure. We also wish to acknowledge the kindness of the following people: in Kanazawa, Yumiko and Kazuo Kadonaga; in Kyoto, Jo Ann and Akira Hirose; in Nagoya, Yamashita Hiroko; in Osaka, Yagi Akiko; in Tokyo, Kobayashi Keiko, Elaine Lipton and Terry Gallagher, Daniel Sneider and Elisabeth Rubinfien, Malinda Marr Cox and Tom K. Ryan, Chieko and Shigeo Matsumoto, and especially Nagasaki Yasuko.

In the United States crucial initial support came from Watanabe Taizō, former consul general of Japan in Los Angeles. Former consul for cultural affairs, Fukuda Susumu, guided us at an important stage of the project. Kamikawa Harumi, Japan Economic and Trade Organization, assisted in promoting the exhibition. Tsukada Akira, Kawahito Takashi, and Takeda Masanori, Japan Business Association, were instrumental in supporting the exhibition and its educational components, for which we are very grateful. Hayano Takeo, Toppan Printing Co., Ltd., coordinated the donation of research books by The Japan Forum in the start-up phase of the project and has been supportive ever since. Mochizuki Kōhei and Matsuura Akira, Toppan Printing Co. (America), Inc., took special interest in the printing of this book. Faranak van Patten, Asia Society of Southern California; Steven C. Clemons, Regan Kibbee, and Jamie Simon, Japan America Society; and Lea Sneider and Dr. Ernest T. Nagamatsu have been very helpful as this project moved forward.

Our counterparts at American institutions lending to this exhibition were particularly supportive. Gratitude is extended to the staff of the Metropolitan Museum of Art, including Dr. Barbara Ford and Jean Mailey, Asian art department, Nobuko Kajitani, textile conservation, and Dr. Alice Zrebiec and Arlene Cooper, European sculpture and decorative arts; Valrae Reynolds and the staff at The Newark Museum; and Bruce Brooks Pfeiffer, Penny Fowler, and the staff of the Frank Lloyd Wright Archives, Taliesin West, Scottsdale, Arizona.

We wish to extend our thanks to colleagues in the United States and Europe who gave useful suggestions, allowed us access to their collections, and shared information: Rand Castile, Richard Mellott, and Yoko Woodson, Asian Art Museum of San Francisco, The Avery Brundage Collection; Angela Lakwete and Laurie E. Barnes, Detroit Institute of Arts; Lotus Stack and Robert Jacobsen, Minneapolis Institute of Arts; Leanne Klein,

Minnesota Museum of Art; Anne Nishimura Morse and Deborah Kraak, Museum of Fine Arts, Boston; Cameran G. Castiel, National Gallery of Art; Richard S. Schneiderman, Dale Pixley, Kerry Boyd, and Peggy Jo Kirby, North Carolina Museum of Art; Susan Anderson Hay and Pamela A. Parmal, Museum of Art, Rhode Island School of Design; Richard L. Wilson, Rice University; Felice Fischer, Philadelphia Museum of Art; Robert Mowry, Arthur M. Sackler Museum, Harvard University; William J. Rathbun, Seattle Art Museum; and Verity Wilson, Victoria and Albert Museum, London. Special thanks go to Brigitte Menzel, Textile Museum, Krefeld, Germany; Milton Sonday, Cooper-Hewitt National Museum of Design, Smithsonian Institution; and Louise Allison Cort, Freer Gallery and Arthur M. Sackler Gallery of Art, Smithsonian Institution.

We also wish to thank Jeffrey Hunter, Weatherhill, Inc., whose initial interest in the concept of this catalogue led to Weatherhill's participation in its publication.

At the Los Angeles County Museum of Art we wish to thank Earl A. Powell III, director, and the Board of Trustees for their unfailing support. The Costume Council deserves special mention for its exemplary support of this project and the Department of Costumes and Textiles. A special thanks goes to the head of the department, Edward Maeder. His faith in us and belief in the importance of the project never flagged despite numerous obstacles and the longevity of the process. Our deepest appreciation goes to the members of the department who helped with the exhibition and catalogue: Sandra L. Rosenbaum, Kaye Durland Spilker, Susan F. Ogle, Alice A. Wolf, Alison Zucrow, Julianne Fischer, and Janine Seyhun. Research assistant Mara Grossman and student interns Flora Ito, Elaine Lou, Minako Oka, and Gary Baras gathered the mass of information required for a project of this size. Translators Etsuko Kuroda Douglass, Usui Sachiko, Hiroko Johnson, Kanekubo Hiroko, Martin Bagish, Sugisaki Kazuko, Shimatsu Yumiko, Anita Stahl, and Cindy Yee facilitated communications and research. Volunteers Evelyn Ackerman, Ethel Bliven, Siuin Morrissy, Ninoska French, Vi Hayashi, Mary Kefgen, Chieko Matsumoto, Terri Niwayama, Ann Notehelfer, May Routh, Jo Schacter, Peggy Stauffer, Gertrude Schwartz, Jo Sobel, Marcia Watanabe, and Betty Zucker provided much appreciated staff support.

Our appreciation is extended to Elizabeth Algermissen and John Passi of the exhibitions department, who often found a way when there seemed to be none. Arthur Owens, assistant director, exhibition operations, and his exhibition and technical services staff made a complex installation proceed quickly and efficiently. Exhibition designer Bernard Kester generously contributed his creative energies to the realization of a truly outstanding environment for the art. Pieter Meyers, Catherine McLean, Cara Varnell, and Victoria Blyth-Hill of the museum's conservation center contributed their expertise and collective wisdom in problem solving. Julie Johnston, Tom Jacobson, Lynn Terelle, Dana Hutt, Connie Hood, Talbot Welles, and Leo Tee, development department, worked tirelessly on behalf of the exhibition, catalogue, and symposium. Eleanor Hartman, Carl Baker, and Anne Diederick, art research library, expedited the search for resource materials. Public information officers Pamela Jenkinson and Anne-Marie Wagener contributed to the success of the exhibition. Renée Montgomery and her registrarial staff smoothly and professionally performed their tasks.

We thank Mitch Tuchman, publications department, for overseeing the production of this catalogue. Gregory A. Dobie did a skillful editing job, keeping us gently on track and never losing his sense of humor. Editor Joseph Newland made invaluable suggestions. Nancy Carcione and Randy Jacks carried out any task required of them with efficiency. Graphic designer Amy McFarland captured the spirit of the subject in an outstanding book design. Head graphic designer Sandy Bell contributed useful suggestions, for which we are grateful. Peter Brenner, Barbara Lyter, and Elliot Shirwo, photographic services department, were a pleasure to work with. Barbara's photographs of the museum's collection added to the beauty of the catalogue. The interest of William Lillys, head of museum education, is greatly appreciated, along with the efficient work of Jane Burrell and Lori Jacobson.

George Kuwayama and June Li, Far Eastern art department, offered special guidance and enthusiasm for the project. The participation of the Far Eastern Art Council in the events surrounding the exhibition is also appreciated. The enthusiasm of the Docent Council is gratefully acknowledged as well.

Our heartfelt appreciation goes to our husbands, Jonathan S. Gluckman and Peter Telford Shelton, families, and friends, without whose patience and constant encouragement we would not have been able to bring this project to completion.

Finally we thank Ambassador Arafune Kiyohiko, who during his tenure as consul general in Los Angeles kindly consented to create the beautiful calligraphy that graces the half-title page of this volume. His deft brushstrokes masterfully express the unity of art and dress that are at the heart of this exhibition.

Chronology

PERIODS AND ERAS	EARLY HISTORICAL PERIOD		MEDIEVAL PERIOD		EARLY MODERN PERIOD								
						Momoyama period				Edo (Tokugawa) period			
											††Early Edo period		
	Asuka-Nara period	Heian period	Kamakura period	Muromachi period			†Tenshō era	Bunroku era	Keichō era		Kan'ei era	Meireki era	Manji era	Kanbun era
*HISTORICAL	c. 550–794	794–1185	1185–1333	1333–1568	1568–1600	1573–92	1592–96	1596–1615	1600–1868	1624–44	1655–58	1658–61	1661–73
**ART-HISTORICAL	552–794	same	same	1333–1573	1573–1615	same	same	same	1615–1868	same	same	same	same

EARLY MODERN PERIOD (CONTINUED)													MODERN PERIOD
Edo (Tokugawa) period (continued)													
††Early Edo period (continued)			††Mid-Edo period							††Late Edo period			Meiji period
Enpo era	Tenna era	Jōkyō era	Genroku era	Shōtoku era	Kyōhō era	Hōreki era	Meiwa era	An'ei era	Tenmei era	Kansei era	Bunka era	Tenpō era	
1673–81	1681–84	1684–88	1688–1704	1711–16	1716–36	1751–64	1764–72	1772–81	1781–89	1789–1801	1804–18	1830–44	1868–1912
same	same	same	1680–c. 1730	same	same	same	same	same	same	same	same	same	same

*Excerpted and adapted from Kodansha 1983, s.v. "history of Japan."

**Excerpted and adapted from Shimizu 1988, 53.

†Only those *nengō* (imperial reign dates) mentioned in the text are provided.

††Stylistic divisions that correspond roughly to the eras indicated.

CATALOGUE NO. 34

Kosode with Scene of Horse Racing

(detail)

Mid-eighteenth century

Kyoto National Museum

Selected Shogunal Life and Reign Dates

MINAMOTO	ASHIKAGA	TOKUGAWA

MINAMOTO

Yoritomo
(1147–99, r. 1192–99)

ASHIKAGA

Takauji
(1308–58, r. 1338–58)
Yoshimitsu
(1358–1408, r. 1367–95)
Yoshimasa
(1435–90, r. 1449–74)
Yoshiaki
(1537–97, r. 1568–73)

TOKUGAWA

Ieyasu
(1542–1616, r. 1603–5)
Hidetada
(1579–1632, r. 1605–23)
Iemitsu
(1604–51, r. 1623–51)
Ietsuna
(1641–80, r. 1651–80)
Tsunayoshi
(1646–1709, r. 1680–1709)
Ienobu
(1662–1712, r. 1709–12)
Ietsugu
(1709–16, r. 1712–16)
Yoshimune
(1684–1751, r. 1716–45)
Ieshige
(1711–61, r. 1745–60)

Ieharu
(1737–86, r. 1760–86)
Ienari
(1773–1841, r. 1786–1837)
Ieyoshi
(1793–1853, r. 1837–53)
Iesada
(1824–58, r. 1853–58)
Iemochi
(1846–66, r. 1858–66)
Yoshinobu
(1837–1913, 1866–67)

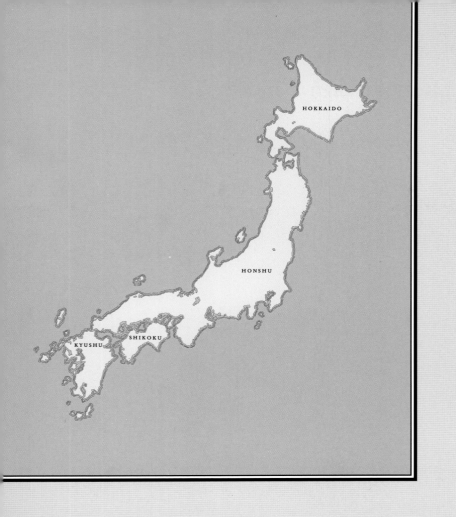

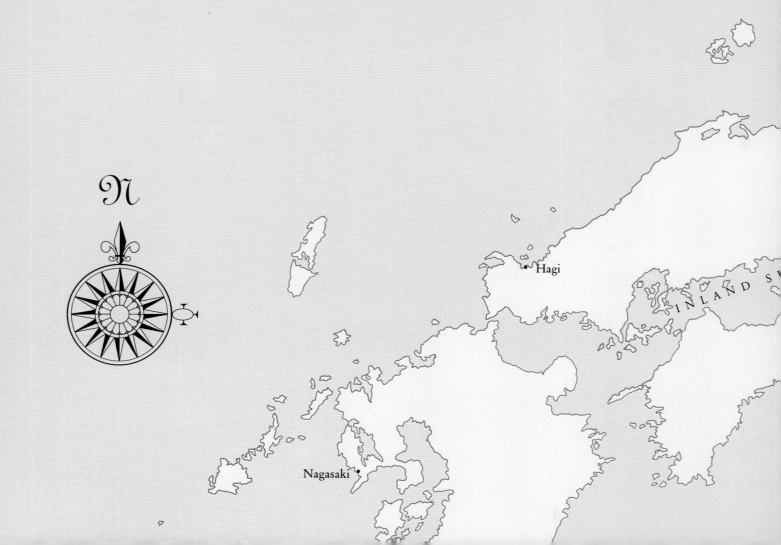

HOKKAIDO

HONSHU

KYUSHU

SHIKOKU

Hagi

INLAND S

Nagasaki

SEA OF
JAPAN

PACIFIC OCEAN

DEWA

Sakata

Mogami River

Nikko

Kiryū

Mito

Isezaki

KANTŌ

Hachiōji

Edo (Tokyo)

Kamakura

KAGA

Tsuruga

Gifu

Nagahama

TANGO

Lake Biwa

Kyoto

ŌMI

OWARI

MIKAWA

Otsu

Tōkaidō

KANSAI

Osaka

Nara

Sumiyoshi

Sakai

Waka no ura

KII

Note to the Reader

1. Japanese terms, with some exceptions, are italicized the first time they occur in the text. A definition is usually provided at that point. These terms are generally listed in the index as well. The reader is urged to consult the glossary for expanded definitions of Japanese textile terms. Words that have entered the English language from the Japanese are treated as English. All such terms, however, will not be pluralized, in keeping with Japanese usage. Translations of terms, titles, and quoted passages in the text, when not credited to a particular source, are the authors' own.

2. A chronology of historical and art-historical periods and eras is provided on pages 20–21. Life and reign dates for the fifteen Tokugawa shogun and other shogun mentioned in the text are supplied on page 23.

3. In accordance with Japanese custom, Japanese names are listed with the surname first and given name second. Prominent individuals were often referred to by their given name.

4. Dimensions for all artworks in the exhibition are provided in both inches and centimeters in the checklist (where all such works not illustrated in the essays are shown).

Measurements for different media are given as follows:

KOSODE
Measurement of center back from base of collar to hem
by measurement of sleeve edge to sleeve edge along shoulder line

•

OBI
Height by length

•

FOLDING SCREENS
Height by width of complete screen (measurements of kosode
fragments on screens are provided in Appendix B)

•

KOSODE FRAGMENTS
& WOODBLOCK-PRINTED BOOKS
Height by width

•

PAINTINGS
Height by width of painting surface, excluding mount

•

CERAMICS
Height by diameter

•

LACQUERWARE
Height by width by depth

Introduction

The primary garment of both men and women in Edo-period Japan was the kosode, the predecessor of the modern kimono. Its evolution reflects the interaction of dress, art, and society in early modern Japan. This catalogue analyzes the aesthetic and cultural context of the Edo-period kosode from the viewpoints of both Japanese and American scholars, providing insight into the significance of this distinctive contribution to the world's textile arts. ❧ During the two-and-a-half-century Edo (Tokugawa) period a dynamic and creative popular culture developed on a scale previously unknown in Japan.[1] This culture grew in an environment of economic expansion and political stability that enriched the *chōnin* (urban merchant and artisan classes) while maintaining the status and prerogatives of the samurai.[2] William B. Hauser, in his essay "A New Society: Japan under Tokugawa Rule," gives a concise account of the socioeconomic milieu of the Edo period and the far-reaching effects of improvements in agriculture, commerce, transportation, and education. In the sophisticated urban centers that grew up or expanded during the rule of the Tokugawa shogun, fashionable dress became an important indicator of material wealth and aesthetic sensibility for the chōnin and was no longer the exclusive privilege of the elite. ❧ In the West expressions of individual style in dress are primarily manifested in variations in the cut and construction of clothing. In Tokugawa Japan these expressions were indicated by the choice of surface decoration: color, design, and technique. Until this period the most desired fabrics were silks patterned on the loom, restricted by decree and cost to the highest levels of society. By the middle of the sixteenth century, however, the rising affluence of the chōnin greatly increased the market for luxurious clothing. In order to satisfy this new demand, textile designers focused on the embellishment of monochrome silk kosode. Exploiting the possibilities of a limited range of techniques—tie-dyeing, embroidery, gold leaf, and painting—they developed a new style, *tsujigahana*, that ushered in the beginning of the ascendance of surface decoration over woven patterning. The essay "Toward a New Aesthetic: The Evolution of the Kosode and Its Decoration" traces the emergence of the kosode and changes in its patterning from the Heian period to the Kanbun era. ❧ By the third quarter of the seventeenth century the stage had been set for an unparalleled development of textile artistry in Japan. Technical advances in dyeing and the graceful simplicity of the kosode, with its clean, straight lines and unbroken surfaces, combined to create a union of decoration and form, an integrated approach to garment and textile design. The

CATALOGUE NO. 67
Uchikake with Cherry Blossoms,
Water, Ducks, and Characters
(detail)
First half nineteenth century
Bunka Gakuen Costume Museum

functions of the textile designer and garment designer became one during the Edo period. Approaching the decoration of a kosode was akin to a painter approaching a blank surface.[3] In "Designs for a Thousand Ages: Printed Pattern Books and Kosode" Nagasaki Iwao studies the effect this new aesthetic had on both clients and producers of luxury kosode and discusses how conceptual changes in the relationship of pattern to ground led to the creation (and 150 years later the demise) of printed design books.

The final fusion of painting and fashion took place in the early years of the eighteenth century, following the development of *yūzen* dyeing, a paste-resist technique that permitted considerable artistic freedom through the direct application of dyes with a brush. Kirihata Ken, in his essay "*Yūzen* Dyeing: A New Pictorialism," examines the development and rapid perfection of this method and the way it both met and encouraged a desire for pictorial imagery and less-embellished decoration.

Fashion as a means of conspicuous consumption had become prevalent among all classes by the Genroku era.[4] The popular literature of the time is filled with detailed descriptions of the attire of both men and women.[5] For urban merchants and artisans—and even the military elite—courtesans and kabuki actors (particularly *onnagata*) set the fashion in obi, hair styles, and the colors and patterns of kosode (see cat. nos. 192–93).[6] Contriving to outdo each other, the wives of wealthy merchants lavished enormous sums of money on clothing. Some even brought ruin to their households by the extravagance of their dress.[7]

Throughout the period the shogunate attempted to curb excess and ensure appropriate class display[8] by repeatedly issuing sumptuary laws: seven were issued on the subject of dress in 1683 alone.[9] Efforts to comply with or circumvent these regulations contributed to further changes in fashion and the introduction of new dyes and decorative techniques. Monica Bethe's essay, "Reflections on *Beni*: Red as a Key to Edo-Period Fashion," considers, among other things, the impact of sumptuary laws on the use of *beni*, a red dye that was one of the most expensive of the period.

The Japanese of the Edo period did not distinguish between the so-called fine and decorative arts; the textile arts were not isolated from calligraphy, ceramics, lacquer, painting, or sculpture.[10] Thus a remarkable cohesiveness existed between the various visual art forms in Japan during this period, making any study of them incomplete without an understanding of the kosode and its decoration. The essay "Clothed in Words: Calligraphic Designs on Kosode" surveys the utilization and placement of words on kosode and explores the thematic sources of such designs. "A Wearable Art: The Relationship of Painting to Kosode Design,"

CATALOGUE NO. 192

Miyagawa Isshō (fl. 1751–63)

Procession of a Courtesan

Mid-eighteenth century

Entrusted to the Azabu Museum of
Arts and Crafts

by Robert T. Singer, examines how identifiable artists, schools, subject matter, and formats crossed over from one medium to another. Maruyama Nobuhiko presents an interesting perspective on the depiction of kosode in genre paintings in his essay "Fashion and the Floating World: The Kosode in Art."

The Japanese classify certain garments by the configuration of their *sode* (sleeves). The word *kosode* (literally, small sleeves) refers to a robe with a small wrist opening; in the Heian period it was worn primarily by commoners.[11] The aristocracy wore the *ōsode* (literally, large sleeves), which had a wide sleeve fully open at the wrist. Large-sleeved garments were essentially the prerogative of the nobility; edicts regulating sleeve size were frequently issued in the Heian period. Even after the aristocracy adopted the kosode as an undergarment, the name had connotations of low social status. It was not until the late Muromachi period, when

CATALOGUE NO. 193

Nishikawa Terunobu (fl. 1716–35)

*Kabuki Actor Specializing in Female
Roles* (Onnagata)

Early eighteenth century

Entrusted to the Azabu Museum of
Arts and Crafts

the upper classes began to wear the kosode as outer attire, that the word took on the meaning of something attractive.[12]

Designed to wrap around the body, the kosode was a constructed but unfitted garment secured by a sash without the aid of other fastenings. It was made to standard dimensions using the entire width of a length of fabric with as little waste as possible.[13] Essentially the kosode consisted of two fabric lengths draped over the shoulders and sewn together with straight seams at the center of the back and at the sides. An additional piece of fabric was added at each front edge to ensure adequate overlap. The collar and sleeves were then added (see Appendix A).

Well suited for a culture where many activities were performed while seated on the floor, the Edo-period kosode facilitated ease of movement.[14] It also proved adaptable to Japan's extreme climatic variations: a single, thin, unlined kosode of silk or bast fiber (usually ramie) could be worn in hot weather; padding the kosode with silk or cotton wadding or wearing several layers of robes afforded protection against the cold.

The few surviving kosode from the last decade of the fifteenth century through the third quarter of the seventeenth century are considered "early kosode."[15] During this period a typical loom width of plain weave silk measured approximately forty-two centimeters. Early kosode had two forms, both with a relatively wide body: one had wide sleeves, the other, narrow (measured from shoulder to wrist). In the first half of the seventeenth century the narrow-sleeved style disappeared, but the other continued, giving a loose, somewhat cumbersome aspect to the kosode readily discernable in paintings of the period (see cat. no. 181). A more slender form of kosode, made from a narrower width of fabric,

was introduced at about this time by women of the pleasure quarters. By the Genroku era the width had decreased to thirty-four centimeters, approximately the measurement maintained today.[16] As the loom width diminished, so did the dimensions of the kosode, until by the late eighteenth century the sleeve width equaled half the width of the back, as it does in the modern kimono.

Prior to the Genroku era the obi took the form of a narrow, flat sash (see cat. nos. 149–50) or a ropelike braid called a *Nagoya obi* (see cat. nos. 178, 180a).[17] Although sometimes elaborately arranged, it was usually tied simply in front, back, or on the side with hanging ends. During the Genroku era the obi began to widen, reaching its maximum width in the first decades of the nineteenth century, when it extended from under the bust to below the abdomen (see cat. nos. 160, 202). The widening obi broke the visual continuity of the garment design. Kosode designers responded by creating a break in the motif at the waistline or by patterning the upper and lower halves of the robe differently (see cat. nos. 30, 90, 94, 130; see Appendix A for diagrams of how kosode patterning changed over the course of the early modern period).

The extravagant silk and fine ramie garments produced for the military elite and the upper levels of chōnin society are the principal focus of this study. Notable exceptions are two *katabira* (ramie

CATALOGUE NO. 160
Obi with Diamond Pattern and Flowers (detail)
First half nineteenth century
Tokyo National Museum

summer robes) that belonged to women of the nobility in the early nineteenth century (cat. nos. 45–46). They illustrate how simple the daily dress of the aristocracy had become by the latter part of the Edo period.

The majority of the kosode in this exhibition belonged to women.[18] A woman's real property was primarily her clothing, which frequently represented a substantial financial investment. By the second half of the eighteenth century it had become the practice among wealthy samurai and chōnin to amass a great quantity of kosode as part of a bride's dowry. Despite repeated sumptuary regulations, enormous sums were spent on elaborate garments and bedding for the trousseau. These kosode were often handed down to daughters and loyal attendants who carefully preserved the expensive treasures.[19] Garments might also be donated to a temple or shrine on the death of the owner to increase the efficacy of prayers for the repose of the deceased's soul.[20] Occasionally preserved intact, more often than not they were cut up and made into *ban* (banners), *kesa* (priests' robes), or *uchishiki* (altar cloths).[21] Several of the kosode in the exhibition were reconstructed from such items and mounted on two-panel *byōbu* (folding screens; see, for example, cat. nos. 93, 127, 132).[22]

Another factor contributing to the preservation of women's kosode in the Edo period was the convention that prescribed changes in the sleeve length, patterning, and coloration of a

woman's garments as she grew older. Young, unmarried women wore the *furisode*, a version of the kosode with long, hanging sleeves. After marriage, Edo-period custom required shortened sleeves. Consequently, many kosode (including several in the exhibition) were remade to conform to a woman's change in marital status. Custom also dictated darker colors and more subdued patterning as a woman aged, thus leading to the retirement of garments.[23]

In general the robes in this exhibition were worn for special occasions. Chōnin women were relatively free to go out in public either in pursuit of their domestic responsibilities or for a limited range of leisure activities. The wealthiest of them, however, looked to the households of the daimyo and shogun for models and led more restricted lives. Yet even the women of the aristocracy and the upper echelons of the military elite did occasionally go out into the world as well as participate in a variety of public and private observances, all opportunities for wearing decorative kosode.

Seasonal outings—particularly spring cherry blossom and autumn maple leaf viewings, summer boating parties, and winter New Year's Day visits to shrines and temples—allowed both commoners and samurai to show off their elegant clothing.[24] The spring and fall viewings were eagerly anticipated events at which the finest kosode were worn and where private spaces were sometimes created around the merrymaking of friends and family by the hanging of additional beautiful robes. By the Genroku era fashionable Edo women were wearing their new kosode while cherry blossom viewing instead of at the New Year (the usual custom) in order to parade unencumbered in the more temperate climate of spring (see fig. 1).[25]

Respectable women were also permitted to attend the kabuki theater (provided they were discreet). There one could see and be seen; even the less affluent wore their best attire.[26] From at least as early as the Genroku era it was the custom for wealthier patrons, both male and female, to change clothing several times during the daylong performances, thus enabling them to display a maximum number of fashionable outfits. Teahouses adjacent to the theater accommodated this activity as well as supplying regular customers with food, tea, tickets, and other amenities (see fig. 2).

The kosode evolved into a highly expressive means of personal display, becoming a vehicle for the graphic representation of the world of its wearers. These images typically portrayed scenes of interest to the chōnin: views of Edo and Kyoto, ordinary objects, famous places in literature, and visual puns. The use of auspicious motifs also increased and became associated with specific occasions, most notably weddings and the New Year. For example, rolls of silk were traditional wedding presents (see cat. nos. 83–84); pairs of mandarin ducks connoted conjugal bliss (see cat. no. 67). Pine, bamboo, plum blossoms, and cranes became associated with the New Year because of their symbolic representation of good fortune and longevity (see cat. nos. 58, 76–78). Other motifs, reserved by convention for the samurai class, recalled heroic tales and an idealized Heian court (see cat. nos. 49–50, 116, 126). Despite the sumptuary laws—which gave increasingly detailed specifications for each social class, regulating colors, cost, materials, and techniques—motifs were never officially restricted.

FIGURE 2
Attributed to Hishikawa Moronobu
(c. 1618–94)
Screen with Kabuki Scene (detail)
Late seventeenth century
Pair of six-panel screens; ink, color, and gold leaf on paper
Each: 66 15/16 × 152 3/8 in.
(170.0 × 387.0 cm)
Tokyo National Museum
Important Art Object

CATALOGUE NO. 83
Kosode with Rolls of Silk and Pines
Late eighteenth–early nineteenth
century
Kanebo, Ltd.

Donald Shively has written: "It would seem that throughout Japanese history, fabrics have excited more interest than any other aspect of the material culture."[27] A greater understanding of that intense and abiding interest can be gained from an examination of the relationship between dress, art, and society in Edo-period Japan. It is hoped that this volume will give Western readers new insight into the beauty and importance of kosode while deepening their appreciation of the rich heritage of modern Japan.

CATALOGUE NO. 76
Katabira with Isle of the Immortals
(Hōrai-san)
First half nineteenth century
Kanebo, Ltd.

NOTES

1. Nosco 1990, 16, defines the expression *popular culture* as being "those forms of secular urban culture that are self-supporting and sustaining, that is those forms that require neither the financial patronage nor independent wealth of the producer of the culture."

2. According to Shively 1965, 123, chōnin, although officially two separate classes, with artisans superior to merchants, "were not, in fact, thought of as two classes, but were called *chōnin* (townsmen), that is, the non-samurai population of the castle towns and cities." For a fuller discussion of chōnin and urban life see William B. Hauser's essay in this volume and Kodansha 1983, s.v. "chōnin."

3. The kosode, especially its back, is sometimes referred to as a canvas. Because of its vertical format, a more appropriate comparison might be with a hanging scroll, the Japanese equivalent of the Western artist's canvas, or with the panels of a folding screen. This is particularly true of Kanbun-era kosode. By the Genroku era greater attention was paid to the relationship between the kosode's front and back, with the whole garment being considered the canvas. See Robert T. Singer's essay in this volume.

4. Although officially the Genroku era lasted from 1688 to 1704, its cultural span was from 1680 to the early 1730s. See Young and Smith 1966, 8.

5. Popular literature focused on the realities of everyday life, the *ukiyo* (floating world). In the Heian period this term referred to the Buddhist awareness of the suffering and transitoriness of life. In the 1680s it was employed to refer to the licensed pleasure quarters, with their momentary diversions. *Ukiyo-zōshi* was the literature of this world; *ukiyo-e* were pictures, in the form of paintings and woodblock prints, of the pleasure districts and their inhabitants. The greatest exponent of ukiyo-zōshi was the Genroku-era novelist Ihara Saikaku (1642–93).

6. The pleasure quarters were highly organized: a formal code of etiquette existed between clients and those who served them; a strict hierarchy existed among the denizens of the houses of pleasure. An *oiran* (or *tayu*) was the highest-ranking courtesan. She was a woman of high principles, sophisticated tastes, and skill in the refined arts (achieved through long and rigorous training). Her customers were mainly wealthy merchants and samurai. The oiran served as an ideal both in and out of the quarters; she was the frequent subject of popular literature, painting, and woodblock prints. See Raz 1983, 142–43. Onnagata, male actors who specialized in women's roles, studied the art of feminine dress, manner, movement, and speech. They became, like the highest-level courtesans they often portrayed, models of ideal femininity and arbiters of fashion. According to Raz 1983, 163, however, after the Genroku era an interesting reversal occurred: "In the past [prior to the eighteenth century], the actors who had played women's roles endeavoured to shape their style after high-born [women] or courtesans, who in turn modelled their appearance and behavior on those of court ladies. Now, as one of the contemporary writers said, the ladies themselves imitated the actors and formed their manners after them." Even as early as the beginning of the seventeenth century women of the court imitated courtesans and kabuki actresses (the kabuki began with women performers; see Hauser essay, note 24): "In 1608–1609 five ladies of the Imperial court, of whom two were favorites of the Emperor, went strolling about the city after the manner of prostitutes and *kabuki* actresses." As this behavior was frowned upon by the imperial household and the shogunate, the women were severely punished. See Shively 1955, 329–30.

7. Shively 1965, 128, cites the fashion competition between the wives of the wealthy merchants Ishikawa Rokubei of Edo and Naniwa-ya Jūemon of Kyoto. Ishikawa's wife won with an apparently simple, black *habutae* (lightweight silk) kosode embroidered with a pattern of *nanten* (nandina) in gold thread, the deep red berries of which, on close examination, were seen to be rare Chinese coral. Ishikawa and his family were eventually banished from Edo because of the extravagance of his wife's clothing. See Monica Bethe's essay in this volume for additional discussion of this event and its relation to the sumptuary laws.

8. Shively 1965, 143, 153, points out that the government was as concerned about display appropriate to one's social standing as it was about controlling extravagance. He writes: "The Tokugawa authorities viewed society as consisting of dozens and dozens of status layers piled in hierarchal order. Each individual was expected to play the type-role assigned by birth and occupation; his [or her] behavior and consumption should be according to his [or her] level" (143).

9. Shively 1965, 126. Saikaku described kabuki actors on a theater holiday (usually an opportunity to parade in their finest clothing) in 1683: "They walked about freely in groups, but their dress was quite subdued in observance of the recently promulgated clothing regulations." See Saikaku 1990, 301. See also Bethe essay for a discussion of the limited effectiveness of these laws.

10. This distinction has been made in the last hundred years as a result of Western influence. See Singer essay and Smith and Harris 1982, 9, for a more detailed discussion of this issue.

11. Kamiya 1971, 18, reports that the oldest record of the use of the word *kosode* is found in the *Seikyuki* (Records of official ceremonies), which was compiled in the mid-Heian period.

12. See Noma S. 1974, 13–14. In the Meiji period the more general term *kimono* (literally, thing to wear) was adopted to distinguish traditional Japanese dress from the newly popular Western attire (*yōfuku*); the new term replaced the word *kosode*.

13. While the fabric width was standardized, the length was proportional to the height of the wearer. The practice of adjusting the kosode's length by making a fold at the wearer's waist did not begin until the Meiji period, when this dimension also became standardized. See Yamanaka 1982, 39, and Kamiya 1971, 18, 55, no. 89.

14. The Edo-period kosode should not be confused with the tight-fitting, movement-restricting (by Western standards) kimono of modern Japan. Although essentially the same garment, the way in which the robe wrapped around the body was quite different. In fact, the kosode, unlike Western clothing, had to be fitted to the body each time it was put on; its look changed depending upon the skill of the dresser and the fashionable silhouette at the time.

15. So named in Kamiya 1971, 28. Kamiya studied both clothing depicted in paintings and garments of known provenance and date. The following discussion is drawn from Kamiya 1971, Maruyama 1988, 21, and Stinchecum 1984, 24–25.

16. Maruyama 1988, 31.

17. Much of this discussion is drawn from Kamiya 1971, 94.

18. It is pointed out in Kamiya 1971, 24, that the majority of surviving kosode are women's. Almost all of those that can be firmly dated, however, belonged to men. Because robes were often presented as gifts by lords to vassals (and thus treasured), buried with prominent male owners, or preserved among the effects of famous warlords, their age can be extrapolated from the life dates of their owners.

19. Saikaku 1965, 47, recounts the story of a man who tried to recoup a debt by arranging a marriage between his daughter and a merchant's son: "And I almost forgot to mention those sixty-five sets of [kosode], still in as brand-new condition as the day they were made. She's the only one who can possibly inherit them in the future [i.e., from her mother]." Sugimoto 1934, 85, relates that "when the young princess [the daughter of a daimyo] bade farewell to my grandmother [her governess], she presented her, as the highest token of grateful and affectionate appreciation, something which she herself had worn—a dress bearing her own crest."

20. Itō 1985, 156.

21. Saikaku 1956, 211, describes a widow about to become a Buddhist nun: "Among the things she must leave behind is a gown with fawn-spot designs [tie-dyeing] and beautiful embroidery. 'I shall not need this anymore. It should be made into a canopy or an altarcloth or a temple pennant.' "

22. Paul 1984 gives an account of the life of Nomura Shōjirō (1879–1943), who collected many of the pieces on display in this exhibition and directed the reconstruction of those kosode now mounted on screens.

23. See Stinchecum 1984, 26.

24. Nishikawa Joken (1648–1724), the author of a practical Edo-period guide for chōnin, suggested the extravagance of their attire on such visits by his admonishment: "When lowly townsmen wear fine clothes and go on outings to temples and imitate the behavior of their superiors, they will bring ruinous misfortune on themselves." As quoted in Shively 1965, 157.

25. Minnich 1963, 207.

26. Much of this discussion is drawn from Raz 1983, 174–77.

27. Shively 1965, 133.

A New Society:
Japan under Tokugawa Rule

WILLIAM B. HAUSER

The Tokugawa period represented a new stage in the development of Japanese society. A highly structured form of military-bureaucratic government, the *bakufu*, under the leadership of fifteen successive shogun from the Tokugawa family, provided a degree of centralized control and political stability previously unknown in Japan. Centered in Edo (renamed Tokyo in 1868), the Tokugawa bakufu consolidated its control over the daimyo during the reigns of the first three shogun. Thereafter, despite variations in the character and competence of shogunal successors, the system continued to represent political and military authority until the resignation of the last shogun in 1867.

❖ ❖ THE POLITICAL CONTEXT ❖ Characteristic of Tokugawa dominance was its control of the largest private domain in Japan. This included approximately 25 percent of the agricultural lands, the major cities of Edo, Osaka, Kyoto, and Nagasaki, and rights to the products of the primary gold and silver mines. In addition, as the national hegemon, the shogun controlled most aspects of Japan's relations with the outside world. This resulted in the exclusion of Portuguese and Spanish traders due to their association with Catholic missionary efforts, the violent suppression of Christianity, and the restriction of most foreign trade to the port of Nagasaki.[1] The Tokugawa house also maintained the largest army and on paper was able to call to arms 80,000 of its own vassals and subvassals as well as reinforcements provided by its regional daimyo allies and relatives. While rarely needing to display this military might after the battles of Osaka Castle in 1614 and 1615, in 1634 the third Tokugawa shogun, Iemitsu, paraded an army of 307,000 men through the streets of Kyoto. This massive display of power in the imperial capital symbolized the dominant position of the Tokugawa house over both the daimyo and the emperor. As the power behind the throne, the shogun was unassailable. ❖

Several innovations reinforced the position of the shogun. First, Tokugawa Ieyasu (see fig. 3), the founder of the Tokugawa line, created three branch houses at Kii, Owari, and Mito to provide adoptive candidates for the office of shogun (if the main line failed to produce a son). They were given strategically located domains to help defend against attacks on Edo or Kyoto. This acknowledged the failure of Oda Nobunaga (1534–82) and Toyotomi Hideyoshi (1536–98), Ieyasu's predecessors in the drive to unification, to assure the succession of their heirs. Next, Tokugawa succession assured, the shogun took control of daimyo succession. Each new daimyo required the approval of the shogun to take office and gain title to his ancestral lands. As evidence of shogunal

FIGURE 3
Portrait of Tokugawa Ieyasu
After 1642
Hanging scroll; ink and color on
paper
44 7/8 × 22 3/16 in. (114.0 × 56.3 cm)
National Museum of Japanese
History, Chiba Prefecture

authority, during the first half century of Tokugawa rule many daimyo were moved to new domains, had their lands increased or decreased, or saw their houses abolished. While this power was utilized less frequently by later shogun, it reflected the dominant authority of the Tokugawa regime.[2]

Another source of support for the centralized position of the Tokugawa shogun was the system of *sankin kōtai* (alternate attendance). This required the daimyo to maintain their immediate families and some of their most important vassals in the shogunal capital, spend every other year in attendance at Edo, and participate in elaborate and costly processions back and forth between Edo and their domains (see fig. 4). In the late seventeenth century the processions of the Maeda family of Kaga Province reflected the wealth and power of the largest daimyo domain. Other daimyo were hard-pressed to compete with the pageantry and display of the Maeda marches, which included more than 4,000 retainers as well as porters, packhorse men, and transport personnel. By the eighteenth century most daimyo processions averaged 150 to 300 persons as a means of limiting expenditures, and the Maeda had cut back to only 1,500 attendants.[3] After vassal salaries, sankin kōtai expenses were the largest item in daimyo budgets.[4]

FIGURE 4
A Daimyo's Procession through Seta
(detail)
Late seventeenth–early eighteenth century
Six-panel screen; color and gold leaf on paper
66 × 145 in. (167.6 × 368.3 cm)
Shin'enkan Collection

This subordination of the daimyo to the shogun was amplified in the *buke shohatto* (laws for military households) issued by the bakufu in 1615 and elaborated thereafter. These laws regulated such things as status-appropriate dress, stating: "There should be no confusion in the types of clothing of superiors and inferiors. There should be distinctions between lord and vassal, between superior and inferior."[5] The laws specified which kinds of clothing were appropriate for which members of the samurai class and made it clear that variations in social status were to be reflected in differences in dress. The shogun also called on the daimyo for periodic contributions to castle construction, public works projects, and the like, but after the death of Iemitsu in 1651 this became less common. The emphasis of the buke shohatto was to maintain discipline and decorum among the daimyo and members of the samurai class.

Further strengthening the dominant position of the Tokugawa were daimyo oaths of loyalty to the shogun. In addition, newly asserted ideological criteria distinguished the shogun from potential rivals for power. This ideology included Confucian theories of natural hierarchy and proper governance reinforced by elements of the Buddhist and Shinto religions. A new religious cult that worshipped the spirit of Ieyasu was established at the Tōshōgū Shrine at Nikko by his grandson Iemitsu. Ieyasu was worshipped as the "divine founder" of the Tokugawa house. As Herman Ooms notes in his analysis of Tokugawa ideology, "Shogunal rule became sacralized as an incarnation of the Way of Heaven."[6] The cult of Ieyasu was in fact a political one, directed at the daimyo and Tokugawa bannermen, not at commoners. Ieyasu qualified as a deity because of his political achievements; through his deification his political authority took on a religious character.[7]

Tokugawa control was far from absolute, however. Except for the restrictions mentioned previously and irregular service obligations, within their domains daimyo ruled autonomously. Additionally, their incomes were not subject to Tokugawa taxes. The bakufu supported its expenses with revenues received directly from Tokugawa lands. While shogunal laws provided models for regional administration, each province created its own legal codes based on daimyo house laws and pragmatic responses to local conditions. When daimyo economic policies conflicted with those issued by the bakufu, it was increasingly the daimyo who prevailed, especially after 1700. Territorial autonomy, despite the demands of the sankin kōtai system and the laws for military households, provided considerable leeway for provincial policy. In the eighteenth and nineteenth centuries many daimyo issued currencies, created commercial monopolies, and aggressively asserted their own economic interests. Even the land surveys that measured the agricultural wealth of the domains did not always conform to Tokugawa standards and procedures. So long as the bakufu was not directly challenged, daimyo autonomy was respected.[8]

URBANIZATION

A major feature of Tokugawa society was urbanization. In the late medieval period the expansion of interregional trade resulted in an increase in temple and port towns, but Kyoto was the primary city in Japan. With a population of more than two hundred thousand residents by the mid-fifteenth century, it was one of the world's great metropolises. Kyoto provided most of the luxury goods for both the aristocratic and military elite and also held the biggest concentration of commercial wealth.[9]

One result of the unification of Japan between 1560 and 1600 was an increase in urban centers, many of which developed from the former temple or port towns or were newly created as the castle towns of the daimyo. Regional and national military leaders created new cities and towns as a means of concentrating their forces in heavily fortified castles and providing the goods, war matériel, and services necessary to support their armies. This also helped to separate the samurai from other members of Tokugawa society and break their ties to the land, making them increasingly dependent on their leaders for their livelihood and more available for military and administrative assistance. Urbanization was thus a conscious policy designed in part to concentrate the power of the daimyo and reinforce his authority over his vassals.[10]

In addition to the regional network of towns and cities, about which more will be said later, were three main urban concentrations: Kyoto, Osaka, and Edo. Kyoto continued as the center of aristocratic culture and high-quality craft production. Its most important commodities included sumptuous silk textiles woven in the Nishijin district and embellished by the city's artisans, providing a substantial portion of the wardrobes of the wealthiest and most powerful members of Tokugawa society. Kyoto also prospered through the manufacturing of other kinds of luxury goods, including specialty foods, lacquer, and ceramics.

Osaka, located near Kyoto, emerged in the late sixteenth century as a major commercial city. Initially a temple town, Osaka developed under Hideyoshi as a center of military power, with a great castle to symbolize its importance. Under the Tokugawa, Osaka served as the seat of military authority in western Japan. Because of its access to waterborne trade routes along the Inland Sea, it expanded as a mercantile center in the seventeenth century. Daimyo from western Japan built warehouses in Osaka, where

both rice received as tax income and other domain products were shipped. This enabled them to exchange tax revenues received in kind for the cash needed to support the expenses of the alternate attendance system. In Osaka, canals and rivers were used to move domain rice cargoes and other goods, a rice market was created, and banking facilities were developed. It soon eclipsed Kyoto as the main trading city of western Japan. Osaka was also an important center of consumption, handicraft production, and processing industries. By the mid-eighteenth century both Osaka and Kyoto included populations of about four hundred thousand and were major metropolitan areas.[11]

Edo, the capital of the Tokugawa bakufu, was the largest Japanese city. With a population of more than one million in 1720, it ranked among the most sizable in the world (see fig. 5). Resident in Edo were the shogun and his immediate retainers, the families of the approximately 264 daimyo with many of their samurai vassals and attendants, and the merchants, artisans, and service personnel required to support the needs of the metropolis. Although the shogun, daimyo, samurai, and their households made up about half of the city's residents, they were allotted approximately 80 percent of the land for their residences. As a result of the system of alternate attendance, Edo emerged as a center of both government and consumption. It was the focal point of a commercial network in eastern Japan and was well provided with consumer goods of all sorts from other regions of the country. Most commodities came by water; some came overland on the backs of draft animals and men. Merchant houses from the Osaka-Kyoto region and elsewhere in western Japan established branch stores in Edo, with the Mitsui house and their Echigoya clothing stores being a prominent example (see cat. no. 109). Many modern department stores, such as Mitsukoshi (the former Echigoya), Takashimaya, Daimaru, Matsuzakaya, and Matsuya, are the successors of prominent Edo-period drapers (see fig. 6). With the largest concentration of wealthy daimyo and samurai, it was an important market for elegant kosode.

Complementing the three great central cities were the dozens of provincial cities and towns mentioned earlier. Ranging in size from more than a hundred thousand to less than a thousand residents, they served the needs of the daimyo and their samurai retainers as regional centers of handicraft industrial production and trade. The removal of most samurai from the land, attempts to separate trade and handicraft production from agriculture by concentrating merchants and artisans in urban areas, expansion of trade and travel between regional centers and Edo, associated improvements in waterborne and overland transportation systems,

FIGURE 5
Bushū Toshima-gun Edo shō-zu
(Toshima area of Edo)
c. 1632
Woodblock print; ink and color on paper
38 3/16 × 50 3/4 in. (97.0 × 129.0 cm)
National Diet Library, Tokyo

and population growth all contributed to increased urbanization. By the mid-eighteenth century as much as 10 percent of the total population lived in cities of ten thousand residents or more. As a result, the medieval trade networks focused on Kyoto and satellite religious centers expanded in the Tokugawa period into a system linking all areas of the country, first to regional towns and cities, then to Osaka and Kyoto in the west and Edo in the east. By the mid-Tokugawa period Japan was transformed into an integrated, preindustrial economy with well-regulated systems of shipping, banking, commodity marketing, and handicraft industrial production.[12]

CATALOGUE NO. 37
Kosode with Agricultural Scenes of the Four Seasons (detail)
First half nineteenth century
Tokyo National Museum

SOCIAL CHANGE

In theory Tokugawa society placed most people in one of four classes. At the top were the samurai, including the shogun and the daimyo. Next were the farmers, the primary producers of the rice crop (see cat. no. 37), which was taxed to support the needs of the ruling class. Then came the artisans, followed by the merchants. The artisans were viewed as essential, for they produced vital goods. The merchants were regarded as a necessary evil, necessary because they distributed food and other commodities required for urban life, but evil because they appeared to profit from the labor of others and produced nothing of their own. Confucian doctrine did not elaborate on distinctions within social classes. Each was characterized, however, by differences in wealth and status that made for significant variations within each group. Outside the four classes were the emperor and the Kyoto court aristocrats, the Shinto and Buddhist clergy, certain professionals like physicians and some teachers, and the outcastes, including actors, prostitutes, leather workers, grave diggers, and members of other suspect professions. Just as each class had its own function within society, each was expected to conform to different norms of behavior.

Fashion was a means of publicly displaying status. Despite Tokugawa efforts to regulate dress, people continued to flaunt their wealth through clothing. Ihara Saikaku noted this in his discussions of merchant society. For example, in *Nihon eitaigura* (The Japanese eternal storehouse) he remarks:

> Fashions have changed from those of the past and have become increasingly ostentatious. In everything people have a liking for finery above their station. Women's clothes in particular go to extremes. Because they forget their proper place, extravagant women should be in fear of divine punishment. Even the robes of the awesome high-ranking families used to be of nothing finer than Kyoto habutae. . . . But in recent years, certain shrewd Kyoto people have started to lavish every manner of magnificence on men's and women's clothes and to put out design books in color. With modish fine-figured patterns, palace style hundred-color prints, and bled dapple tie-dye, they go the limit for unusual designs to suit any taste. . . . Prostitutes make a daily display of beautiful clothes toward earning a living. But beautiful wives of commoners, when they are not blossom-viewing in spring or maple-viewing in autumn or going to weddings, should forego these many layers of conspicuous garments.[13]

Whereas Saikaku only approved of fine dress for commoners on ceremonial occasions, he believed it was appropriate for samurai at all times. He went on to note: "Fine clothes are essential to a samurai's status, and therefore even a samurai who is without attendants should not dress like an ordinary person."[14] For Saikaku the laws on dress helped distinguish people of different status and social function. It was thus appropriate for the government to regulate clothing as one means of preserving the order of society. Tokugawa governance was characterized by rule by status.[15]

Confucian conceptions of the natural order of society and Tokugawa-period social realities became increasingly inconsistent. While urbanization efforts of the sixteenth and seventeenth centuries concentrated the samurai, artisans, and merchants in castle towns, this effort did not prove lasting. For one thing, Japanese cultivators were farmers, not peasants. As the urban demand for goods increased, village residents found crops other than rice very profitable. While legally limited in their choice of crops, farmers evaded controls and used rice fields for growing vegetables, tobacco, cotton, rapeseed (for pressed oil), and other market-oriented products. Over the course of the Tokugawa period fields were reclaimed, probably doubling the arable land, while population grew more slowly and leveled off after about 1720. The result was an increased quality of rural life that included improvements in housing, diet, clothing, and the general level of material culture. For example, during the seventeenth century cotton cloth replaced bast fiber as the staple fabric for commoner clothing and bedding. Cotton was warmer, more comfortable, and easier to process, dye, and wash. As demand for cotton textiles increased, so did the growing of cotton as a cash crop in agricultural villages. The cultivation of such crops expanded commercial agriculture and changed socioeconomic conditions in rural Japan.[16]

Changes in crop selections, evident in the provinces around Osaka and Kyoto in the early Tokugawa period, gradually spread elsewhere. Initially cash crops like seed cotton, rapeseed, and tobacco were sold to urban merchants for processing and sale. As demand expanded in the mid-Tokugawa period, however, farmers began to process more of their crops than they needed for household consumption. Semi- or fully processed goods like ginned cotton, cotton thread, and cotton textiles were increasingly produced for sale by farm households. Urban guilds asserted their monopoly rights to purchase and process goods like cotton to limit the growth of rural competition. By the late eighteenth century, however, these rights proved difficult to enforce, and farmers aggressively competed for the extra income available from by-employments in processing and trade. Farmers who initially changed crop patterns to profit from metropolitan consumption now actively competed with chōnin as suppliers of consumer goods. Daimyo also recognized the economic benefits of increased domain trade and used monopoly buying and distribution systems to enhance the value of their revenues.[17]

Changing crop patterns and the diffusion of spinning and weaving technology to rural areas also affected the silk industry. Although the best silk thread was imported from China, by the late seventeenth century domestic production flourished in northern Japan and the Kantō region around Edo. The Nishijin district of Kyoto had long been the center of the silk-weaving industry in Japan. By 1706 there were more than two thousand households of weavers in the city (see fig. 7). As domestic sericulture expanded, so did provincial silk spinning and weaving. Gifu, Hachiōji, Isezaki, Kiryū, Nagahama, Tango, and other regional centers competed with the Nishijin silk industry. By 1730, when fire destroyed three thousand of the estimated seven thousand looms operating in Kyoto, much of the thread supplied to the weavers was produced in Japan. The Kyoto fire only accelerated the diffu-

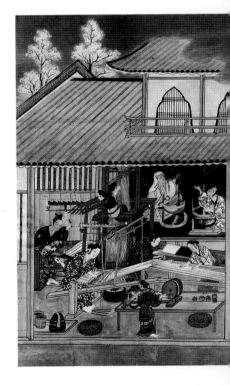

FIGURE 7
Craftsmen at Work: Weavers (detail)
Early eighteenth century
Set of four six-panel screens
Each screen: 45 ½ × 123 1/16 in.
(115.5 × 312.6 cm)
Suntory Museum of Art, Tokyo

sion of spinning and weaving technology to the provinces. Many weavers and their apprentices were displaced from the city and moved to outlying sericulture centers. Although much of the finished cloth was shipped to Kyoto for dyeing and decoration (see fig. 8a,b), the impact of rural silk production on the Nishijin weavers was significant. The Kyoto guilds attempted to curtail competition from the countryside, but their efforts failed to check such production.[18]

FIGURE 8 a,b
Pages from *Shinpan tōfū
on-hiinakata*
1684

The diffusion of processing industries and trade, combined with new crop patterns, resulted in dramatic changes in the character of village life. No longer isolated from the monetized economy of urban centers, small rural towns now offered many of the same employment opportunities available in cities. Villagers with inadequate land resources to support themselves by farming engaged in craft production or trade to supplement their incomes. Wealthy farmers hired workers to tend their fields, spin thread, weave textiles, and engage in a host of other forms of handicraft industrial production. The idealized Confucian society with clean functional lines separating classes no longer represented the social reality of villages on major trade routes or in the vicinity of cities like Osaka and Kyoto. Farmers functioned as merchants and artisans in the off-season, and some village residents never engaged in agriculture at all. Others worked as hired hands for wages in either the fields or workshops or in both. The excess population of the villages, formerly attracted to cities in search of economic opportunity, could now find comparable work at comparable wages in the countryside. While seasonal or permanent migration to cities and towns was still common in remote areas, others found work closer to home.[19] Even those at the lowest economic levels of the samurai class often turned to handicraft production or teaching to supplement their meager stipends. In economic and social terms, official Tokugawa class distinctions were artificial and misleading. However, class distinctions kept out of the samurai class all but the few commoners who purchased entry or were awarded the privilege, despite the fluid movement among the three lower classes of society.

Changes in village life reflected the increased monetization of the Japanese economy during the Tokugawa period. While taxes were largely paid in bales of rice, most private transactions involved cash. Urban merchants developed complex credit relationships, but both goods and services were exchanged for money, and accounts were in cash. This significantly affected the lives of urban residents, including members of the military class. While paid in bales of rice, they needed cash to buy household necessities and pay the wages of their maids, cooks, and other servants. Although samurai incomes remained stable for most of the Tokugawa period, their wants increased. Incomes that were adequate in the seventeenth century were less and less sufficient as demand for goods and services increased in the eighteenth and nineteenth centuries. This led to increasing poverty for many of the military elite and greater dependence on loans from urban merchants and bankers. Legally superior to the chōnin, samurai found it increasingly difficult to match the quality of life of their more successful inferiors.[20]

Urban life changed substantially over the Tokugawa period. Places like Osaka and Edo expanded as newcomers flocked to them in search of work and as the commercial, handicraft industrial, and cultural life of metropolitan areas increased in complexity. Large and small merchant and artisan houses rose and fell, property was bought and sold, and the turnover in the occupants of rental property was especially dramatic. Studies of Edo and Osaka merchant houses, neighborhoods, employment patterns, social mobility, and cultural activities all testify to the instability of urban life. Fires, famines, natural disasters, and economic booms and busts all affected the nature of city living in Tokugawa Japan.[21]

Demographic patterns also changed. Village data indicate that the population was relatively stable from the 1720s. Recent interpretations of this evidence suggest that many families limited their offspring to enhance the quality of their lives. Family limitation is seen as evidence of rational decision making by farmers confident that smaller households could still ensure succession for another generation, provide sufficient labor to till the fields, and achieve a better standard of living for all. Evidence of improvements in material culture, greater investments in irrigation systems, draft animals, and tools, and more rationalized and systematic approaches to farming support these conclusions. In rural Japan shrewd choices about crop patterns, by-employments, and family size improved the quality of village life.[22]

POPULAR CULTURE

Urbanization and improved material conditions resulted in the emergence of a new popular culture in Tokugawa Japan. This complemented the elite culture of the samurai and the Kyoto aristocrats. Two crucial features of this process were improvements in printing technology and the establishment of licensed entertainment districts in major cities.

The diffusion of printed books and woodblock prints revolutionized access to information. Before the seventeenth century most literature circulated in handwritten copies; only Buddhist materials were printed. In the late sixteenth century movable type was first used for printing nonreligious books, but the primary technology for the diffusion of printed materials was woodblock printed books and prints in which pages of text and illustrations were carved onto single blocks. Suddenly, in the seventeenth century, many books that had circulated privately among the elite became available in multiple copies. Initially readership was limited, but by the late seventeenth century most samurai were literate and more merchants and artisans gained access to education in private academies and temple schools. The increased commercialization and monetization of the economy required written records. Urban and rural administration demanded literate functionaries who came from the commoner classes. Chōnin had better access to education than did farmers, but wealthy village residents found ways to educate their sons so they could keep family records and serve as village leaders. By the late

FIGURE 9
Katsushika Hokusai (1760–1849)
Five Beautiful Women (detail)
Early nineteenth century
Hanging scroll; ink and color
on silk
34 × 13 ½ in. (86.4 × 34.3 cm)
Seattle Art Museum, Margaret E.
Fuller Purchase Fund, 56.246

CATALOGUE NO. 110
*Kosode with Views of Yoshiwara
Pleasure Quarters* (detail)
Second half eighteenth century
Kanebo, Ltd.

Tokugawa period it is estimated that 40 to 50 percent of boys and 15 percent of girls received some formal schooling outside their homes and had basic literacy skills. As the reading public expanded, so did the number of publishers, booksellers, and lending libraries. This greatly expanded access to information in Tokugawa Japan (see fig. 9).[23]

The social and cultural implications of widespread literacy were dramatic. Confucian ideology was spread throughout Tokugawa society as the content of the curriculum of most schools. Many samurai and some commoners engaged in serious scholarship of Confucian and neo-Confucian theory, classical prose and poetry, or religious materials. Much of this was written in Chinese, not Japanese, and the educated elite continued to compose scholarly commentaries and poetry in Chinese. Nativist scholars probed the earliest Japanese texts in search of the essence of Japanese cultural traditions that existed before the arrival of mainland culture from China and Korea. From the mid-eighteenth century, "Dutch Studies" provided limited access to Western science and geography from European books imported by Dutch traders at Nagasaki. More important for the development of popular culture were printed collections of fiction and poetry, guidebooks, miscellanies, and instruction manuals, many with extensive illustrations, all written in Japanese. Woodblock printing enabled the diffusion of graphic art (ukiyo-e) and literature (ukiyo-zōshi) to a growing public with interests in theater, style, and the attractions of the brothels and teahouses, the so-called floating world (ukiyo) of urban entertainment. The monochrome prints of the early Tokugawa period could be hand-colored; later, multiblock prints enabled colored illustrations of actors, courtesans, and patrons of the entertainment quarters.

The establishment of licensed brothel districts encouraged the
concentration of theaters, teahouses, restaurants, and other components of entertainment in specific areas of major cities. Edo had
Yoshiwara (see cat. no. 110), Kyoto had Shimabara, and Osaka
had Shinmachi as centers of popular culture. Kabuki and *bunraku*
(puppet) theaters flourished (see fig. 10), actors, courtesans,
geisha, and others competed to create elegant costumes that provided models of taste and fashion, and new forms of extravagance
came to characterize the aspirations of many artisans and merchants.[24] Style was an important feature of urban sophistication
for both samurai and chōnin. Sumptuary laws restricted the outward display of wealth by commoners, but some challenged the
restrictions by wearing plain kosode with luxuriant linings. Others used elegant accessories to show their refinement.

Saikaku was not the only writer who decried extravagant clothing. Ishida Baigan (1685–1744), the author of social and ethical
teachings for commoners, noted in *Seikaron* (Essay on household
management; 1744): "Ostentatious people of the present world
not only wear fine clothes themselves but dress their maids in

clothing made of thin damask and figured satin with embroidery
and appliqué. . . . Lowly townsmen who are so ostentatious are
criminals who violate moral principles. . . . They put in disorder
the propriety of noble and humble, of honored and despised."[25]
Yet efforts to regulate elaborate clothing were ineffective. As is
evident from the garments displayed in this catalogue and exhibition, dramatically patterned and colored kosode were among the
most flamboyant examples of Tokugawa-period textile art.

Those who could not participate directly in the floating world
could read about the entertainment districts in fiction by Saikaku
or Ejima Kiseki (1666–1735) or enjoy images of the costumes,
theater, and brothels in woodblock prints. Playwrights like
Chikamatsu Monzaemon (1653–1724) also portrayed the delights
and dangers of hedonistic enjoyment and the conflicts between
desire and obligation that confronted the chōnin. The popular
literature of the Genroku era set standards of literary achievement
and creativity that later writers rarely attained. More explicit
works like *Shikidō ōkagami* (The great mirror of the art of love;
1678) by Fujimoto Kizan (1626–1704) detailed the pursuit of sensual pleasure in the brothel districts. Wealthy and not-so-wealthy
chōnin faced daunting choices. Was guarding the profits of the
family business more important than sensual pleasure? Were luxury and personal fulfillment inconsistent with family obligations?
Did life have to be dutiful and dull? These questions typified the
themes in popular plays and literature and added to the range of
experience of commoners and samurai alike. Some of this material
appealed to women, but entertainment districts primarily catered
to men, who composed the majority of city populations. Bakufu

FIGURE 11
Attributed to Tosa Mitsuoki
(1617–91)
Entertainment Quarter Scenes
(detail)
Third quarter seventeenth century
Album; ink and color on paper
13 1/4 × 9 1/2 in. (33.7 × 24.1 cm)
Los Angeles County Museum of
Art, gift of Caroline and Jarred
Morse, M.81.61.6–.17

and domain officials condoned (but did not approve of) the activities of the pleasure quarters, because they recognized their value for relieving social tensions (see fig. 11).[26]

Not all popular culture was flamboyant, sensual, and extravagant. Poets like Matsuo Bashō (1644–94) and Yosa Buson (1716–84) distilled aesthetic experience into *haikai* (haiku; seventeen-syllable poems); others wrote *renga* (linked poetry) or *kyōka* (humorous poetry). The brightly colored paintings of the Kano and Tosa schools were contrasted with the more muted and contemplative works of the *bunjinga* (literary painters). In addition to Confucian and literary classics, commoners studied the tea ceremony, flower arranging, music, dance, poetry, and accounting. Merchant house codes encouraged good business practices, frugality, and responsibility. Baigan created the ethical philosophy of Shingaku, including elements of Confucianism, Buddhism, and Shinto, to encourage merchants to take pride in their social importance and excel in business. Pilgrimages—for religious purposes and sight-seeing as well as a means of evading restrictions on travel—took people to distant shrines and temples, exposed them to regional specialties of all kinds, broadened the markets for local products, and provided a range of cultural and social experiences. Physical, social, and cultural isolation, typical of peasants and most chōnin before the seventeenth century, was no longer universal. While each region was typified by local dialects, specialty products, and a sense of local identity, Tokugawa Japan was a far more integrated society than anything that preceded it. By the mid-nineteenth century socioeconomic changes provided the Japanese with many elements that would ease the transition to modernity after the Meiji Restoration of 1868.

CATALOGUE NO. 100
Kosode on Screen (detail)
Kosode fragment with folding
screens depicting the fifty-three
stages of the Tōkaidō
Second half eighteenth century
National Museum of Japanese
History, Nomura Collection

A New Society

Japanese society in 1850 was very different from what it had been in 1600. It was more urban and literate, better able to provide a range of goods and services to residents of cities, towns, and villages than ever before. The self-sufficient agrarian community was displaced by villages incorporated into elaborate marketing systems that gave them access to goods from a wide range of sources. Farmers could purchase books, paper and writing materials, metal tools, hair and cooking oils, specialty foods, fertilizers and seeds, and a host of other commodities in their own communities or nearby market centers. Communities closer to major towns and cities or along trade routes had better access to consumer goods than did isolated villages, but virtually all parts of the country were tied into some kind of marketing system.

Regular shipping routes transported goods and people from

coastal Hokkaido to Kyushu. Dried seaweeds and other marine food products from Hokkaido were consumed in Osaka, Edo, and other cities, while dried fish from eastern Japan and herring meal from Hokkaido fertilized cotton fields in the Osaka region. Osaka commodity prices influenced the cost of goods in urban areas throughout Japan. The highways and coastal transport systems were used not only by daimyo and samurai on their processions to and from Edo but also by merchants, peddlers, transporters, pilgrims, and pleasure seekers (see cat. no. 100). Commoners traveled to cities in search of employment or just to see the sights and sell some regional specialties they carried with them. Vacation travel in the off-season increased in popularity as farmers and chōnin went to famous temples and shrines, explored urban entertainment districts far from home, or viewed famous sights they had read about in travel guides. Constraints still existed and limited the choices available to many Japanese, but they were far less inhibiting than the law codes and sumptuary edicts suggest. Farmers altered crop choices in response to market demands, engaged in trade and handicraft production as forms of village by-employment, and sent their sons and daughters to work for wages on farms, in village workshops, or in nearby or distant towns and cities.

The consumers of such luxury goods as elegant silk kosode and fine ramie katabira were the daimyo and upper-level members of the samurai class, rich merchants and artisans, and the courtesans and stars of the entertainment districts. The wealthiest members of Tokugawa society could wear silk daily, but most people wore cotton clothing, not elegant silk kosode, which were reserved for special occasions. Kosode of the quality displayed here were the designer clothing of the Edo period. They reflected the utmost in elegance, refinement, and splendor. As a result, they were extraordinarily expensive. Most people, if they saw them at all, saw them from afar or in woodblock prints illustrating beautiful women, courtesans, or actors. We can safely assume that this kosode exhibition provides better access to the highest-quality kosode than enjoyed by most Tokugawa-period Japanese.

1. For a discussion of foreign relations see Toby 1984. For Japanese reactions to European missionary activities see Elison 1973.

2. Bolitho 1974, 34–36.

3. Tsukahira 1966, 76–80.

4. Bolitho 1974, 13–14.

5. Shively 1965, 144. See also 145–47.

6. Ooms 1985, 57.

7. Ibid., 60–61.

8. Bolitho 1974, 19–36. Information was also drawn from "Domain Formation in Early Modern Japan," an unpublished book manuscript by Philip C. Brown.

9. Yamamura 1990, 376–83.

10. Hall 1968.

11. See Hauser 1974b, especially chapters 2 and 3, Hauser 1977, and Hauser 1985.

12. Rozman 1989, 533–48; Moriya 1990, 97–114.

13. As quoted in Shively 1965, 124–25.

14. Ibid., 125.

15. Hall 1974.

16. Hanley 1991.

17. Hauser 1974a.

18. Gotō Y. 1960; Sawada 1967.

19. Smith 1988.

20. Yamamura 1974, 26–48.

21. See Hauser 1977, Hanley and Yamamura 1977, Saitō 1987, and Inui 1977.

22. Hanley and Yamamura 1977; Hauser 1983.

23. Moriya 1990, 114–23.

24. Kabuki and bunraku were theatrical forms developed during the Tokugawa period. Kabuki was restricted to male actors after its use by women and young men to advertise their sexual services offended the government. Bunraku is a form of puppet theater using marionettes that are one-half to two-thirds life-size and are manipulated by one to three operators who are visible to the audience. Geisha were female entertainers who provided singing, dancing, conversation, games, and companionship to male customers. They were artists and not the same as the courtesans and prostitutes found in Tokugawa cities, although the distinction was often blurred. See Kodansha 1983, s.vv. "bunraku," "geisha," and "kabuki."

25. As quoted in Shively 1965, 158.

26. See Hibbett 1960 for a discussion of the culture of the floating world.

Toward a New Aesthetic:
The Evolution of the Kosode and Its Decoration

DALE CAROLYN GLUCKMAN

Kosode of the Edo period exhibit an integration of design and form, technique and color, pattern and ground unprecedented in the history of dress. Behind this flowering of the Japanese textile arts lies more than seven hundred years of formal and stylistic development. Tracing the evolution of the kosode provides a fascinating glimpse into the interplay of historical and aesthetic forces that shaped this quintessential Japanese garment. ❧ At the beginning of the Heian period the bast-fiber kosode was the principal attire of commoners. The succeeding centuries of political turmoil, economic dislocation, and technical innovation eventually brought the kosode to the forefront of fashion as the primary outer garment of all classes. By the latter part of the Muromachi period the complex process of shifting from cloth-oriented, continuous patterning to whole-garment design had begun.[1] This culminated in the Kanbun kosode, the boldly graphic starting point for Edo-period dress (see cat. no. 11).[2] ❧❧ A LAYERED AESTHETIC ❧ Heian court life centered on Heian-kyo (Kyoto), where an aristocratic minority pursued increasingly refined aesthetic ideals. In the words of Sir George Sansom, "What most occupied the thoughts of the Heian courtiers were ceremonies, costumes, elegant pastimes like verse-making and amorous intrigue conducted according to rules."[3] ❧ The form of women's dress that developed at the Heian court was a multilayered combination of garments (*kasane shōzoku*) often referred to today by the sixteenth-century term *jūni-hitoe* (literally, twelve unlined garments).[4] The actual number of layers varied, reaching a maximum of twenty in the early eleventh century; after this time sumptuary laws limited the number to five. The usual costume worn by a woman of the Heian court consisted of an unlined undergarment (*hitoe*) closest to the skin; a bifurcated lower garment (*hakama*), a cross between full-cut trousers and a divided skirt; and variable layers of lined robes (*uchigi*). These formed the basic combination over which several types of robes or jackets could be added for formal occasions. At official court functions the outermost article of clothing was the *mo*, an apronlike skirt that trailed behind the wearer. ❧ The aristocratic Heian woman spent much of her life seated on the floor, concealed behind bamboo shades and silk curtains. The sleeves and hems of her garments, exposed at the edges of these screening devices, were often all that revealed her physical presence (see fig. 12). Those visible portions of the costume inevitably became the focal point of the layered colors that encoded the poetic, literary, and emotional allusions "as necessary to social life as air is to breathing."[5] In this rarified atmo-

CATALOGUE NO. 4

Kosode on Screen (detail)

Left: Kosode fragment with grapevines and lozenges

Momoyama period, late sixteenth– early seventeenth century

Right: Kosode fragment with mountains, waves, roundels, fan papers, and flowers

Early seventeenth century

National Museum of Japanese History, Nomura Collection

FIGURE 12

Genji monogatari emaki (Tale of
Genji handscroll)

Heian period, twelfth century

Color on paper

8 5/8 × 18 15/16 in. (21.9 × 48.1 cm)

Tokugawa Art Museum, Nagoya

National Treasure

sphere of a shared literary-aesthetic system the color combinations a woman chose were based neither on personal preference nor fashion but were selected from a predefined body of "color sets" intended to reflect her sensibilities through the appropriate combining of "season, occasion, classical allusion, [rank,] and personal sentiment."[6] It was by her manipulation of subtle nuances within this highly restricted vocabulary that a woman expressed her aesthetic sensitivity and emotional character, qualities by which her individuality and desirability were judged. A glimpse of calligraphy or of a sleeve, a poetic response, or a passage of koto music were often the things that caused a man to desire one woman over another.[7]

The billowing layers of fabric that surrounded the wearer in undulating folds of silk discouraged the development of unified, large-scale textile designs. Woven or embroidered patterns on kasane shōzoku continued earlier motifs such as roundels and scattered geometric repeats, but on a smaller scale than in the previous Nara period. In addition to woven patterns several types of dyeing techniques became popular, among them monochrome-shaded dyeing from dark to light (or vice versa) and several qualities of *shibori* (resist dyeing). *Yūhata* and *narabi-sakume* were finely executed types of shibori apparently restricted to the garments of high-ranking women; cruder forms of shibori and stenciled shibori (*dai-kechi suri*) are thought to have been worn by soldiers and servants, respectively, in the tenth century.[8]

Unfortunately very few Heian-period textiles or garments have survived;[9] the same is true of the period's narrative picture scrolls (those from succeeding eras provide valuable textile and dress information). A useful visual source that has come down to us from the late Heian period is a group of Buddhist texts (sutra) inscribed over genre scenes in a fan-shaped format. Several of these present images of both courtiers and their servants. In one (fig. 13) the courtiers' garments are decorated with woven geometric designs or fine tie-dyeing (*kanoko shibori*), while the palace servants appear to be wearing garments patterned with several types of simple shibori and an irregularly spaced decoration resembling scattered leaves. The latter may have been achieved by dye or ink painting, by stamping, or by the *itajime* resist technique.[10] Another possible explanation for the technique depicted is stencil dyeing, seen on the leather components of armor from the late Heian-early Kamakura period. Despite the absence of surviving examples, the technique may have been used on clothing in the same period.[11] All show continuous patterning.

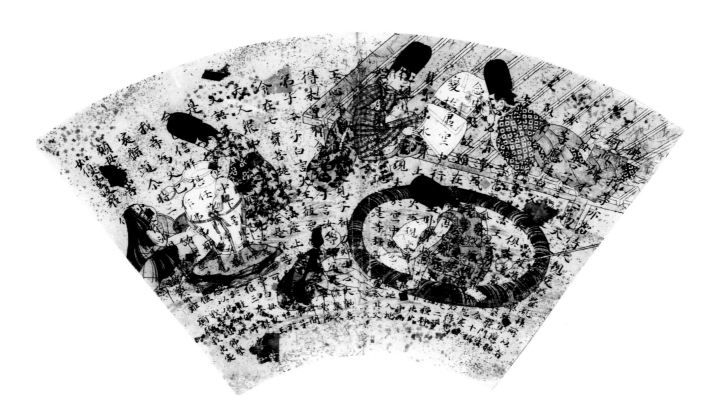

The common people in Heian Japan, forbidden to wear (and unable to afford) kasane shōzoku, silk fabrics, or elaborate woven patterns, wore simple attire of bast fiber: the unlined kosode. Male laborers wore loose trousers gathered at the ankle (*kukuri-bakama*) over the kosode. Some historians speculate that aristocratic women began to wear a silk version of the kosode in the mid-Heian period as the undermost garment of the kasane shōzoku.[12]

FIGURE 13
Hoke-kyō (detail)
Heian period, twelfth century
Book of twenty-two leaves; ink and color on paper
Each leaf: 10 1/16 × 19 7/16 in.
(25.6 × 49.4 cm)
Tokyo National Museum
National Treasure

The early twelfth century marked the political and social emergence of the samurai. At the beginning of the Kamakura period political power shifted from the imperial court to the military elite, remaining there until 1867. The shogun, however, never displaced the emperor, because of the samurai's profound respect for the cultural traditions the court maintained. Thus for more than six hundred years the imperial household, despite periods of extreme poverty, continued to practice state rituals and engage in genteel pursuits, while de facto political power remained in the hands of the military.

In keeping with the warrior's code, the Kamakura regime was characterized by austerity and simplicity (although this spartan behavior slowly eroded after the death of its first shogun, Minamoto Yoritomo, in 1199). The city of Kamakura was chosen as Yoritomo's capital to escape the social rivalries, refined luxuries, and lavish spending on dwellings, attire, and entertainment that constituted upper-class life in Kyoto, the imperial capital. Yet the military elite admired, even envied, the learning and accomplishments of the court. A blend of these opposite life-styles occurred as aristocrats were brought to Kamakura to train the soldiers, their sons, and retainers in noble skills. Kamakura culture, particularly as it developed in the thirteenth century and early fourteenth century, may therefore be seen as a product of the diffusion of Heian court culture throughout the warrior class, leading to a synthesis of the courtly tradition and samurai principles.[13]

Zen Buddhism was introduced from China during the Kamakura period; its simplicity, discipline, and lack of scripture appealed to military minds. The same characteristics that united samurai ideals and Zen philosophy were also expressed in matters of dress. Although the court initially maintained the clothing styles of the preceding era, under the austere influence of the military regime the number of robes was gradually reduced. By the Edo period the five-layered jūni-hitoe had become purely ceremonial in use; even court ladies wore the kosode for daily attire (see cat. nos. 45–46).

Toward the end of the Kamakura period samurai women, perhaps to emphasize their new position, adopted the attire of court attendants: a skirtlike combination of the mo and hakama (*mobakama*) worn over several kosode.[14] On formal occasions an additional kosode, the embroidered or brocaded silk *uchikake*, was worn as an outer cloak, at times slipped off the shoulders and held with a narrow sash. By the Muromachi period the uchikake had become a garment for special occasions; it has remained so to the present day. In the Edo period its use spread from the samurai

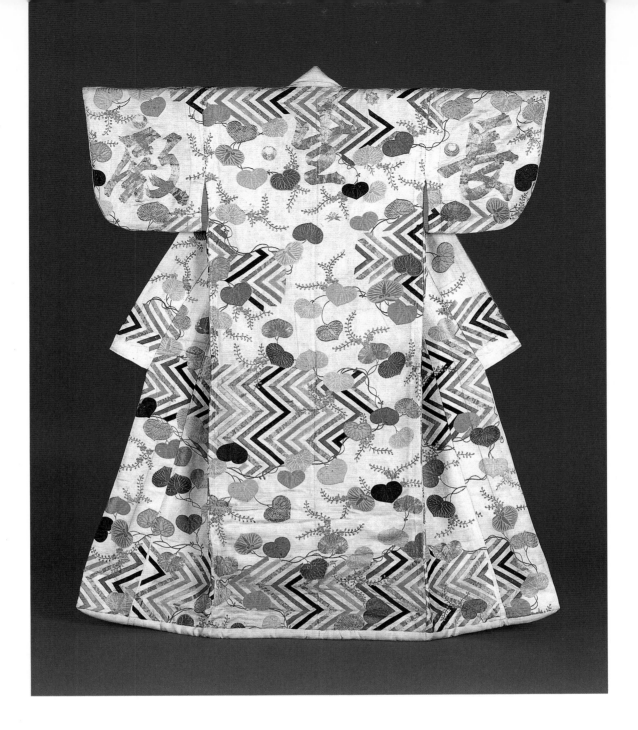

class to wealthy chōnin and high-ranking courtesans; it was worn
unbelted and became an important vehicle for elaborate decoration
(see cat. nos. 47–48, 53, 64, 144).

The establishment of the samurai as the ruling class, newly
privileged to wear silk garments, began the expansion of the circle
of people who were able to dress in fashionable attire. This was
one of the factors contributing to the flowering of decorative
motifs and techniques in the Edo period. Another factor was the
appearance, in the late Heian and early Kamakura periods, of
representational designs on the dress of commoners in contrast
with the stylized, repeating geometric woven patterns of the silks
of the aristocracy.[15]

Evidence of these new motifs can be found in the narrative

CATALOGUE NO. 144
*Uchikake with Wild Ginger,
Chevron-filled Clouds, and
Characters*
Late eighteenth–early nineteenth
century
Kanebo, Ltd.

14a

picture scrolls of the Kamakura period. They provide modern textile historians with surprisingly detailed information about the patterns (and in some cases even the techniques) used to decorate garments worn by the various classes. Scrolls such as the *Kasuga Gongen reigen-ki*[16] (Miracles of the deities of Kasuga Shrine; 1309; fig. 14a) depict samurai-class men and women wearing plaids, stripes, geometric patterns, and small dots (created by kanoko shibori) as well as representational motifs of flying geese, hawk feathers, small flowers, and horses possibly resisted in white on a dyed ground.[17] The same handscroll (fig. 14b) also shows laborers wearing clothing with large, scattered designs of fans, bamboo, hemp palm leaves, and half-submerged oxcart wheels, probably executed by block printing or painting.

Another significant factor in the development of the kosode is the appearance at this time of parti-colored garments separated into design areas concentrated either at the shoulder and hem (*katasuso*), on the right and left halves (*katami-gawari*), or in quarters (*dan-gawari*), indicating an elementary change in decora-

FIGURE 14a,b
Takashina Takane (fourteenth century)
Kasuga Gongen reigen-ki (detail)
1309
Set of twenty scrolls; ink and color on silk
h: 16 1/4 in. (41.2 cm)
Imperial Household Collection

14b

FIGURE 15

Hōnen Shōnin eden (detail)

Second half thirteenth century

Set of two handscrolls; color on
paper

Second scroll: 12 7/8 × 436 13/16 in.
(32.8 × 1,109.5 cm)

Zōjō-ji, Tokyo

Important Cultural Property

tive conception: a simple form of patterning the garment rather
than the cloth (see Appendix A). The latter two divisions could
easily be achieved by sewing together different fabrics. This may
have begun as a simple, economic expedient—the replacement of
worn or soiled sections of a garment with fabric from a second
garment—or as a means of achieving design variation with limited
financial expenditure.[18] Katasuso with irregularly shaped edges
(*suhama*), however, required the use of stitch-resist (*nuishime
shibori*). The earliest known depiction of this type of patterning is
found in the *Hōnen Shōnin eden* (Life of the monk Hōnen
Shōnin) handscroll in the Zōjō-ji, Tokyo, from the second half of
the thirteenth century (fig. 15). The suhama katasuso patterning
illustrated (see lower left) is evidence that the technique of
nuishime shibori, which would play an important role in later
textile development, was in use prior to the fourteenth century.

A DECORATIVE AESTHETIC

In 1333 the city of Kamakura was destroyed during a civil war,
and Kyoto was again made the capital. The years from 1336 to
1392 are known as the Nanbokuchō (the age of the northern and
southern courts). The Emperor Kōmyō (1322–80) reigned in
Kyoto with the support of Ashikaga Takauji, while the Emperor
Go-Daigo (1288–1339) established a rival court to the south in
Yoshino. The Ashikaga family secured its hegemony in 1392,
when the two rival imperial courts were united. Thus began the
Muromachi period, named after the section of Kyoto in which the
Ashikaga shogun established their residence. By 1400 Kyoto and

its environs were again torn by civil strife. The ten-year Ōnin War (1467–77) led to the near destruction of the capital and the collapse of the central government. The dawn of the sixteenth century saw the fighting spread throughout Japan as independent feudal lords contested for territorial control.

Despite almost constant warfare and major interruptions in the supply of goods and services in the Muromachi period, the arts flourished. The Ashikaga were generous in their patronage, particularly the third Ashikaga shogun, Yoshimitsu, and the eighth, Yoshimasa. Nevertheless the devastation of Kyoto further weakened an already declining court culture. As the period progressed, the military elite could no longer look solely to the Kyoto aristocracy as the source of cultural inspiration.[19] Increasingly China was turned to for models of philosophy, art, and literature, while at the same time lower-status retainers and artisans were relied upon as arbiters of aesthetic taste and sources of artistic innovation.[20] Among the notable developments during this period were Nō drama, which developed as a blend of popular dance-oriented performing arts; renga, the linked verse of commoners, which replaced *waka* (court verse); and the new, more austere form of the tea ceremony, which possibly began among the lower classes.[21]

The Ōnin War had a profound effect on Japanese society in general and the development of textiles and dress in particular.[22] The destruction and chaos caused by the war, especially in Kyoto, blurred class boundaries, enabling greater social mobility: a few men and women of modest beginnings rose to powerful positions (including the warlord Toyotomi Hideyoshi, who began his career as a foot soldier), farmers moved into the samurai class, and many of the urban Kyoto elite were scattered to rural areas and the port town of Sakai (near Osaka).

The unsettled times affected craftsmen in several ways. A relaxation of restrictions by the weakened central authority permitted the formation of guilds for mutual protection; these in turn provided greater influence and prestige for the artisans. Both artisans and merchants were called upon to supply competing lords, stimulating the economic rise of the chōnin. Artists and craftsmen, freed from almost total dependence on aristocratic or ecclesiastical patronage, began to cater to this new class of patrons.

The weavers of Kyoto, producers of the luxury silks consumed by the upper classes, were also affected. The widespread destruction of the city during the Ōnin War forced some of them to flee to outlying castle towns, while the majority relocated to Sakai, joining a large community of Chinese weavers already there.

This social and demographic upheaval affected dress by accelerating the simplifications that had begun in the Kamakura period and hastening the adoption of the kosode as the primary outer garment of the elite. By the end of the fifteenth century the kosode was the principal garment of both genders and all classes.

With the widespread acceptance of the kosode the concept of clothing changed. The kasane shōzoku style, with its voluminous, layered garments appropriate for the sedentary life of a leisured aristocracy, hid the body and submerged the individual while expanding the space around the wearer. It is estimated that a complete fifteen-layer ensemble required about 480 yards of silk (approximately forty modern *tan*). The kosode, by contrast, revealed the body (relative to earlier styles) and was better suited to more active lives. A single-layer kosode required slightly more than 12 yards of silk (approximately one modern tan).[23] Aesthetically the two types of dress were quite different as well. The expressive quality of the kasane shōzoku was in its form—color and motif were distinct entities functioning independently. Virtually the sole emphasis of the kosode was on its decoration—motif and color working together.

The disruptions of continuous warfare and natural disasters in the late Muromachi period simultaneously contributed to the popularity of the kosode and crippled the means of its production. The Ōnin War, which leveled much of Kyoto, was followed by disease, famine, and more fighting. Yet some weavers returned to the capital, settling in a former military encampment called Nishijin. In 1575 Oda Nobunaga, in a dispute with the Kami-kyo ward, put seven thousand houses to the torch, destroying in the process the stores of silk yarn intended for the looms of Kyoto's still-recovering weaving industry.[24]

Neither the demands of upper-class patrons replenishing wardrobes nor the desires of wealthy guildsmen and urban merchants, now able to afford luxury silks, could be met by Chinese imports and domestic production. To emulate these expensive textiles, whose intricately woven patterns were not yet widely mastered, new interest arose in the use of surface techniques for the decoration of silk kosode. The influx of painted, printed, and dyed textiles from India and Southeast Asia in the latter part of the Muromachi period also contributed to the interest in surface techniques.[25] As a result, the Muromachi period produced a uniquely Japanese form of dyed textile decoration, tsujigahana, the first step in freeing kosode design from cloth-oriented, continuous patterning.[26]

Surviving garments and textile fragments from the late Muromachi period through the early Edo period that are called tsujigahana by most textile historians[27] manifest the following combination of surface techniques: shibori (nuishime and kanoko), *kaki-e* (painting), *surihaku* (metallic leaf), and nui, usually executed on *neri-*

nuki (thin silk). This plain-weave fabric made possible the balance of decorative methods found in tsujigahana.[28] It enhanced the contrast between the metallic leaf and embroidery and made it possible to create sharper outlines with nuishime shibori even when motifs were very close together. It is difficult to know, however, whether the demand for surface-dyed decoration spurred the use of nerinuki or if its greater availability during and after the Ōnin War encouraged the development of these techniques.

All of these methods were long established in the dyer's repertoire. Kaki-e, surihaku, and nui were used on upper-class clothing in the Heian period;[29] shibori (particularly nuishime) and kaki-e appeared on the garments of lower-ranking samurai from at least as early as the late thirteenth century. Today tsujigahana is defined as the use, on textiles from the period under discussion, of any combination of these techniques that includes shibori (see cat. nos. 1 left and right, 2 left, 4 left, 147, 163).

A dearth of firmly dated examples and the lack of precise literary references make the establishment of a clear chronology for the development of tsujigahana impossible at present. Compounding the difficulty are factors affecting dating whose precise nature is not yet known: widely varying production costs and skills, overlapping stylistic trends, and diverse centers of manufacture. It is generally agreed, however, that tsujigahana, born of the social flux of the Muromachi period, came to maturity in the succeeding Momoyama period.[30]

A Bolder Aesthetic

The rule of the Ashikaga shogunate, growing increasingly ineffectual, was finally brought to an end in 1573 by Nobunaga. He began the work of reorganizing the country and rebuilding Kyoto, tasks continued by his successor, Hideyoshi.[31] Wendell Cole described the thirty years between Nobunaga's triumphal entry into Kyoto in 1568 and Hideyoshi's death in 1598:

> The imperial capital was the center of an unprecedented transformation of Japanese society. Peasants and serfs, freed from the land, flocked to the cities where they became artisans and merchants. Commerce and industry increased immeasurably. Religious life, no longer dominated by Buddhism, was diverted toward Confucian rationalism. Castles and palaces of unparalleled magnificence were constructed in Kyoto, Fushimi, Azuchi, and Osaka. There was an explosive outburst of brilliant color and bold design in painting, sculpture, ceramics, and weaving. It was a time of national glory and artistic achievement—the starting point for the history of modern Japan.[32]

CATALOGUE NO. I

Kosode on Screen

Left: Kosode fragment with
scattered floral motifs
Momoyama period, late sixteenth–
early seventeenth century
Right: Kosode fragment with
horizontal bands of squares and of
camellias and wisteria
Momoyama period, late sixteenth–
early seventeenth century
National Museum of Japanese
History, Nomura Collection

CATALOGUE NO. 2

Kosode on Screen

Left: Kosode fragment with
Chinese bellflowers and camellias
Momoyama period, late sixteenth–
early seventeenth century

Right: Kosode fragment with
flowers and clouds

First quarter seventeenth century

National Museum of Japanese
History, Nomura Collection

CATALOGUE NO. 4

Kosode on Screen

Left: Kosode fragment with grapevines and lozenges Momoyama period, late sixteenth– early seventeenth century

Right: Kosode fragment with mountains, waves, roundels, fan papers, and flowers Early seventeenth century National Museum of Japanese History, Nomura Collection

Momoyama artistic expression reflected several influences: warrior and merchant tastes, European culture, and tea ceremony aesthetics. First, the samurai elite contributed a new interest in large-scale decorative statements often made even more striking by the incorporation of gold (a symbol of military and political strength).[33] Chōnin lived in a world that placed a strong emphasis on the here and now. Townsmen were bent on experiencing, and having portrayed in art, the temporal diversions offered by the burgeoning cities of Kyoto, Osaka, and Sakai, particularly their flourishing pleasure quarters.

Second, the arrival of three Portuguese sailors near Kyushu in 1543 began a century of direct contact with Europeans.[34] Portuguese and Spanish Jesuits were the first to arrive, intent on both conversion and commerce. Merchants and adventurers soon followed. Their unusual appearance sparked a fad for European dress among Japanese men of all classes, who sported capes, velvet hats, ruffs, full breeches, and crucifixes well into the early decades of the seventeenth century. *Nanban* art, encompassing depictions of the "Southern Barbarians" and objects made to their taste, was one outcome of this contact; the exchange of Japanese silver for European woolens, Chinese silks, and Indian and Southeast Asian cottons was another. Father Francisco Pasio commented in 1594 that Hideyoshi "has become so enamored of Portuguese dress and

CATALOGUE NO. 147
Obi with Snowflake Roundels,
Spring Plants, and Characters
(detail)
Third quarter seventeenth century
Sendai City Museum
Important Cultural Property

costume that he and his retainers frequently wear this apparel as do all the lords of Japan . . . with rosaries of driftwood on the breast above all their clothing, and with a crucifix at their side, or hanging from the waist."[35]

Third, the austere aesthetic of simplicity and appreciation of the imperfections of nature associated with *wabicha* (the informal cult of tea) influenced the samurai class and well-to-do chōnin, eventually permeating all levels of society. Substantially shaped by the taste of the famous tea master Sen no Rikyū (1521–91), wabicha used Korean kitchenware and kiln "accidents." It contrasted sharply with the lavish and competitive tea ceremonies, with their solid gold utensils and priceless Chinese porcelains, held by the Ashikaga and continued by Hideyoshi and wealthy daimyo. These extremely expensive and extravagant tea ceremonies began in the Muromachi period among wealthy daimyo in Kyoto. They rapidly became a means of flaunting wealth, and therefore power, among the military elite. The most extreme example of public ostentation was Hideyoshi's portable solid-gold tearoom, in which he served tea to the emperor in 1586. At the same time, Hideyoshi, with Rikyū as his advisor, privately practiced wabicha.[36]

The military leaders of this period indulged in other extravagant displays as well: Nobunaga built his magnificent castle at Azuchi and was fond of exotic dress; Hideyoshi loved entertaining on a grand scale and had enormous stores of expensive fabric and clothing. Luis Frois (1532–97), a Portuguese Jesuit, was given a personal tour of the castle in Osaka by Hideyoshi in 1586. Frois was shown a room full of gold and silver, another of silver, a third of bales of silk, and a fourth filled with robes. He noted: "In one of the chambers through which we passed there were ten or twelve new cloaks, dyed a scarlet hue and hanging on silken cords—a most unusual sight in Japan."[37]

It is no surprise that in this climate of unrestrained luxury the textile arts flourished. João Rodrigues (c. 1561–1633), a Portuguese Jesuit who lived in Japan from 1577 to 1610, observed: "Usually the people wore garments woven from linen. . . . but since the time of *Taikō* [Hideyoshi] there has been a general peace throughout the kingdom and trade has so increased that the whole nation wears silk robes; even peasants and their wives have silk sashes."[38] Domestic and imported brocades, embroidery, metallic leaf, and nuihaku continued to be worn by those who could afford them, particularly the military elite. At the same time, delicate tsujigahana on thin nerinuki seems to have reached its peak of popularity with both the samurai (see fig. 16a) and the chōnin (see fig. 16b).

16a

FIGURE 16a,b
Attributed to Kano Hideyori
(fl. c. 1540)
Maple Viewing at Takao (details)
Sixteenth century
Six-panel screen; color on paper
58 11/16 × 143 5/16 in.
(149.1 × 364.0 cm)
Tokyo National Museum
National Treasure

16b

Growing interest in the graphic potential of the kosode impelled advancements in the mastery of the techniques used in tsujigahana.[39] For example, inked outlines enhanced the representational qualities of nuishime shibori (see cat. no. 1 right). Ink painting was also used alone to create a delicate pictorialism incorporating natural elements (see cat. nos. 147, 163). Yet the treatment in these three examples remains essentially the same: isolated motifs placed on a neutral ground. The impetus toward representationalism would further push technical refinements and ultimately contribute to the unique pictorial qualities of Edo-period kosode design.

A New Aesthetic

The power struggle following the death of Hideyoshi concluded with Tokugawa Ieyasu established as the sole ruler of Japan. His new shogunal dynasty provided more than 250 years of peace and stability (see Hauser essay). At the inauguration of Tokugawa hegemony, Japanese society was still being transformed by the cultural momentum of the Momoyama period, driven by the increasing wealth of the chōnin and the relatively free mingling of social classes.[40] The years from the Keichō era to the Kanbun era form a continuum in which kosode patterning made the final transition to the unified design field characteristic of the fully developed Edo-period kosode.

CATALOGUE NO. 163
Kosode Fragment with Fan Roundels, Flowering Vines, and Wild Ginger Leaves (detail)
Momoyama period, late sixteenth–early seventeenth century
Los Angeles County Museum of Art, gift of Miss Bella Mabury, M.39.2.304

·

CATALOGUE NO. 2
Kosode on Screen (detail)
Left: Kosode fragment with Chinese bellflowers and camellias
Momoyama period, late sixteenth–early seventeenth century
Right: Kosode fragment with flowers and clouds
First quarter seventeenth century
National Museum of Japanese History, Nomura Collection

During those years, from the late sixteenth century to the mid-seventeenth century, chōnin prosperity created a widening market for decorated silk kosode. In meeting this upsurge in demand, producers focused on greater technical facility and stylistic innovations stimulated by new materials and a growing interest in graphic representation on clothing. Owing to the relatively greater number of extant examples from this time span, it is possible to trace in detail the evolution of a new aesthetic.

The first innovation, known today as the Keichō-Kan'ei style, appeared on kosode worn by women of the military elite (see cat. nos. 2 right, 3, 4 right, 5–6).[41] Perhaps its most striking feature was a radical change in coloration. Whereas tsujigahana utilized a wide variety of colors, giving a light, airy effect, the new mode used a consciously restricted palette of deep crimson, black, purple, and brown, creating an impression of somberness and solidity. The introduction of *rinzu*, a monochrome figured silk, coincided with the appearance of the Keichō-Kan'ei style and may even have brought it about.

CATALOGUE NO. 5
Kosode with Abstract Shapes, Birds, Plants, and Flowers
Early seventeenth century
Tabata Collection
Important Cultural Property

CATALOGUE NO. 3
Kosode on Screen
Kosode fragment with mountains, snowflake roundels, wisteria, and plants of the four seasons
Early seventeenth century
National Museum of Japanese History, Nomura Collection

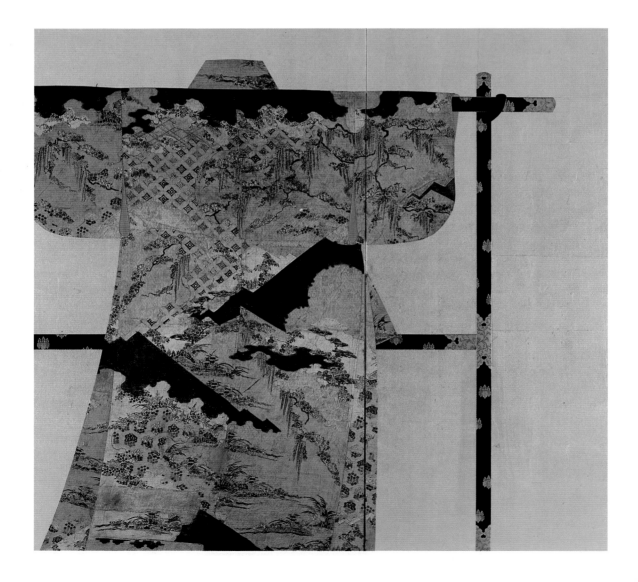

CATALOGUE NO. 6

Kosode on Screen

Kosode fragment with leaves, fans,
and plants

Second quarter seventeenth century

National Museum of Japanese

History, Nomura Collection

First imported from China toward the end of the sixteenth century, by 1615 rinzu was being produced by the Nishijin weavers. It gradually replaced the thinner but stiffer nerinuki (although nerinuki continued to be used for embroidered *koshimaki*, part of the formal summer attire of samurai women; see cat. no. 52). More luxurious in look and feel, rinzu satisfied the desire of fashion-conscious patrons for a softer, more relaxed silhouette, remaining popular throughout the Edo period.[42]

The textural quality of rinzu shattered the unity and balance of tsujigahana, leading to the establishment of new roles for some decorative techniques and the elimination of others. Kanoko shibori, a previously minor technique in tsujigahana, replaced nuishime shibori as the primary means of delineating and filling specific shapes; on rinzu, nuishime shibori was better suited to defining larger areas. This newly established relationship continued throughout the Tokugawa period.

Neither metallic leaf nor ink were compatible with the new ground. Small stenciled diaper patterns replaced the fine outlines and broad "washes" of the thin leaf of tsujigahana (compare cat. nos. 6, 163). The dark, saturated colors typical of the Keichō-Kan'ei style would have shown the tiny, geometric patterns of surihaku to best advantage. These dark colors also would have minimized the light-reflective (and distracting) qualities of the self-figured ground. This may explain, at least in part, the rather dramatic shift in coloration in this period. By the Kanbun era surihaku was largely replaced by couched metallic thread. The domestic manufacture of metallic thread began during the Keichō-Kan'ei eras and can occasionally be found on kosode of that time (see cat. no. 6). Some use of surihaku continued in fashionable dress in the Edo period (see cat. nos. 66, 82, 92), but it survived primarily as decoration, with or without embroidery, on Nō costumes. Ink painting, virtually impossible on the textured surface of rinzu, became an independent technique on unpatterned silks and was seen on some Edo-period robes (see cat. nos. 101, 108, 115).

Embroidery also changed, becoming minute in scale with short, sparse stitches. In contrast, Momoyama embroidery featured relatively large motifs and long, parallel stitches (*ura-nuki*). In the Keichō-Kan'ei style, embroidery was often used to create tiny landscapes of flowers and autumn grasses. Since the needle is almost as flexible as the brush, the pictorial function of ink painting in tsujigahana may have been transferred to embroidery. As the period progressed toward the Manji and Kanbun eras, embroidery gradually became more dense and precise with increasingly realistic detail, foreshadowing the mature Edo-period style (compare cat. nos. 6, 164).

CATALOGUE NO. 6 (detail)

CATALOGUE NO. 164
Kosode Fragment with Mountains, Snowflake Roundels, Wisteria, and Plants of the Four Seasons (detail)
Early seventeenth century
Los Angeles County Museum of Art, Costume Council Fund, M.85.188

From the introduction of the Keichō-Kan'ei style to the appearance of the developed Kanbun style the concept of kosode decoration underwent a gradual evolution: asymmetry, motion, interactive pattern and ground, and boldness of scale distinguish the early Edo-period kosode from its predecessors.[43] Yet the garments of the Keichō-Kan'ei years should be seen not as purely transitional but as forming a distinct and striking style in which the emergence of a new aesthetic can be seen.[44] Devastating fires in Edo (1657) and Kyoto (1661), once thought to have brought about the Kanbun style, merely accelerated an established trend.[45]

As indicated above, two general categories of pattern organization had dominated kosode design since the Kamakura period:

CATALOGUE NO. 8
Kosode with Noshi and Flowering Plants
First half seventeenth century
Kanebo, Ltd.

continuous patterning and geometrical sectioning (katasuso, katami-gawari, and dan-gawari), each of which might also contain smaller design units. Keichō-style patterning introduced irregularly shaped divisions, the first departure from the symmetry and rigid compartmentalization of earlier decoration. The flat plane of the ground began to break up, creating visual ambiguity. However, with rare exception (and cat. no. 5 is a very early one), even on the most complex somewake ground the rigid dividing lines are carefully maintained, with no portion of the embroidered or gilded leaf design crossing over into an adjacent space despite clever impressions of movement. Although the first hint can be

CATALOGUE NO. 7
Kosode with Waterfall,
Chrysanthemums, and Footed Tray
Mid-seventeenth century
National Museum of Japanese
History, Nomura Collection

seen in the above-mentioned kosode, it was not until the Kanbun era that motifs began to overlap ground divisions. This style is called *jinashi* (without ground), because the ground and pattern are indistinguishable (see cat. no. 3).[46]

Gradually the somewake shapes became recognizable forms—mountains and waves (see cat. no. 4 right) and leaves (see cat. no. 6), for example, with sweeping curves and angular lines that impart a sense of movement to the surface. This motion, fully exploited in the Kanbun and Genroku eras, marks another break with the static quality of prior patterning. Combining asymmetry with the movement of curved lines, the surface of the kosode appears to open, revealing a relatively blank space containing smaller elements (see cat. no. 8). Positive and negative spaces work together as elements of the same design; no longer is a motif simply sitting on a neutral ground (see Nagasaki essay).

The final transformations are of color and scale. By the Kanbun era a lighter and more colorful palette returned (see cat. no. 14). A new boldness appeared, often in the form of a single large motif spreading asymmetrically across the back from one shoulder to the hem against a monochrome ground still covered with gold leaf in some of the transitional pieces (see. cat. nos. 7, 9–10). A subtle but significant change took place with the introduction of a single motif: the weight of the decoration shifted to the back of the garment. Maruyama Nobuhiko proposes that this reflects the influence of the clothing of certain elements of the chōnin population: kabuki actors, courtesans, and rogues, whose self-assertive life-styles demanded oversized, easy-to-read, and prominently placed images. Such realistic images[47] as water wheels, bridges, and fans, echoing the taste of the chōnin class, were drawn from the objects and activities of everyday life.[48] By contrast, the motifs preferred by the upper classes consisted of the natural phenomena (for example, flowing water, seasonal plants, and floral roundels) so closely associated with literature and heightened emotional response since the Heian period (see fig. 17).[49] These motifs also grew in size, echoing developments in chōnin dress (see cat. nos. 12, 131).

Thus a new aesthetic made its appearance in the third quarter of the seventeenth century, as static and compartmentalized patterning gave way to whole-garment decoration focused on a unified, dynamic motif (see cat. no. 11). The foundation was laid for the extraordinary stylistic diversity of the Edo-period kosode.

FIGURE 17
Honda Heihachirō and Princess Senhime (detail)
First half seventeenth century
Two-panel screen; color on paper
28 ⅝ × 62 in. (72.7 × 157.5 cm)
Tokugawa Art Museum, Nagoya

CATALOGUE NO. 11
Katabira with Chrysanthemums
Third quarter seventeenth century
Kyoto National Museum

NOTES

1. Cloth-oriented, continuous patterning refers to textile decoration in which design units are placed in a regular or scattered fashion on a neutral ground. The patterning of the cloth becomes the decoration of the garment. In contrast, whole-garment patterning refers to the conceptualization of the finished garment as a single design unit. The decoration of the garment becomes the patterning of the cloth.

2. Although well into the Edo period, it wasn't until the Kanbun era that the true Edo-period kosode style actually emerged. Nagasaki Iwao has been instrumental in directing the author's attention to this crucial point.

3. Sansom 1978, 241.

4. Dalby 1988, 5. The author is indebted to Dalby's excellent article.

5. Dalby 1988, 3.

6. Ibid.

7. This approach to beauty, so antithetical to Western ideas of physical "perfection" as the trigger of romantic love, survives in present-day Japan. Haak 1973, 113, records the comments of an obi wholesaler, who explained that "the Japanese choose their women by their graces and by their taste in kimono," not by their figure or personality. It is against this background of what Haak calls "invisible beauty" that the kosode in this exhibition should be viewed.

8. Wada, Rice, and Barton 1983, 15–16.

9. See Kirihata 1983a for a discussion and illustrations of most of the extant Heian textiles, all loom-patterned silks.

10. For a discussion of itajime see Yamanobe 1966, 54–55.

11. Yamanobe 1966, 44.

12. Notably Imanaga 1983a, 112, and Kubo 1972, 6.

13. Sansom 1978, 341–42.

14. Hinonishi 1968, 68. It is often stated that the kosode "emerged" from under the jūni-hitoe toward the end of the Kamakura period (Noma S. 1974, 13–14; Okada 1958, 16). This may have been true for the nobility; as commoners, however, samurai women would have been wearing the kosode as a matter of course.

15. Earlier, in the Nara period, pictorial designs had appeared on imported luxury textiles in the so-called "Continental Style" of Tang China (618–906), a blend of Mediterranean, Iranian, Chinese, Indian, and Central Asian elements. See Matsumoto 1984. See also Yamanobe 1966, 25–37, for a discussion of their patterns within the context of Japanese textile development.

16. For excellent details and discussion of the clothing portrayed see Ogasawara 1988, 64–65.

17. Yamanobe 1966, 44–46, suggests that these white-against-blue (indigo) patterns may have been executed with starch-paste resist and stencils. He points to the evidence of starch-paste-resist dyeing of family crests on samurai garments of the Kamakura period.

18. Noma S. 1974, 116–19. See also Stinchecum 1984, 40.

19. Sansom 1978, 371, points out that the samurai themselves began to replace the court as arbiters of fashion. When Nawa, the constable of Hōki, escorted the emperor into Kyoto in 1333, his style set off a fad known as the "Hōki manner."

20. See Toyoda and Sugiyama 1977, 144, and Hayashiya, Nakamura, and Hayashiya 1974, 15–31.

21. See Ienaga 1979, 95–109, and Varley 1977.

22. The following comments were drawn from several sources, including Stinchecum 1984, 24, 27; Toyoda and Sugiyama 1977; and Hayashiya 1977.

23. Extrapolated from Imanaga 1983a, 110, and Yamanobe 1966, 39.

24. See Haak 1973, 132–34.

25. See Kirihata 1988b, 23.

26. Another response was the addition of haku (metallic leaf) to nui (embroidery), creating nuihaku, a luxury textile that was popular throughout the Momoyama period. In the Edo period it was used almost exclusively for Nō theater costumes.

27. Professor Yamanobe Tomoyuki has stated that the term was initially associated with these textiles by historians in the Meiji period. See Itō 1985, 187. The word itself, however, first appears in a fourteenth-century poem; there are also scattered references in works from the succeeding two centuries. These sources give no description of what is meant by the term; no documented relationship exists between it and either the extant textiles or shibori technique associated with it. For a thorough discussion of this see Itō 1985, 19–33, and Stinchecum 1984, 34–35, 211–12, note 28.

28. The importance of nerinuki to tsujigahana is suggested in Kirihata 1988b, 23; see also Wada, Rice, and Barton 1983, 26.

29. See Kirihata 1980, 307–10.

30. Kirihata 1988b, 58, speculates that tsujigahana reached its peak of development in the Tenshō-Bunroku era, immediately preceding the Keichō era, which introduced a new style. Ishimura and Maruyama 1988, 9, however, asserts that the height of tsujigahana development cannot be ascertained.

31. Nobunaga conquered Kyoto in 1568 but did not depose Yoshiaki, the last Ashikaga shogun, until 1573. The Momoyama period took its name from a hill where Hideyoshi built his castle, at Fushimi near Kyoto. Some scholars refer to the time as the Azuchi-Momoyama period in recognition of Nobunaga's great castle built at Azuchi in 1576. By either name the period formed a cultural continuum with the Edo period; the two together constitute the early modern period.

32. Cole 1967, 27. One might add that it was in dyed as well as woven textiles that new levels of expression were achieved.

33. See Shimizu 1988, 26–27.

34. See Cooper 1971 for a good overview of the early contacts between Japan and Europe that focuses on mutual exchange.

35. As quoted in Cole 1967, 84. Francisco Pasio (or Paez), a Portuguese Jesuit, arrived in Japan at an unknown date and left in 1612.

36. See Hayashiya, Nakamura, and Hayashiya 1974, 12–14, and Meech-Pekarik 1975, xvi.

37. As quoted in Cooper 1965, 136–37.

38. Rodrigues 1973, 133. The availability of silk, the bulk of which was in Chinese silk cloth or silk yarn, was greatly increased in the second half of the sixteenth century by European trade. See Cooper 1971, 19, and Boxer 1959. In addition, domestic production reached new heights owing to Hideyoshi's strong patronage of Nishijin weavers during his rule. See Haak 1973, 134–35.

39. See Ōsone 1989, 25–28. Imanaga 1983a, 113, also proposes that a new demand for pictorial expression came first and was responded to by craftsmen with the techniques at hand.

40. Meech-Pekarik 1975, xv, suggests Momoyama culture extended into the Kan'ei era. Ienaga 1979, 116, extends this even further: "In terms of culture, however, it is better to think of the Momoyama period as lasting for eighty years, well into the middle of the seventeenth century."

41. Kawakami 1982, 34. Once believed to have been confined solely to the Keichō era, the style's extension into the Kan'ei era is now recognized. See Stinchecum 1984, 43–44. It is also referred to as *Keichō somewake*, because many examples exhibit a ground divided into several color areas (somewake).

42. See Stinchecum 1984, 43.

43. Maruyama 1986, 196, argues on the evidence of extant pattern books that the so-called "Kanbun style" actually appeared in the Manji era. As the conventional terminology is "Kanbun kosode," that term will be used here, but it is to be understood as encompassing both the Manji and Kanbun eras.

44. It should be pointed out, however, that both woven decoration and continuous patterning continued as conservative kosode styles throughout the Edo period.

45. See Stinchecum 1984, 53. See also Kawakami 1982, 34, Maruyama 1986, and Nagasaki essay.

46. A variant of the Keichō-Kan'ei style termed "black background" in Stinchecum 1984, 47, was characterized by a dark, solid ground, often continuously patterned, and used nerinuki or glossed silk rather than rinzu (see cat. no. 2 right). Whether the style predated the introduction of the somewake ground or paralleled it cannot be determined. A dearth of firmly dated examples permits no more than speculation on the chronology of the Keichō-Kan'ei style.

47. According to Lee 1983, 2, "the confusion between realism of subject and realism of style plagues the study of both Eastern and Occidental art." The concern here is for the subject.

48. Maruyama 1986, 219, suggests that these motifs began to appear on the kosode of chōnin between the end of the Keichō era and the beginning of the Kan'ei era.

49. Maruyama 1986, 198.

Designs for a Thousand Ages: Printed Pattern Books and Kosode

NAGASAKI IWAO

Kosode moyō hinagata-bon are sample books of kosode designs that were published in the Edo period. The term *hinagata* refers to a miniaturized object or something created to serve as a model. During a period of about 150 years, from 1666 to 1820, approximately 170 to 180 kosode design books were published.[1] Nearly all of these included an issue date, thus providing a very important means of tracing the stylistic development of kosode decoration. Naturally the designs were the main focus of the sample books, but appended notes on colors and decorative techniques have proven to be extremely significant. They supply specific details about contemporary kosode colors and dyeing and weaving methods. ❖ ❖ PUBLICATION OF KOSODE MOYŌ HINAGATA-BON ❖ *On-hiinakata* (Design patterns; 1666)[2] is considered the first kosode pattern book,[3] but two types of publications similar in format already existed prior to its issuance. One is the type exemplified by the two *On'e-chō* (Picture book) volumes, well known because of their relation to the kosode merchant house Kariganeya, owned by the family of the painter Ogata Kōrin (1658–1716). These works, produced in 1661 and 1663, were formerly in the collection of the Konishi family and are now in that of the Osaka Municipal Museum of Art (see Takeda essay, note 10).

They were, in all likelihood, *kosode hinagata-chō* (kosode order books), composed as compilations of memoranda made when clothing was ordered. They depict hand-drawn ink designs within the outlines of kosode forms and record in the margins both the techniques in which the garments were to be executed and the dates they were to be completed (see fig. 18). When the kosode were actually to be dyed, working specifications based on these notations were probably written up and passed on to the craftsmen. There are also Kariganeya order books without illustrations that predate the *On'e-chō*, but those accompanied by illustrations first appeared after the mid-seventeenth century, when the composition of kosode design had become too complicated to be conveyed in words alone. It is reasonable to suppose that all the garments depicted in the *On'e-chō* volumes were manufactured; through them we can visualize actual kosode of the time. Although these books are similar to the kosode moyō hinagata-bon in form and method of depiction of design, the object and manner of their use differed greatly. ❖ The other type of publication that preceded kosode design books is represented by *Onna shoreishū* (Compilation of manners for women; 1660). It depicts folded kosode draped on *ikō* (clothes racks); around the illustrations are notes on the colors and patterns of the garments

FIGURE 18

Page from *On'e-chō*

1663

(see fig. 19). Such publications resembled kosode moyō hinagata-bon in form, but they contained no more than about ten design leaves. Their use was rather different as well, serving as educational manuals for women.

Thus in the strictest sense the appearance of kosode design books had to wait for the publication of *On-hiinakata*. In 1667 this work was reprinted, with only slight changes in content.[4] In the second edition the composition of each page consists of the outline of the back view of a kosode, on which a design has been drawn, surrounded by notes on pattern and background color (see fig. 20).

This basic form continued in succeeding printed design books, but in the process a number of changes came about. For example, in *On-hinagata manjoshū* (Design book: Collection of ten thousand women), probably published during the Enpo or Tenna eras, figures of women wearing kosode are shown (see fig. 21). The preface explains:

> Since the time kosode designs were first reproduced as small-scale drawings called hinagata, kosode moyō hinagata-bon have spread throughout society. In recent years, however, there have been many kosode made from these design books that were not flattering or suitable to the people who were to wear them, because of their age or appearance. Accordingly, in this publication we have included a drawing of a particular type of woman wearing kosode, so that the customer can choose one that suits her own appearance.

Details of the background color, design, and execution are written across the top of the page. The same style of expression also occurs in *Onnayō kinmō zui* (Collection of illustrations for the enlightenment of women; 1678), where each page of the third volume includes a picture of a woman dressed in a kosode, with an explanation of the pattern in the space next to the figure. *Kosode no sugatami* (Reflections of kosode), thought to have been published during the Genroku era, and *Toshi no hana* (Blossoms of the year), published in 1691, continue this idea. The right-hand pages of *Kosode no sugatami* display the figures of one or two women (except for one page that depicts young men), while on the left-hand pages the pattern is illustrated within the outlines of a kosode. The surrounding space contains notes on color, etc. The pattern of the kosode worn by the figure on the right-hand page, however, bears

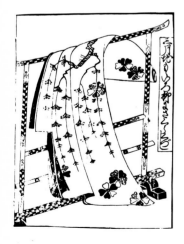

FIGURE 19

Pages from *Onna shoreishū*

1660

FIGURE 20

Page from *On-hiinakata*

1667

no relation whatsoever to the illustration on the left. *Toshi no hana* shows on the right-hand pages the figure of a kabuki actor and notes his full name and the name of his guild; the left-hand pages illustrate the back view of a kosode as a hinagata picture. There are exceptions, but as a rule depictions of full figures show a front view, while hinagata illustrations display the back.

These four books (*On-hinagata manjoshū*, *Onnayō kinmō zui*, *Kosode no sugatami*, and *Toshi no hana*), as revealed by their prefaces and texts, can be included within the range of kosode moyō hinagata-bon and regarded as an advancement over the simple forms of representation current before their publication. Despite the fact that the purpose of depicting figures was ostensibly to enable the prospective purchaser to envision a harmony between the design and her own age and appearance, the artistic depiction of the human figure became the hinagata illustrator's primary objective. These figures clearly exhibit features of the type of work known as *bijinga* (pictures of beautiful women). The books are closer in character to today's fashion magazines than to collections of sample patterns; they seem to have existed simply for the pleasure provided by thumbing through them rather than for any practical purpose.

FORM AND CHARACTERISTICS OF HINAGATA-BON

Most of the printed kosode design books had dark blue covers, on which the book title was displayed in the center or on the left side (see cat. nos. 203–6). The pages were bound in a sleeve-type fold. Small books contained about twenty designs; larger ones may have had two hundred illustrations bound together or divided among two or more volumes. Three-volume sets with about one hundred designs were the most common type. A preface or postscript mainly noted the reason for publication or for the selection of the name of the collection, but earlier publications sometimes provided information that has since proven valuable to textile historians. The introduction to the three volumes of *Genji hinakata* (Genji patterns; 1687), for example, lists twenty-seven types of dyeing.

Most of the hinagata designs depicted the back view of the kosode with the pattern executed in black ink, but some contained front views, illustrations of the top or bottom half of the front of the garment, or depicted figures wearing kosode. Some were also printed in color.[5] In the kosode designs themselves there was a considerable degree of variation in the representation of the neckband, sleeves, hem, etc. Each design book had its own characteristic manner of depiction. Because almost all of the hinagata-bon were printed in black and white, the pattern and background colors, inseparable from the design itself, were indicated, along

FIGURE 21
Page from *On-hinagata manjoshū*
c. 1673–84

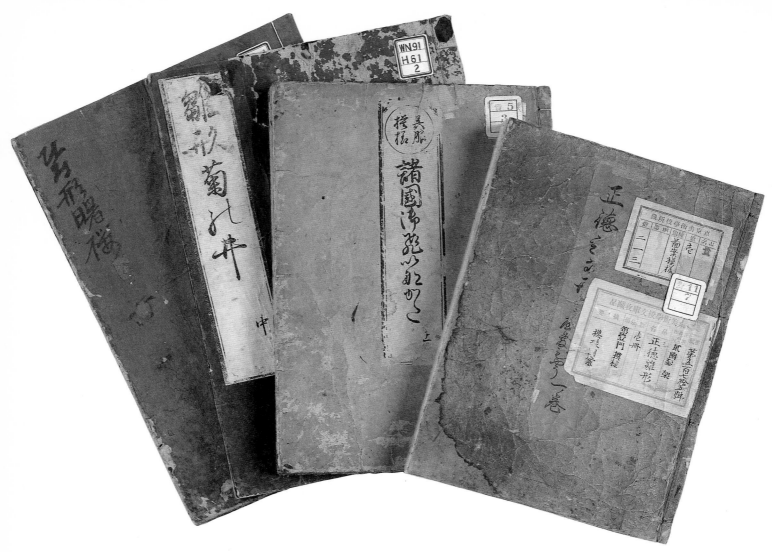

CATALOGUE NOS. 203–6

From left to right:

203

Shin hinagata akebonozakura, 1781

•

206

Hinagata kiku no i, 1719

•

204

*Gofuku moyō shokoku
on-hinakata*, 1668

•

205

Shōtoku hinagata, 1713

Tokyo National University of Fine
Art and Music

with the decorative techniques to be used, in the empty spaces of each composition. The content and position of these notations varied from book to book. The designs collected in the printed pattern books were mainly of kosode for adult women, but there were also design books of katabira, *yogi* (padded nightclothes), *yukata* (informal kimono worn after the bath), *katsugi* (kimono-shaped women's garments draped over the head for outdoor wear), kimono for young people and children, and infants' robes.[6] There were also design books organized according to the social position or age of the wearer, the places where kosode could be worn, or the background color of the kosode. *Shinpan kosode on-hiinakata* (Newly published kosode pattern book; 1677), for instance, is organized according to age and social position of the wearer and contains sections of designs for girls and boys, designs in the style of grand courtesans, and designs with short, rounded sleeves for matrons. *Shōtoku hinagata* (Patterns for the Shōtoku era; 1713) is divided into sections for various types of people: aristocrats, samurai, chōnin, courtesans, lower-ranking courtesans, bathhouse girls, young male prostitutes, and youthful rogues. The designs in *Shokoku on-hiinakata* (Patterns for many provinces; 1686) and *Hinagata sankōchō* (Pattern book: Finch; 1732) are grouped according to place or region: Gosho, Edo,

98

Owari, and Chūgoku in the former, and Miyako, Naniwa, and Azuma in the latter. In *Imayō on-hiinakata* (Up-to-the-minute patterns; 1685), volumes one and two contain designs for the four seasons, while *Miyako hiinakata* (Miyako patterns; 1691) is organized by background color into sections of scarlet, black, yellow ocher, gold, purple and light blue, and blackish brown.

In examining next the creators and "consumers" of kosode moyō hinagata-bon, it may be noted that with the rare exception of the appearance of the names of artists like Nishikawa Sukenobu (1671–1751), all the designs were drawn by anonymous illustrators. We can see, however, that the creation of the designs was sometimes allotted to separate craftsmen who acted as technical coordinators or pattern designers. For example, at the end of the table of contents for *Imayō on-hiinakata* the names of "Shigetsugu, technical coordinator for dyeing, resident of central Kyoto" and "Masanori, pattern designer" are noted. Although there are the names of a very few provincial artists included among the pattern designers, publishers are limited to Edo, Osaka, and primarily Kyoto, the center not only of textile weaving and dyeing but also of publishing.

The readers of kosode pattern books were the makers and purveyors of kosode as well as the women who wore them. One of the most important things to consider when making a kosode was the design: theme and motif and the method of fashioning the two into a unified composition. These elements always had to be new and consistent with current taste. Kosode moyō hinagata-bon must have been indispensable in choosing designs that were up-to-date. Among printed kosode pattern books, those in which the designs were colored by hand, those with specially decorated covers, and those with particular inscriptions inside the front cover may have been presented or lent to customers to encourage them to place orders.[7] This idea is supported by the illustration, in the first volume of *Nishikawa hinagata* (Nishikawa patterns; 1686), of three women sitting in a drawing room making selections from a pattern book, exclaiming, "What an unusual design," "Find one you like," and "I think I'll have this one."

Among the legacies of the period are a number of kosode that might have been made from particular hinagata-bon illustrations. Very few, however, follow faithfully the notations on color or decorative techniques. Here we might suppose that when the garment was actually made, the customer's personal taste was given full consideration. For example, the plain weave silk kosode patterned with camellias and weeping willows (cat. no. 99) corresponds almost exactly with the forty-first illustration in the *Hinagata kiku no i* (Printed patterns: The well of chrysanthemums; 1719; fig. 22). It is clear that the kosode was produced

based on this hinagata illustration, but whereas the latter indicates a white background, the garment itself is brown.

Similarly the dark blue chirimen kosode decorated with a pattern of wisteria and shoji screens (cat. no. 35) appears to have been adapted from number 159 of the *Kōrin hinagata wakamitori* (Kōrin-style printed patterns: Young green; 1727; fig. 23). Although the design illustration, entitled "Yoru no fuji" (Wisteria by night), indicates simple white forms created by paste resist and detailed with ink painting, the actual decorative techniques used include embroidery in various colors with pigments brushed in as

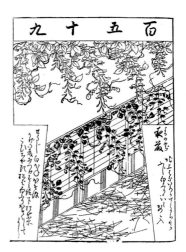

a substitute for the ink drawing. Comparing the light purple chirimen kosode with a design of blossoming plum branches seen through a window (cat. no. 26) with the hinagata illustration on the right-hand side of the second leaf of the second volume of *Ogurayama hyakushū hinagata* (Designs from one hundred poems of Mt. Ogura; 1688; fig. 24), we can see similarities in the cloud forms and in the way the branches of the plum tree hang down to the window. The Chinese characters for *old*, *village*, and *past*, included in the hinagata design, have been omitted from the kosode, however, and the plum blossoms have been exaggerated.

CATALOGUE NO. 26
*Kosode with Plum Tree and
Architectural Motif*
Late seventeenth–early eighteenth
century
Kanebo, Ltd.

•

FIGURE 24
Page from *Ogurayama hyakushū
hinagata*
1688

The preface to the fourth volume of *Onnayō kinmō zui* confirms that customer taste was taken into account. It notes: "By interchanging the right side of the design with the left or left with right, or top and bottom according to the imagination of the wearer, it is possible to change the design significantly to suit her taste." In general we can surmise that after the merchant received an order, made on the basis of a kosode moyō hinagata-bon, he would make a memo of technical details or enter them into an order book from which specifications for production would be written up and passed on to each artisan involved in the work.

CHANGES IN KOSODE STYLE AND
KOSODE MOYŌ HINAGATA-BON

It is possible to discern a connection between the rise of kosode design books and the ascent of so-called Kanbun designs or the Kanbun style (named for the Kanbun era, when the look was at its peak). According to one theory the Kanbun style was necessitated by historical events. As a result of the Great Fire of Meireki (1657), which destroyed more than half the city of Edo, there was, this explanation states, a sudden increase in the demand for new kosode that were not only beautiful but that could be quickly executed using simple techniques, abbreviating the complicated methods and processes of earlier decoration. In looking at the development of kosode during the early Edo period, however, it seems likely that the emergence of the Kanbun style was not a consequence of historical conditions, but a result of the aesthetic tastes of the newly wealthy chōnin exerting their influence on fashion. Regardless of which of these causes bears greater weight, it cannot have been an easy matter for clothing merchants to contrive large numbers of new garments fulfilling complex specifications as embodied in the Kanbun style. The rise of the kosode moyō hinagata-bon, then, which illustrated many different designs within a kosode form, precisely fulfilled the societal demands of the time. Moreover, while costly robes featuring the multicolored pictorial imagery of the preceding era had been created mainly for women of the ruling military elite, around the time of the Kanbun era an increasingly wealthy merchant class became consumers of fashion as well. It is easy to imagine that this factor contributed to the appearance of publications that could provide large numbers of kosode designs. Another factor might have been the dramatic change in the relationship of pattern to ground.

Until the Keichō and Kan'ei eras there was a tendency to decorate kosode by filling the surface with evenly distributed pattern elements (jinashi). From about the Kanbun era, however, both ground and pattern began to change. The ground became much like the canvas of a painting, occupying even the space under the pattern and acting as its support. Accordingly even the unpatterned areas had a positive meaning as necessary space within the design field of the kosode. In earlier styles color was generally subordinate to pattern; with the Kanbun style the decorative function of color came to play an important role as background, supporting the pattern and bringing it into relief.

At this point in the stylistic development of the kosode, when a design for a particular garment was determined, many factors had to be taken into consideration, including the overall balance of the composition, the harmony of background color with the color of each part of the pattern, and the choice of decorative techniques. Kosode design books must have been conceived so that they could be relied upon in making these decisions. It was probably in response to such considerations that, from the Kanbun era onward, in the majority of printed pattern books kosode designs were indicated by depicting the pattern within the outline of an unfolded kosode (usually a back view) with details of ground color and decorative techniques noted in the surrounding space. It should be recalled that in *Onna shoreishū*, one of the forerunners of the kosode moyō hinagata-bon, patterns were represented within the outlines of kosode folded and hung over the bars of ikō. This was an infelicitous mode of depiction from the viewpoint of showing the overall design composition of the garment. It was acceptable, however, because most of the patterns collected in this work were either of the katasuso type or jinashi type prevalent before the Kanbun era, in which the concept of ground in opposition to pattern was not yet clearly formed.

In contrast, we can see from the careful considerations outlined in the following passage from *On-hinagata manjoshū* that the kosode moyō hinagata-bon were actually used in determining the harmony of the ground color with the color scheme of the pattern:

> When the ground is red, dyed with safflower, the kanoko shibori should be medium blue. The tail of the phoenix is embroidered with black floss and outlined with gold thread. The leaves of the paulownia are executed in purple kanoko shibori, and the plum blossoms are dyed and embroidered with gold thread. But if the ground color is to be white, there should be both red and light blue kanoko shibori; the dyeing and embroidery are the same as in the former case. If the ground is to be blackish green [*tokusa*], it would be appropriate to embroider it in scarlet, purple, and peach.

The publication of kosode pattern books began to decline in the Tenmei era, and it is believed that their production ceased in 1820 with the *Banzai hiinakata* (Printed designs for ten thousand years). The causes for this can be summed up in the following three points. First of all, we can see stagnation in kosode design and dyeing techniques around this time. As the prefaces to hinagata-bon often noted, the purpose of the pattern books was to present the newest and most fashionable kosode designs and to introduce the techniques of dyeing, embroidery, and other methods that were employed in carrying out these designs. The *Banzai hiinakata*, a reprint of a hinagata-bon from a hundred years before, provides clear evidence that kosode design had become formulaic. In terms of techniques, already established methods gained in popularity. After the middle of the Kyōhō era more than half the designs in the vast majority of kosode moyō hinagata-bon were for kosode decorated by the *shiro-age* method of paste-resist dyeing. The use of embroidery as the sole means of decoration also showed a marked increase during this period.[8] From the latter half of the eighteenth century through the first

half of the nineteenth century, patterns of small, stylized motifs covering the entire kosode and conventionalized landscapes called *goshodoki* (both executed in shiro-age and/or embroidery; see cat. nos. 49–51) as well as allover patterns worked in kanoko shibori were favored (see cat. nos. 55–58). The dearth of new fashion ideas or techniques weakened the need for hinagata-bon.

The second reason for the decline of the pattern books lies in the trend toward concentration of the patterned area of the garment just below the waist, around the hem, or on the skirt, which accompanied the increased width of the obi. Because of this there was little leeway for variations in the composition of the design and little necessity for kosode design books that presented compositions of large-scale patterns covering the entire garment.

The third source of decline can be found in the periodic issuance, from the Shōtoku and Kyōhō eras onward, of sumptuary laws that made the wearing of luxurious and gorgeously decorated kosode increasingly difficult. At the same time, under the influence of these laws there was a drift toward a more restrained taste. As often seen in popular art and literature of the period, subdued patterns and colors, such as stripes and *komon* (very small-scale

CATALOGUE NO. 56
Furisode with Cranes, Boats,
and Pine Trees
First half nineteenth century
Kanebo, Ltd.

CATALOGUE NO. 57
Furisode with Plum Tree
Late eighteenth century
Tokyo National Museum

stencil motifs), came to be used for kosode. Thus there was not necessarily a need for hinagata-bon, with their wealth of dazzling designs.

All the design books published toward the end of the hinagata-bon era were mainly collections of skirt or hem patterns. These included *Shinpan tsuma moyō azuma hinagata* (Newly published skirt patterns in a design book of eastern Japan; 1769), *Tōsei miyako hinagata* (Contemporary designs from the capital; 1785), and *Shin hinagata chitose sode*. As noted above, these reflected contemporary fashion in kosode design; their publication was based on the demands of society. The fact must not be overlooked, however, that although kosode decorated only on the hem or skirt continued to be made long after this period (see cat. nos. 59–60), kosode moyō hinagata-bon featuring hem and skirt patterns were not. What caused their decline?

Scanning other sources on textiles while considering this issue, a group of bound materials very similar in composition to the kosode moyō hinagata-bon comes to mind: painted design books. Their printed kosode outlines are nearly the same as those in the kosode pattern books, but the designs are painted in with a brush instead of being printed (see fig. 25). Another difference is that most have no annotations on ground color or decorative techniques. The covers of the painted design books are decorated with stamped or stenciled patterns; the kosode designs are generally for hem, skirt, or waist-level decoration. That the books were used for kosode selection can be seen from statements printed on the inside cover or elsewhere. *Some hinagata* (Dye patterns), for example, includes the following inscription: "We would like each of you to select many patterns from this book and return it to us as quickly as possible." Hand-written notes on an illustration, apparently corresponding to a customer's wishes, also suggest that they were used to facilitate taking orders. This is supported by the first leaf of *Hinagata-bon*

FIGURE 25

Pages from *Uchikake hinakata*

1791

(Design book), which depicts two women, one looking at a sample book of hem patterns, the other scrutinizing a roll of undyed cloth (see fig. 26).

Although the names of the kimono merchants and dyers who must have used these painted design books are inscribed in them, there is no clear record of any of those involved in their publication, including the artists. Few are dated, but some contain publication information.[9] *Kamejirushi tōsei on-hinagata* (Tortoise-brand fashionable design book), for example, contains the following postscript: "Bunka 13 hinoe-ne chūshun" (mid-spring, the second month, nineteenth year of the sexagenary cycle, thirteenth year of Bunka [1816]). *Takejirushi on-hinagata* (Bamboo-brand design book) includes the postscript: "Bunsei 12, ushi 10 shinchō, Kyōshi Tachiuri Higashimachi, Naraya Hachibei, Rihei" (newly made in the tenth month of the twelfth year of Bunsei [1829], Kyoto, Tachiuri Higashimachi, by Naraya Hachibei and Rihei). The first leaf of *Uchikake hinakata* (Design book of outer robes)

FIGURE 26

Page from *Hinagata-bon*

Early to mid-1800s

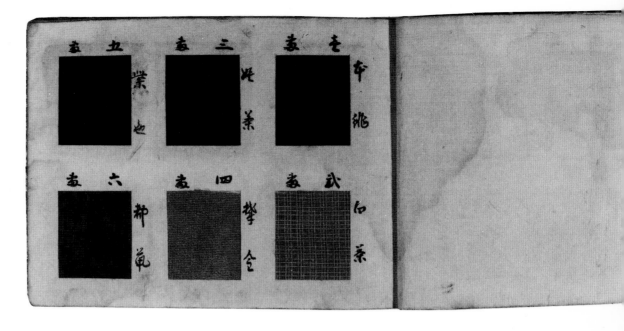

FIGURE 27
Page from *Fuku jirushi*
Mid- to late 1800s

notes: "Kansei 3, chūshun, kore wo utsusu Kyoto Emori Shige-yuki" (the third year of Kansei [1791], mid-spring, second month, Emori Shigeyuki of Kyoto copied this). From the latter example we can tell that the original must have been made before 1791.

Another group of bound materials also took the place of printed pattern books: dye-color sample books. Clearly these were made available to customers who were ordering kosode. Used by kimono merchants and dyers, they were smaller and more horizontal in format than kosode moyō hinagata-bon. The covers are similar to those of the painted design books; on each page are pasted four or six rectangular swatches of fabric with numbers above and color names to the right (for example, see *Fuku jirushi* [Marks of happiness], fig. 27). Also similar is the inclusion on the inside cover of the name and address of the merchant or dyer. Unlike the hand-painted design books, however, none are dated, making it even more difficult to determine when they were produced. From the similarity of their format to the hand-painted books, as well as from the close relationship between them and the color terms collected in *Tekagami moyō setsuyō* (Models of patterns for economical use), a kind of color lexicon published in 1789, it seems likely that the dye-color sample books were produced between the Kansei and Bunka eras.

Although there are divergences in designs and coloring, insofar as intended use is concerned, there is little difference between the hand-painted design books and the dye-color sample books, both of which seem to be similar to the printed pattern books. The fact that they originated at a time when the printed hinagata-bon were coming to an end makes it possible to propose the following hypothesis: hand-painted design books and dye-color sample books emerged as replacements for the kosode moyō hinagata-bon because there was a change in the relationship of the decorative function of pattern and ground. When the integral relationship between the two disappeared, a development that had its beginnings in the middle of the eighteenth century, kosode moyō hinagata-bon lost their essential purpose. On the occasion of ordering a kosode, painted design books were used to select a design, while dye-color sample books functioned primarily to provide the background color choices. The harmony between pattern and ground color was still taken into consideration, but attention was focused on a pattern or a color, rather than the two together. When choosing a design, the customer's eye was drawn to the details of the pattern and its expression. This idea is supported by the fact that a significant number of the hand-painted design books show, along with an allover view of a kosode with patterned hem or skirt, a detail of the pattern itself. Some even consist solely of enlargements of pattern details. In selecting the ground color, interest would be concentrated on subtle differences in shade or tone. Surviving dye-color sample books contain a great number of colors, finely distinguished one from another.

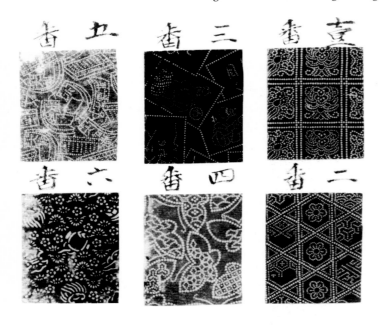

The popularity of komon during this period is also a result of this trend. In komon stencil dyeing, pattern and ground bear absolutely equal weight in decorative function but do not interact. Furthermore, the close similarity in organization and use between extant komon sample books (see fig. 28)[10] and dye-color sample books demonstrates that the two were employed together.

The change in the relationship between kosode pattern and ground color can be seen as a major cause for the decline of the kosode moyō hinagata-bon. During their life span, however, they sensitively reflected shifts in fashionable taste. For this reason, kosode moyō hinagata-bon are invaluable resources for tracing developments in Edo-period kosode design.

NOTES

1. Ueno 1974, 1:11.

2. *On-hiinakata* is also known as *Shinsen on-hiinagata*. *Hinakata*, *hiinakata* and *hiinagata* are variations on the spelling of *hinagata*. Hinagata-bon were published in multiple copies, like today's fashion magazines. Existing copies vary in their rarity. Marks made by the producers or users of the books contribute to their value.

3. Ueno 1974, 1:22.

4. Ibid.

5. Front views and representations of the top or bottom of the front of the kosode were often included in pattern books like the *Shin hinagata chitose sode* (New design book of sleeves for a thousand years), issued in 1800, toward the end of the period of hinagata publication. *Saishiki hinagata kokonoe nishiki* (Colorful patterns for multiple brocades; 1784) and *Some moyō gokusaishiki shin hinagata chiyo no sode* (Colorful dyed patterns: New design book of sleeves for a thousand ages; 1786) are examples printed in color.

6. For example, the first and second volumes of *Yūzen hiinakata* (Yūzen patterns; 1688) contain yogi, katabira, and yukata, while the fourth volume contains *fukusa* (gift covers) and obi.

7. Hand-colored hinagata illustrations can be seen in fig. 1 of *Toryū moyō hinagata Kyō no mizu* (Printed patterns in the style of the times: Waters of Kyoto; 1705). Quoted inscriptions can be found in the second volume of *Tōsei moyō hinagata hahakogusa* (Up-to-date printed patterns: Hahako grass; 1754) as well as at the back of the first volume of *Hinagata Kasuga-yama* (Printed patterns: Mt. Kasuga; 1768).

8. During this period both shiro-age and a style of embroidery known as *su-nui* were used to imitate ink drawing. They were characterized by fine lines, a limited color range, and a monochrome ground.

9. While most are undated, the author has sought and provided examples of dated volumes.

10. *Tōsei komon-chō* (Book of fashionable komon) consists of two volumes in a horizontal format between covers of thick paper decorated with a stamped pattern. On the inside cover of the first is the question, "Which is your favorite pattern in this book of komon designs?"; the second asks that "each of our customers please choose many patterns from this komon book and then return it to us as soon as possible." Six komon samples are attached to each side of each folded page.

The development of *yūzen-zome* (yūzen dyeing) was essential to the establishment of a new pictorialism in kosode decoration. The technique drew design inspiration from traditional sources and incorporated known materials and methods, yet the old was refashioned to create the new. By discussing the combination of both old and new elements in yūzen dyeing, an understanding of its importance and popularity can be gained. ❧ Resist dyeing, of which yūzen-zome is an example, is a process in which some substance (paper, yarn, wax, paste, etc.) is applied to cloth to prevent dye penetration. The areas covered or compressed by the resist medium remain unaffected by the dye. Yūzen dyeing involves four main steps. The process begins when outlines of a design are drawn on the fabric. Using a cloth tube fitted with a metal tip, a fine ribbon of starch paste is then applied to this drawing. After the paste has dried, dyes of various colors are brushed within the starch boundaries, which prevent the bleeding of one color into another. The paste is then washed away, leaving fine white lines between components of the design. Utilizing the freedom afforded by resist paste and subjecting the fabric to a complex series of other processes results in multicolored, richly varied patterning.[1] ❧ Yūzen dyeing is named for the man traditionally believed to have perfected the process, Miyazaki Yūzen, an artist-monk who was a fan painter active in the late 1600s and early 1700s. He supposedly lived in the Monzen-chō area of Kyoto, in Higashi-yama ward, outside the gate of the famous Chion'in, the main temple of the Jōdo sect of Buddhism. The streets of Monzen-chō were filled with establishments unique to that area, particularly the workshops of makers of Buddhist altars and ritual implements. Also situated there were the inns that took in pilgrims from all over Japan. Once these pious worshippers had completed their obeisances at the Chion'in, the pleasures of Gion-machi, the nearby entertainment district, beckoned.[2] ❧ Painted fans from Yūzen's brush were extremely popular at the time, indispensable for every big spender in the pleasure quarters. Why did these wealthy, hedonistic men, who were highly educated and possessed refined aesthetic sensibilities, take such pleasure in these fans? The answer lies in the subjects Yūzen depicted. His fan paintings did not merely illustrate grasses and flowers, birds and landscapes, but often included allusions to the world of classical literature, such as the poems of the *Kokin wakashū* (Poems of past and present ages) or the *Genji monogatari* (Tale of Genji).[3] For example, one design for a fan painting (fig. 29a) shows a Chinese-style wooden pestle

CATALOGUE NO. 31
Kosode with Screens and Hawks
(detail)
First half eighteenth century
Tokyo National Museum

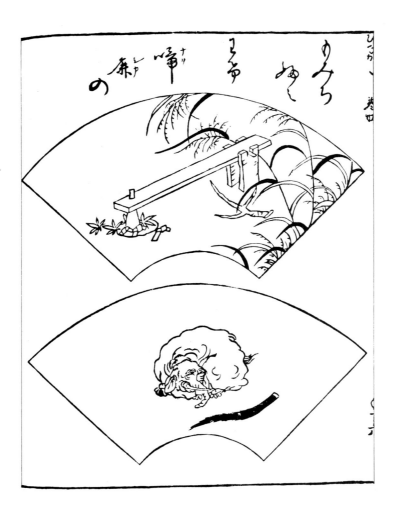

in a clump of autumn grasses. A folded letter and branch of maple leaves spill out of the stone mortar, which is partially buried in the ground beneath the pounding end of the pestle. Near the grasses lies a splendid staghorn. Outside the outline of the fan are the words "momiji fumiwake naku shika no" (Stepping among the maple leaves, the deer cries). This design was inspired by a poem from the autumn section of the *Kokin wakashū*.[4]

What, though, is the relationship between Miyazaki Yūzen and textile design? Evidently the involvement began when he painted illustrations inspired by the *Genji monogatari* in *sumi* (Chinese ink) on a *haori* (half coat) for Wanya Kyūbei, a merchant from Osaka. Yūzen was not alone in painting pictures on clothing for his patrons; it was an accepted practice for popular artists of the day (see Singer essay). It is significant, however, that the subject was the *Genji monogatari*, indicative of Yūzen's special talent in introducing literary themes into decorative designs.

As requests for textile designs gradually increased, they eventually became the mainstay of the artist's work. This may have encouraged him to explore technical possibilities, which in turn may have led to the development of the new dyeing technique.

Yūzen-zome became so popular that other types of dyeing fashionable at the time quickly fell into disuse.

This sudden popularity might be attributed to any number of causes, including the enthusiasm for designs incorporating literary allusions, but the author concurs with the words of Yūjinsai Kiyochika, who is thought to have been a student of Yūzen. He wrote in the preface to *Yūzen hiinakata* (Yūzen patterns; 1688):

> Yūzen dyeing encompasses old-fashioned [*kofū*] but elegant traditions. But if that were all, it would not have achieved its current popularity. On top of emphasizing the exquisite traditions of olden times, yūzen dyeing reflected a fresh sensibility that was always contemporary [*imayō*]. It appealed to the highest and the lowest—from the sheltered lady whose skin was never touched by the sun to the maid with mud-bespattered feet—becoming the fashion of the day.

By explaining the content and manner of kofū and imayō, the old and the new, the essential character of yūzen dyeing should become clear.

KOFŪ

The preface to *Yūzen hiinakata* states: "The images incorporated in yūzen dyeing express the sense or feeling of classical poems or take as their themes the meanings of old sayings." The literary content of yūzen designs is evident here, just as in Yūzen's fan paintings. The practice of taking literary themes and incorporating them in textile or clothing design had a long history in Japan[5] and can be found occasionally in Heian-period works, such as *Eiga monogatari* (A tale of flowering fortunes). It is related in this source that at a spring poetry-reading party at the empress's palace in April 1056, Lady Shin Shōnagon's costume was decorated with a design of a pond surrounded by wisteria, alluding to a poem from the *Kokin wakashū*:

wa ga yado no	Cascades of flowers
ike no fujinami	bloom on the wisteria
sakinikeri	by my garden lake.
yamahototogisu	When might the mountain cuckoo
itsu ka kinakamu	come with his melodious song?[6]

Sometimes Heian court ladies made allusions to Chinese poems from the *Wakan rōeishū*[7] (Collection of Japanese and Chinese poems for recitation) by means of the combinations of colors chosen for their many layers of robes. In the case of designs for yūzen dyeing, an example of using literary allusions for kosode appears in a *Yūzen hiinakata* illustration (fig. 29b). The design is drawn from the ninth section of *Ise monogatari* (Tales of Ise),

FIGURE 29b
Page from *Yūzen hiinakata*
1688

which concerns the courtier Ariwara Narihira's travels in eastern Japan.[8] The passage in question reads:

> Once a certain man decided that it was useless for him to remain in the capital. With one or two old friends, he set out toward the east in search of a province in which to settle. Since none of the party knew the way, they blundered ahead as best they could, until in time they arrived at a place called Yatsuhashi in Mikawa Province. (It was a spot where the waters of a river branched into eight channels, each with a bridge, and thus it had come to be called Yatsuhashi—"Eight Bridges.") Dismounting to sit under a tree near this marshy area, they ate a meal of parched rice. Someone glanced at the clumps of irises that were blooming luxuriantly in the swamp. "Compose a poem on the subject, 'A Traveler's Sentiments,' beginning each line with a syllable from the word 'iris' [*kakitsubata*]," he said. The man recited,

*ka*ragoromo	I have a beloved wife,
*ki*tsutsu narenishi	familiar as the skirt
*tsu*ma shi areba	of a well-worn robe,
*ha*rubaru kinuru	and so this distant journeying
*ta*bi o shi zo omou	fills my heart with grief.

> They all wept onto their dried rice until it swelled with the moisture.[9]

This famous passage is commonly illustrated by a design of irises and plank bridges and often appeared on Edo-period kosode (see cat. nos. 121–22).

CATALOGUE NO. 121
Kosode with Plank Bridges
(Yatsuhashi), *Irises, and Butterflies*
First half nineteenth century
Los Angeles County Museum of Art, gift of Miss Bella Mabury,
M.39.2.9

CATALOGUE NO. 122
Furisode with Plank Bridges
(Yatsuhashi), *Irises, and Swallows*
Late eighteenth–early nineteenth century
Los Angeles County Museum of Art, gift of Mrs. Philip A. Colman in memory of Philip A. Colman,
M.90.8

FIGURE 29c–d
Pages from *Yūzen hiinakata*
1688

Other illustrations employ allusive imagery from the *Genji monogatari*. One, for example, drawing from the "Suma" chapter, pictures Prince Genji, who has been exiled to the shores of Suma, longing for the capital as he looks out across the water at a boat retreating into the distance (see fig. 29c). From the "Akashi" chapter comes an image of the prince traveling to see a lady he has come to love in his exile. His journey is depicted in a seashore scene (see fig. 29d).[10]

Many of the designs in Yūzen's own *Yosei hinakata* (Patterns of lingering charm; 1692) also employ imagery derived from literature. The sources include the story "Kado itsutsu" (The well crib at the gate) from *Ise monogatari* and a design based on the "Wakamurasaki" (Lavender) chapter of the *Genji monogatari*. A katabira in the exhibition (cat. no. 49) is decorated with imagery from the latter.

In contrast with these designs built on literary allusions are purely decorative motifs of flowers and grasses. It is evident from many objects in the Shōsō-in imperial repository that by the Nara period such designs had already reached a high level of perfection in Japan.[11] In the Heian period, motifs of flowers and grasses developed from an aesthetic sensibility based on an incomparable love of autumn plants. *Yūzen hiinakata* abounds with designs that drew on this tradition (see fig. 29e, cat. nos. 71 left and right, 72).

FIGURE 29e
Page from *Yūzen hiinakata*
1688

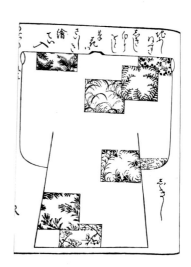

CATALOGUE NO. 71

Kosode on Screen

Left: Kosode fragment with water,
maple leaves, and autumn grasses
Mid-eighteenth century
Right: Kosode fragment with
autumn flowers and plovers
First half eighteenth century
National Museum of Japanese
History, Nomura Collection

CATALOGUE NO. 72

*Furisode with Stream and
Bush Clover* (Hagi)
First half nineteenth century
Kanebo, Ltd.

CATALOGUE NO. 129

Kosode with Vertical Bands of Sedge
Hats, Fans, and Characters (detail)
Mid-eighteenth century
Okajima Collection

FIGURE 30

Page from *Shokoku on-hiinakata*

1686

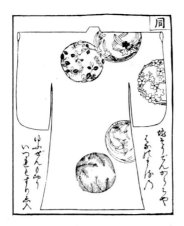

Floral roundels (see cat. no. 13) were among the earliest of yūzen motifs, appearing in *Shokoku on-hiinakata* (Patterns for many provinces; 1686; fig. 30). These too were derived from ancient traditions. They appear in the polychrome patterns of Heian-period Buddhist paintings and on the gold and silver fittings of some of the seven amulets preserved at Shi-tennō-ji monastery in Osaka.[12]

Just as yūzen designs often drew from traditional sources, so did yūzen-dyeing techniques. For example, consider the use of paste resist.[13] When this technique was first used in Japan is unclear, but a box wrapper of tanned leather with a design of grapes and vines in the Shōsō-in collection may have been patterned this way.[14] The preface to *Yūzen hiinakata* makes special mention of the use of paste-resist techniques in yūzen dyeing: "Yūzen dyeing employs underdrawings of the desired design. Then the cloth is divided into separate areas by means of either resist paste or *kukushi*. The picture is painted in, however, without correcting the outlines."

Kukushi, another traditional method, was a shibori technique in which areas of cloth were reserved in white by binding or clamping before dyeing. The crimson chirimen furisode in the collection of the Association for Yūzen History (fig. 31) is a representative example of kukushi. The garment features a bold design of *noshi* (bundled decorative streamers used as offerings). Each strip is embellished with a different pattern. The most likely method of executing this complex work would have involved first reserving in white the broad outlines of the streamers by means of shibori, then applying resist paste to the fine details of the underdrawing, and finally brushing in the dyes. Many examples of shibori appear in the Shōsō-in collection; it is probably safe to say that it is a much older and more basic technique than paste resist. Another method was to accent yūzen-dyed designs with areas of color created by nuishime shibori or *tsuke-zome* (dip-dyeing; see cat. nos. 31–32, 105, 129, 137).

Two further points remain to be discussed concerning the regard for tradition in the techniques associated with yūzen dyeing. The first is the use of embroidery. Highly refined examples dating back to ancient China include those excavated from a Former (Western) Han tomb (no. 1; c. 170 B.C.) at Mawangtui,

FIGURE 31

Furisode with Noshi

Mid-eighteenth century

Paste resist (yūzen dyeing), stenciled gold leaf (surihaku), and embroidery on red figured silk

Center back: 61 ⅝ in. (156.5 cm)

Association for Yūzen History

Important Cultural Property

CATALOGUE NO. 32
Kosode with Fence, Maple Branches,
and Plum Blossoms
Mid-eighteenth century
National Museum of Japanese
History, Nomura Collection

Kosode with Japanese Roses, Rocks,
Water, and Characters
Mid-eighteenth century
Tabata Collection

Changsha.[15] The embroidery accompanying yūzen dyeing fails to fully exploit the already proven potential of the medium. It was introduced merely as a means of adding gold and the particular red achieved by dyeing with safflower (see Bethe essay). Gold was desired because the metallic thread reflected light and gave an opulent effect. The story of red was more complicated. There is a great deal of red in yūzen dyeing, but this was obtained from cochineal. This cold, clear red, with its blue undertones, could not satisfy the aesthetic sensibilities of Edo-period society. Beni-red, however, with its warm, luminous, yellow undertones, was indispensable. It is precisely this shade that represented the Japanese sense of color. Because the beauty of beni could only be achieved by vat dyeing, it was not suited to the yūzen technique, in which the colors, including those of the background, were applied by brush (in order to avoid damaging the delicate lines of resist paste). Thus the device of embroidering with beni-red thread was conceived as a means of introducing this beloved crimson into yūzen fabrics.

The other technique that typically augmented yūzen dyeing was the abundant use of *bokashi* (shading or bleeding). Designs of flower petals, leaves, and feathers could be shaded with two different colors or two tones of the same color by using this technique. It too, like beni, resonated with something in the Japanese aesthetic sense. The decorative arts of the Heian period abundantly utilized bokashi; from the introduction to *Makura no sōshi* (The pillow book) we can see that the courtiers of the day interpreted the beauties of nature as deriving from the beauty of bokashi, from one thing shading into another.[16] These traditions achieved a new prominence with the flourishing of yūzen dyeing.

IMAYŌ

From both *Yūzen hiinakata* and in actual kosode of the eighteenth century it is clear that yūzen dyeing, while drawing from ancient traditions, introduced a "fresh sensibility." The range of themes became significantly broader, with human figures becoming popular as a subject for kosode design (see cat. nos. 34, 37–38). Before the development of yūzen dyeing the effective representation of human forms was extremely difficult, although not entirely absent.[17]

The appearance of fully developed landscapes represents another new trend in design themes. *Murasaki Shikibu nikki* (Diary of Murasaki Shikibu; c. 1010)[18] notes that ladies of the court had designs featuring landscape elements painted on their skirts. As we have seen previously (in the case of Heian-period clothing), however, there was always a literary theme, from poetry or elsewhere, underlying such depictions. The pure rendering of landscapes had to wait for the development of yūzen dyeing, for it was yūzen techniques that made such representation possible. The designs in *Yūzen hiinakata* are still rather literary and cannot really be characterized as realistic scenery, but the previously mentioned images from the "Suma" and "Akashi" chapters of the *Genji monogatari* are examples of this new trend. While serving as examples of kofū themes (literature), they contain an imayō element (pure landscape) as well. In addition, insofar as Prince Genji is represented in the images, they should also be noted as portrayals of the human figure.

All of the following extant examples of landscape designs charm the eye with their technical virtuosity: various scenes of the "Eight Views of Ōmi" (cat. nos. 105, 107), Sumiyoshi (cat. nos. 103–4), famous scenic spots of Kyoto (cat. no. 111), the pleasure quarters of Yoshiwara in Edo (cat. no. 110), and scenes from the fifty-three stages of the Tōkaidō represented as if on folding screens (cat. no. 100). As noted above, these would not be possible without the techniques of yūzen dyeing, without painting directly on cloth with dyes. It was the desires of the fashionable world of the Edo period, a delight in designs featuring human figures and landscapes, that yūzen dyeing satisfied.

These designs also reflected the interest in visiting famous scenic spots and historical places in every region of Japan, an activity that grew increasingly popular beginning in the Genroku era. This interest was demonstrated by the publication in rapid succession of various types of books intended as guides to the Kyoto area. The touristic passion for travel was related to a growing prosperity and capacity for leisure. At the same time, however, it pointed to a desire to approach things objectively, to examine an

CATALOGUE NO. 38
Furisode with Tea-picking Scenes
(detail)
First half nineteenth century
Tokyo National Museum

KIRIHATA

127

object with one's own eyes. There were writers active during the period who might be described as embodying this spirit, including Ihara Saikaku, Matsuo Bashō, and Chikamatsu Monzaemon.[19]

Designs based on literary imagery were previously mentioned as a tradition originating in the Heian period and cited as an

FIGURE 32
Page from *On-hiinakata*
1667

example of the kofū sensibility. Miyazaki Yūzen is credited with their reintroduction. The revival in the early modern period of the practice of using literary allusions predated the emergence of yūzen dyeing, however. A kosode illustration from *On-hiinakata* (Design patterns; 1667; fig. 32) featuring giant characters that read *Waka no ura*[20] demonstrates how Kanbun designs treated classical poetry. Yūzen's achievement, which provides a glimpse of the imayō mentality, was his reintroduction of literary images through pictorial representation, which led to yūzen dyeing.

From comments in the preface to *Yūzen hiinakata* we can see that yūzen dyeing also introduced new techniques: "When the colors are immersed in water, they do not run, and no matter what kind of silk is used, it remains soft." This comment shows that although these two qualities are now, of course, an essential feature of yūzen dyeing (and, in fact, of all types of dyeing),

in those days they were considered amazing new advantages. It also suggests that the colors used in other dyeing methods were unstable and that in order to fix them it was necessary to use some type of oil or other substance that detracted from the original pliancy of the fabric.

CONCLUSION

The essence and appeal of yūzen dyeing at the time it emerged has been explored here, with particular attention being paid to the words "encompasses old-fashioned but elegant traditions . . . [while reflecting] a fresh sensibility that was always contemporary." Today yūzen dyeing is still flourishing in many workshops. Since it first developed during the Genroku era, the technique has changed in response to the tastes of each succeeding period. By its adaptability and beauty yūzen dyeing has continued to blend the old-fashioned with the contemporary, being rediscovered by each new generation.

NOTES

1. For a more detailed description of the yūzen-dyeing technique see Stinchecum 1984, 35–38.

2. The unabashed combining of religious devotion and worldly pleasure was common in Japan. In fact, as C. J. Dunn points out, in the seventeenth century pleasure was the main objective of most pilgrims. Even near the great shrine of Ise, Japan's most sacred Shinto precinct, there was a street of brothels, eating establishments, and souvenir shops; itinerant entertainers added to the attractions. See Dunn 1987, 80–81.

3. The *Kokin wakashū*, the first of twenty-one imperial anthologies, was compiled about 905 by Ki no Tsurayuki (c. 872–945), Ki no Tomonori (fl. c. 850?–904?), Ōshikōchi Mitsune (fl. 898–922), and Mibu no Tadamine (fl. 898–920). This collection of thirty-one-syllable waka was divided into two parts: seasonal and love themes. *Genji monogatari*, a narrative description of life at the Heian court, was written by Murasaki Shikibu (d. 1014) in the early eleventh century. These and other works often provided imagery for the visual arts, particularly in the early modern period.

4. See Takeda essay for an alternate translation of the complete poem.

5. Miyazaki Yūzen revived this tradition after a long period (from the late twelfth century to the mid-seventeenth century) when it seems that literary allusions were not used on clothing. By Yūzen's day the clientele for such clothing had expanded to include the newly wealthy chōnin.

6. The story is from the "Ne-awase" (Root-matching contest) chapter of *Eiga monogatari*, a historical chronicle in narrative form written in the eleventh century. The work, in two parts, describes court life from the mid-tenth century to 1028 and from 1029 to 1092. See McCullough and McCullough 1980 for an English translation of the first part. The poem is from the spring section of the *Kokin wakashū*, no. 135; see McCullough 1985, 437.

7. The *Wakan rōeishū* was an anthology of poems and fragments of poems compiled about 1013 by Fujiwara Kintō (966–1041).

8. *Ise monogatari*, probably compiled in the first half of the tenth century, combines the thirty-one-syllable waka of Narihira (825–80) and some anonymous poems from the *Kokin wakashū* to form a rudimentary narrative framework of more than 120 short sections. See McCullough 1968.

9. McCullough 1968, 74–75. Japanese orthography allows the substitution of *ha* for *ba* for the first syllable of the poem's fourth line.

10. Murasaki 1979, 237–38, 262–64.

11. The Shōsō-in repository, in the precinct of Todai-ji, a temple in Nara, contained a collection of artifacts donated between 741 and 768. The most significant of these objects were associated with the emperor Shōmu (d. 756). They were given by his widow, the empress Kōmyō, in 756 and 757 to commemorate his death. Other treasures were subsequently stored in the wooden structure, lying virtually undisturbed until the nineteenth century. The contents are now preserved in a modern research facility.

12. Illustrated in Okada 1958, 14, fig. 23.

13. Paste resist might be considered the most important technical innovation of yūzen dyeing, but this is not the case. This is evident from the existence at the time of its introduction of other dyeing modes that also employed resist paste, such as *chaya-zome* (see cat. nos. 41–44, 97–98), a method of vat-dyeing with several shades of indigo against a reserved white background, and *sarasa-zome*, an earlier style of patterning derived from Indian and Indonesian fabrics. A passage from *Genji hinakata* (Genji patterns; 1687) confirms that sarasa-zome involved the use of paste resist: "Sarasa-zome is created with resist paste and pigments for coloring."

14. Matsumoto 1984, 142–43, pl. 119.

15. See Hunan Provincial Museum 1973 for several examples.

16. *Makura no sōshi*, a selection of observations of court life, nature, and human character, was written in the early eleventh century by a court lady, Sei Shōnagon (c. 966–c. 1017), known for her astuteness and wit. See Morris 1971.

17. One rare example from the early Edo period is an embroidered textile fragment showing fishermen. See Kyoto Shoin 1985, 8:39, pl. 47.

18. See Bowring 1963.

19. Matsuo Bashō (1644–94) was a haiku poet best known for his travel diaries with embedded poems, the most famous of which was *Oku no hosomichi* (On the narrow road to the far north). Chikamatsu Monzaemon (1653–1724) wrote pathos-filled plays for the Osaka bunraku theater, including *Sonezaki shinjū* (Love suicides at Sonezaki). Their works have been widely translated into English.

20. Waka no ura, in present-day Wakayama Prefecture, is one of the *uta makura* (places celebrated in poetry). Designs based on it appear in many printed kosode moyō hinagata-bon, beginning with *On-hiinakata*, and were very popular during the early and mid-Edo periods.

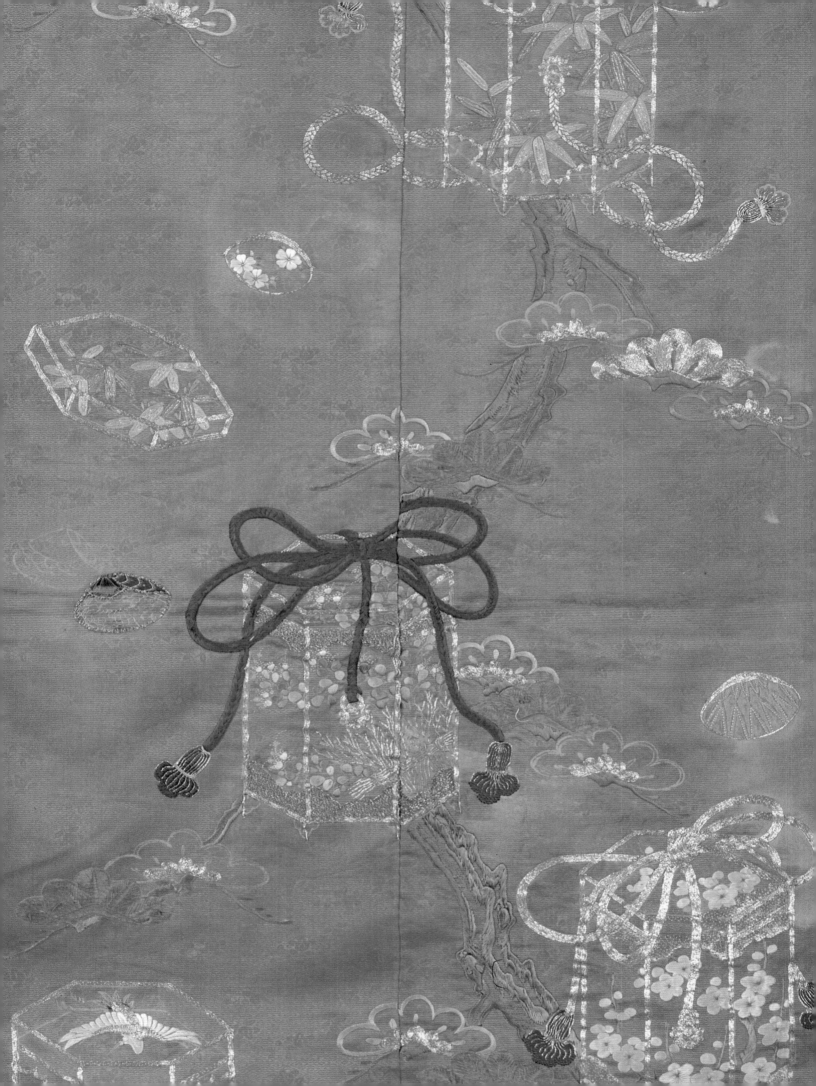

Reflections on *Beni*:
Red as a Key to Edo-Period Fashion

MONICA BETHE

Each of the varied colors and shades of Edo-period kosode has its own history, a story of complex social and economic interaction. The production of each color fluctuated in response to a demand swayed by changing fashion. Influenced by developments in agriculture, trade, transportation, and dye techniques, the colors had their beginnings in the fields where dye stuffs were cultivated. They then passed through the hands of several middlemen and traveled along the roads and waterways of Japan to the dealers, dyers, and tailors in the central cities, who fulfilled the requests of fashion-conscious women, actors, and dandies. ❧ To comprehend the significance of these hues, it is important to understand that the concept of color has strong metaphoric and cultural implications for the Japanese. To begin with, the Japanese word for color, *iro*, refers to far more than tints and hues. Its original meaning, as it appears in eighth-century poems, translates as "love" or "passion."[1] Even today the word carries overtones of intimacy and attractiveness. It can refer to a countenance, a look, a sweetheart, or to sensual pleasure. The Edo dandy was in search of the *iromekashii* (colored) and the *iroppoi* (colorful), which are roughly equivalent to the amorous, fascinating, and seductive. A woman who "has color" (*irokke ga aru*) is sexy. ❧ A garment that "has color" (*iro ari*), however, is one that contains the color red.[2]

Red is felt to be charming, alluring, an evocation of the innate attractiveness of youth. Worn by a young woman, the color brings out the blush in her cheeks. When worn by an older woman, it appears entirely inappropriate, brash and gaudy. Her garments must be *iro nashi* (without red). This equation goes far back in Japanese history and remains even today in women's fashions. A gray-haired woman would be embarrassed to appear in bright red or pink but readily wears lavender, whose soberer tone is considered more appropriate to maturity. *Red* here refers to such colors as *beni*, *kurenai*, and *kōbai*, shades of deepening pink extracted from the petals of the *benibana* (safflower).[3] It is difficult to translate into English the exact range of shades produced by this flower. Some translators have equated it with scarlet, others, with crimson.[4] ❧ The social, cultural, and literary connotations of a color added to its purely optical impact. In prehistoric times many colors were associated with the plant sources, often medicinal, from which they were derived. Colors were seen as embodying the spirit of the plant from which they were extracted. It was believed as well that dye processes transferred the medicinal (magical) potency of a dye plant to the colored cloth.[5] An extract of the yellow dye from the bark of the *kihada* (philodendron), for example, could be imbibed to settle a stomachache; it could be applied externally to treat skin disorders. By extension it was thought that wearing garments dyed in kihada next to the skin served as protection against rashes. Benibana, introduced into Japan from China in about the fifth century, proved effective against fever;[6] as a pesticide it helped preserve the cloth onto which it was dyed.

In the Nara and Heian periods dyers were court attendants and retainers. Poems and novels of the time suggest that dyeing processes as well as peculiarities of the dye plants were general knowledge. Both served as metaphors in the *Man'yōshū*, creating a cultural fund of imagery and associations that persists to this day. For example, beni-red became a symbol of alluring love, but since the dye is light sensitive, it also suggested interest that faded easily.[7] The long roots of *murasaki* (gromwell), which dye purple, became a metaphor for undying love, while the delicate balance of red and blue in the extracted purple dye stood for *yukari* (a true bond of feeling).[8]

In the Nara period the magical importance of color was given cosmological dimensions through the introduction of the Chinese theory of *gogyō*, which associates the primary colors with such things as virtues, animals, grains, organs, tastes, smells, and the points of the compass.[9] In accordance with this the Japanese established a system of court ranks indicated by the color of robes and/or hats (*kan'i*).[10] In this way certain colors were restricted to the uppermost levels of society.

The association of specific colors with court ranks continued through the Heian period. In addition, *kasane iro* (the layering of solid colors) became a refined aesthetic reflecting the sensitivity of the wearer. Most of the combinations that developed were based either on contrast or the juxtaposition of closely related colors, such as dark and light shades of the same hue. These combinations often bore names derived from nature, like *fuji* (wisteria; purple over green) and *ume* (plum; white on dark red). Designated colors came to be considered appropriate for particular seasons: white with green for early spring; pink, lavender, and green for late spring; yellow with maroon for summer; purple or red with white for late fall into winter.[11]

Five centuries later, in the Edo period, similar color combinations drawn from nature were translated into decorative patterning on a single garment. Seasonal appropriateness remained a primary concern. Social ranking reflected in color, which had lapsed during the medieval period, was again reinstated through numerous sumptuary laws.[12] The most frequently restricted colors were murasaki and beni-red, the former to be worn only by the nobility and highest clergy, and the latter, meant for the samurai class and above.

The choice of these colors had an economic as well as historical basis. Dyeing with benibana, for example, was extremely expensive and laborious, requiring as many as twelve pounds of petals for one kosode. This gave rise to the proverb "ikkō, ichigon" (a pound of beni is worth a pound of gold).[13] Material dyed with benibana spoke money. Laws limiting its use were not only an attempt to keep certain classes of society in their place but also were aimed at regulating the economy.

Historically, the Heian-period restriction of deep shades of safflower dye to the very highest court ranks set a precedent. At that time the layered combination of graduated shades from crimson to pink (*kurenai no nioi*), even if considered gaudy by some, was a clear proclamation of high-class status.[14]

When the Heian nobility lost its power to the military, however, restrictions on clothing and colors proved difficult to maintain. In 1471 the government withdrew all laws limiting the use of benibana dye.[15] Young warriors were free to wear red *dōbuku* (a short jacket) and to decorate their armor with red cords.[16] A comment in the fifteenth-century diary of Ninagawa Chikamoto, a retainer of the Ashikaga shogunate, suggests that sporting beni-red garments had become quite common, for he remarks on the restraint of one man at a Hosokawa family dog chase who wore a robe "without red."[17]

By the second half of the sixteenth century, the time of Oda Nobunaga and Toyotomi Hideyoshi, clothing had become more lavish; beni-red robes appeared everywhere. We are fortunate to have examples preserved today, although the bright hues have generally faded to tan, dimming the original effect (see cat. no. 2 left). Beni-red appeared in tsujigahana (see cat. no. 1 right), nuihaku, and *karaori* (brocade). Indeed the ubiquitous presence of this shade in Momoyama-period robes led the textile historian Kirihata Ken to classify the period as the "age of beni."[18]

The transition years into the Edo period were marked by a love of gold and silver foil. To offset these glittering designs, dark grounds were preferred (see cat. nos. 4 right, 6). Their sobriety was relieved by tie-dyed patches of white and beni-red and embroidered highlights of beni-red and other colors. It was at this time that the third Tokugawa shogun, Iemitsu, issued sumptuary restrictions on the use of benibana dye.

Sumptuary laws, by instituting guidelines for and prohibiting excess expenditures by all levels of society, established visible class distinctions and helped maintain the status quo. The proclamations regulated clothing, dye colors, styles of entertainment, and the consumption of goods.[19] As a result, they were in part responsible for setting fashion. They also had the effect of encouraging the use of unrestricted colors and stimulating ways of circumventing the letter of the law.

Since enforcement of sumptuary laws was inconsistent, an appraisal of how they were ignored is as much our concern as how they were followed. Often flouted openly after a few days, as the phrase "mikka hatto" (three-day laws) implies, the regulations required repeated reissuing. Frequent attacks on the same dye color suggest a widespread use of the forbidden substance. In this sense the ineffectiveness of the laws is as telling as their contents.

The inventive imagination of the merchant class came to the fore as its members searched for methods to indulge their tastes and also stay within the law. "Ikazu, korosazu" (don't step out of bounds, and you won't be killed), went the proverb. In the dye world, methods of circumvention included experimentation with complex techniques of top-dyeing and an innovative use of mordants.[20] Dyers found they could imitate forbidden colors without using the prohibited dye plant. *Suō* (sappanwood), imported in quantity on Dutch ships, could be top-dyed with a warm yellow (such as the dye extracted from *kuchinashi* [gardenia seeds]) and mordanted with alum or tin, also a frequent item on Dutch trading ships, to produce a good likeness of the red dyed with safflower.[21] This "fake" beni-red (*nise kurenai*) had as its counterpart "fake" purple (*nise murasaki*), which was also dyed with sappanwood but which used iron as a mordant. Fake purple, of a slightly redder tone than true purple dyed with gromwell roots, became quite popular in Edo and led to redder shades of purple being known as "Edo murasaki." According to the dyer Murakami Tetsurō, a dark shade of fake purple was probably the color the *ninja* (spies) wore.[22]

It is likely that experimentation leading to "fake" colors was implied in the edict of the fifth Tokugawa shogun, Tsunayoshi, when in 1683 he forbade "new and unusual weaving and dyeing."[23] The sumptuary laws of 1683 also specified red as being off-limits to the merchant class, even imported red wool.

Circumvention of sumptuary laws may also be one cause for the mid-seventeenth-century (Kan'ei-Kanbun eras) shift in palette from dark colors to a greater prominence of white. Some scholars

CATALOGUE NO. 21
Kosode with Snowflake Roundels,
Mandarin Orange Tree, and
Scattered Fans
Early eighteenth century
Kawashima Textile Museum

have seen in this a reaction to laws restricting the use of gold and silver, which were particularly resplendent against a dark ground.

The effectiveness of the sumptuary laws, moreover, related directly to the personality of the shogun. While Iemitsu promulgated forty-two sumptuary laws[24] and Tsunayoshi, known for the harshness of his edicts, issued fifty-nine, neither felt constrained to curb their own display of wealth and power nor that of the daimyo class. Despite severe restrictions on merchant-class expenditures, fashions were increasingly ornate. Enforcement of the law tended to be intermittent and exemplary. Particularly famous is the confiscation of property and banishment from Edo of Ishikawa Rokubei after the public appearance of his wife and her attendants in overly ostentatious clothing, including beni-red kosode. Such punishment served as a reminder to others but must have been exceptional, for the incident is singled out by many.[25]

Lax enforcement made possible the flamboyant and luxurious clothing of the Genroku era. The palette blossomed into varied and bright hues. New techniques of decorative dyeing, like yūzen, circumvented the law. Ground colors tended to be of lighter hues, often white. Beni appeared in various ways: embroidered in as a highlight, brushed into the paste-resist design, or dip-dyed to form a background color (for later examples of these uses of beni see cat. nos. 21, 39, 81). A nodding obedience to the law was a cover for indulgence in half-hidden uses of forbidden colors, such as for linings and undergarments. Saikaku's *Seken mune zan'yō* (Reckonings that carry men through the world; 1692) describes women sporting bathing loincloths of a "double layer of silk dyed with benibana" and warns that "in former times such things could not have been afforded even by a daimyo lady. Considering their own status as townsmen's wives, they should fear divine punishment."[26]

In contrast with his ancestors, the eighth Tokugawa shogun, Yoshimune, had a sober and restrained personality. His own taste for dark, cold colors (known in Japanese as *jimi*) helped enforce by example a series of sensible, balanced laws. Taste turned to delicate patterns, often of dark green, dark blue, or brown, occasionally red, on a light ground neatly executed in yūzen dyeing. Fashion leaned toward colors that merchants could wear without fear of prosecution, colors that had been associated with commoners long before the Edo period: shades of brown, blue, and gray.[27] To this period can be assigned many of the numerous flowered robes with light grounds (see cat. nos. 25, 27–28). On Yoshimune's death a reaction to his conservatism set in, yet the years of sobriety left their mark. The popularity of somber shades clearly had deeper roots than just the taste of the ruling personal-

CATALOGUE NO. 25
Hitoe with Bamboo, Plum, Rafts,
and Characters
First quarter eighteenth century
Tōyama Memorial Museum

ity; it also arose from shifts in the social balance and reflected a new economic structure based on extensive provincial development.[28]

In the Hōreki era dark designs on light grounds changed to light designs on dark grounds, often of blues, greens, browns, and grays (see cat. nos. 30, 74, 95). Traces of beni appeared on undergarments and in embroidery (as accents on yūzen-dyed garments such as chaya-zome katabira, for example). As the nineteenth century dawned, grays gained in popularity. In the eighteenth century, literary references, order books for kosode, and hinagata-bon listed as many as ninety-four different colors incorporating

CATALOGUE NO. 27
Katabira with Lattice, Flowering
Plum Tree, Chrysanthemums, and
Bush Clover (Hagi)
First half eighteenth century
Matsuzakaya Co., Ltd.

the word *cha* (brown) and fifty-nine other brownish colors. By the nineteenth century the number of browns had decreased and the number of grays so increased as to give rise to the proverb "yonjūhacha, hyakuso" (a hundred grays to forty-eight browns).[29]

FASHION COLORS AND THE WORLD OF THE KABUKI ACTOR

A major form of entertainment in Edo-period Japan was the kabuki theater. A new role required eye-catching costumes, involving careful consultations between actors and dyers.[30] Novel shades were created by fine adjustments in the dyeing process, innovative uses of mordants to set the dyes, or complex top-dyeing techniques. When the color was successful, the actor set the fashion of the day. Having seen a color onstage, kabuki fans would rush to have their own kosode dyed to match. The color became known by the name of the actor or by the role he played wearing it. The audience, poster makers, ukiyo-e print masters, and critics then popularized it.

Perhaps the actor's color with the most lasting popularity was Rokōcha, a dark yellow-brown. It first appeared when the onnagata Segawa Kikunojō II (Rokō) performed the role of Osugi in the "Yaoya Oshichi" act of *Edo-zome* (Edo style) in 1766.[31] It

remained popular until 1848. Many of the beauties in prints by
the ukiyo-e artist Suzuki Harunobu (1725–70) wear kosode dyed
in Rokōcha. Writings such as the *Shikitei zakki* (Diary of Shikitei
[Samba]; 1810–12) and *Morisada mankō* (Observations of
[Kitagawa] Morisada; 1837–53) mention the color. By contrast,
some other colors lost favor quickly. The color historian Nagasaki
Seiki suggests that the dyers took great pains when creating their
colors to feed into the current fashion. Thus Rokōcha was really a
variation on the already popular yellow-brown *hiwacha*.[32]

Of note is that almost all of these actors' colors were muddy
shades of green or brown—"commoners' colors" through and
through—and that shades of gray (of growing popularity outside
the stage) were missing. The reason for this omission, Nagasaki
suggests, may lie in an alternate meaning of the character for gray
(*nezumi*): rat. The rodent was felt to be dirty; its color inappropriate for the theater.[33] It must also be remembered that the
popularized actors' colors were not the only ones appearing on the
kabuki stage. Red was a must for young women's roles and for
those of young warriors, like the sixteen-year-old Atsumori
(played by an onnagata). These reds, to stay within the law,
would not have been dyed with benibana.[34]

THE WORLD OF BENI

Considering the rise in popularity of commoners' colors during
the eighteenth century, one would expect a decline in the production of benibana. Surprisingly, statistics suggest the opposite.
According to Imada Shinichi, in the Kyōhō era a little more than
1,000 *ta* (horse loads) of benibana was grown, about 40 percent
along the Mogami River in Dewa Province.[35] A century later, at
the end of the Edo period, this had doubled to more than 2,400
ta, of which 50 percent came from Dewa. Was this due to the failure of the sumptuary laws, an overall increase in population and
advance in the standard of living, an improvement of production
methods, or a combination of the above with yet other reasons?

To answer this we must look at the changes in the economic
structure, at various uses of beni dye outside of the dyeing of
kosode, and at the aesthetics that evolved during the mid-Edo
period. These aesthetics can be seen as being in part, although by
no means totally, a response to the sumptuary laws.

First, as discussed in William Hauser's essay, a transformation
took place during the course of the Edo period. Whereas in the
seventeenth century the *ton'ya* (wholesalers; fig. 33a) in Kyoto
and Osaka controlled the whole process, from seeding to tailor-
ing, by the end of the eighteenth century the farmers and dyers

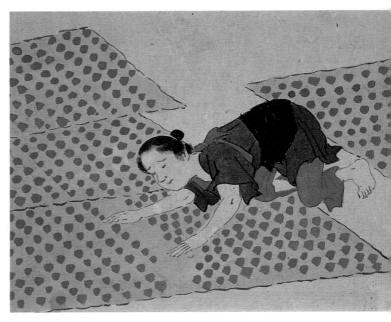

FIGURE 33a,b
Aoyama Eikō (1817–79)
Benibana Screen (details)
Early nineteenth century
Pair of six-panel screens;
pigment on paper
Each: 61 ¹³/₁₆ × 138 ⁹/₁₆ in.
(157.0 × 352.0 cm)
Yamagata City Collection,
Yamagata Prefecture

were independently established.[36] If cotton stands as a model, production became more competitive and local villages gained enough surplus cash to invest in their own product, sometimes with the help of local daimyo.[37] An improved transportation system in turn stimulated greater trade.

By the mid-Edo period benibana passed through some eight or nine different hands on its way to the dye house. The farmers in Dewa were responsible for harvesting and drying the petals. Some were used as is, but much of the harvest was fermented and formed into *benimochi* (beni balls; fig. 33b), a far more concentrated dye that was easier to transport.[38] A local representative tested the product; it was then shipped from Dewa by boat down the Mogami River to Sakata and along the coast to Tsuruga. From here the product went by land to Lake Biwa, by boat to Ōtsu, and by land again over the mountains to Kyoto, where it was collected by one wholesaler, stored by another, and finally sold to the *benizomeya* (beni dye houses; fig. 34).[39] Records show that during the Genroku era the benibana ton'ya in Kyoto formed a guild to serve 9 beni dyers and related middlemen. Outside the guild there worked an additional 152 beni dyers. In 1735 fourteen houses were officially authorized as beni ton'ya.[40] An indication of the importance of the dye is that by the eighteenth century the word for dyer was synonymous with *benishi* (beni-artisan).[41]

The increasing demand for beni was in part due to its multiple uses. By allowing the dye to sediment, a beautiful pigment could be obtained.[42] This became a prized ingredient in makeup as both

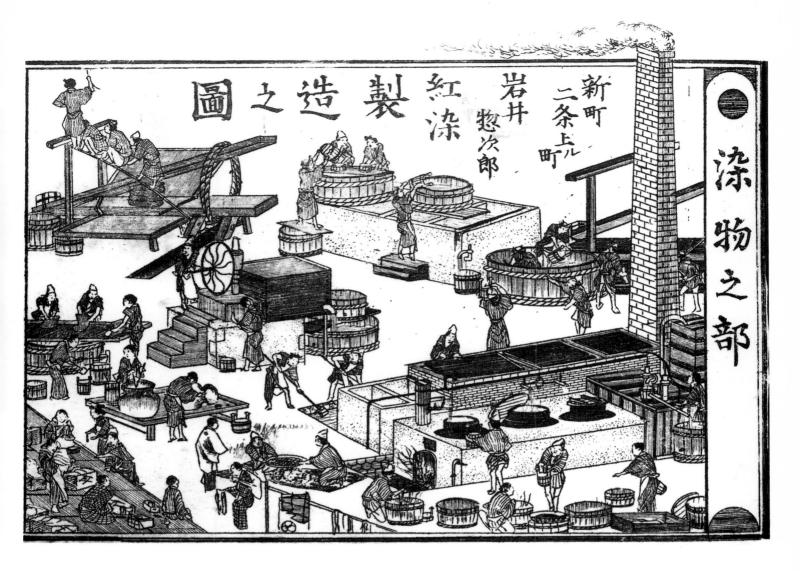

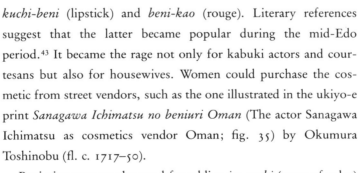

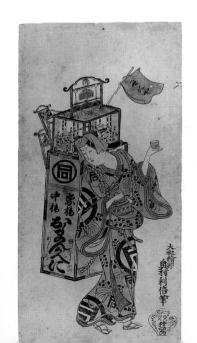

kuchi-beni (lipstick) and *beni-kao* (rouge). Literary references suggest that the latter became popular during the mid-Edo period.[43] It became the rage not only for kabuki actors and courtesans but also for housewives. Women could purchase the cosmetic from street vendors, such as the one illustrated in the ukiyo-e print *Sanagawa Ichimatsu no beniuri Oman* (The actor Sanagawa Ichimatsu as cosmetics vendor Oman; fig. 35) by Okumura Toshinobu (fl. c. 1717–50).

Beni pigment was also used for adding *iro-zashi* (spots of color) to yūzen-dyed cloth. In addition it was a mainstay color of ukiyo-e printers. *Beni-e* (red pictures; woodblock outlines with brushed-in color), *benizuri-e* (red print pictures; woodblock prints using a limited number of color blocks), and *nishiki-e* (multicolored prints; numerous colors printed from many blocks using a color separation system) all used beni pigment as a main color. Paintings also depicted women wearing garments dyed with beni. For example, beni-red appears in slim lines around the neck, hem, and sleeve openings of the garment worn by the standing woman depicted in *Ni bijin-zu* (Two beauties; fig. 36), attributed to Kitagawa Kikumaro (fl. c. 1830).

FIGURE 34
Page from *Miyako sakigake*
(Upcoming fashions from the
capital)
1883
Woodblock-printed book; ink
on paper
4 5/16 × 6 5/16 in.
(11.0 × 16.0 cm)
Kyoto Municipal Library

·

FIGURE 35
Okumura Toshinobu
(fl. c. 1717–50)
*The Actor Sanagawa Ichimatsu as
Cosmetics Vendor Oman*
Mid-eighteenth century
Woodblock print; ink and color
on paper
13 3/16 × 6 1/8 in. (33.5 × 15.5 cm)
Tokyo National Museum,
Matsukata Collection

FIGURE 36

Attributed to Kitagawa Kikumaro
(fl. c. 1830)

Two Beauties

First half nineteenth century

Hanging scroll; ink and color

on paper

49 ⅛ × 21 ⅞ in. (124.8 × 55.6 cm)

Shin'enkan Collection, Los Angeles

County Museum of Art, L.83.50.35

The fashion of sporting the coveted beni-red on an undergarment (known as *beni kakushi ura*), well camouflaged by muddy greens and browns and sober grays worn on the outside, became increasingly popular during the eighteenth and nineteenth centuries. The ladies of the court decorated their underclothing with repeat patterns done in the labor-intensive itajime technique, while commoners often wore undergarments of solid red.[44] This would imply a tremendous demand for the dye.

The beni-dyed underrobe typified the aesthetic of hidden glamor, hinted at but not openly displayed, known as *iki* (loosely translated as "chic"; see fig. 37). Originally iki referred to unpretentious elegance, alluring yet not ostentatious. By the late Edo period the term was popularly applied to a suggestive understatement, whereby attractive beauty arose within the bounds of tradition. Iki was an *iroppasa* (eroticism) arising from a refinement held in tension by the urbane. Kuki Shūzo in his *Iki no kōzō* (The structure of iki) defines it as a combination of "attractiveness, willpower and cynicism . . . a beauty expressing the self with idealism and etherealism."[45] Translated into colors, this meant either a contrast of two or three tones, rather than a wide variety, or a single color in dark and light shades. Single colors, however, could contain all the meanings of iki, from restraint to panache. The colors that fulfilled this most aptly were grays, browns, and blues, all unrestricted colors.[46] Kosode displaying these sober colors on the outside would often be lined with beni-red as a highlight and a contrast.

In examining the aesthetics of beni, there is a continuum from the Heian period to the Edo period. During the former, laws restricted all but the highest-ranking court ladies from wearing kōbai, although lighter shades of pink were permitted. These lighter shades often appeared at the bottom of a layered combination of kasane iro. The appropriateness of burying this highly favored color so that only a small outline showed along the edge of the sleeves and lapel was described as *yukashi*. Although beni was no longer the color of the aristocracy by the Edo period, the same sense of a need for restrained suggestiveness was embodied in the idea of iki. In the eighteenth-century ladies' journal *Joshūhōki* (Important jeweled notes for women) appears the warning to paint one's cheeks, lips, and fingernails only with light beni, for deep scarlet (kurenai or kōbai) would be disgusting. Similarly, deep shades of beni-red were reserved for undergarments and linings, which would be exposed with a seductive flick as a woman walked by.[47]

FIGURE 37
Kunisada (Utagawa Toyokuni III)
(1786–1864)
Beauty Reading a Letter
First half nineteenth century
Hanging scroll; ink and color
on silk
33 ¾ × 11 ⁹⁄₁₆ in. (85.7 × 29.4 cm)
Shin'enkan Collection, Los Angeles
County Museum of Art, L.83.50.39

Summary

In the Momoyama period, the earliest period from which a variety
of whole garments survive, beni-red was a predominant color.[48] It
not only adorned many of the tie-dyed garments known as tsujigahana but also was used extensively in embroidered nuihaku
and brocades like karaori. During the seventeenth century beni-
red was used as a background color with black and white and also
for highlights done in embroidery. By the eighteenth century,
however, the outward display of beni-red was replaced by more
subtle, suggestive statements. At this point beni-red retreated to

undergarments and linings, peeping out at the collars, cuffs, and hem. This did not, however, reduce the market demand. Indeed statistics indicate the opposite.

The increasing popularity of unrestricted colors is the reverse side of the story of beni (see cat. nos. 119–20). Novels and diaries of Tokugawa life illuminate the importance of these commoners' colors and suggest the growing dominance of the merchant class in setting fashion trends from the late seventeenth century on. The garments preserved today do not always reflect contemporary fashion as outlined by literary sources, the reason for this being that the surviving objects primarily belonged to the upper classes, while the writings were by and for the chōnin. During the Edo period fashions moved upwards, coming to the samurai class after they were well established among merchant women and being adopted by the military and finally the nobility years later. Thus we find that by the nineteenth century, although members of the nobility were free to wear restricted colors, even they turned to grays, browns, and blues for many of their kosode.

CATALOGUE NO. 119
Furisode with Symbols from an
Incense Identification Game
(Genji-kō) *and Flowering Vines*
First half nineteenth century
National Museum of Japanese
History, Nomura Collection

Finally the story of beni-red is but one of many similar stories that could be told of murasaki, the esteemed and elegant purple; of *kuro*, the formal yet forever alluring black; of *shiro* (white), kuro's pure, unstained alter ego; and of *ai* (indigo), the staple color for dyeing cotton. Each would reveal another social network tying the provinces into the major cities; each would disclose another aspect of Japanese taste and consciousness supported by another set of proverbs, poems, and prejudices. Yet the overall outlines would be the same. The sensitivity to subtle differences in shades, the respect for the life or spirit of the color, the close connection in the minds of the buyers with the dye plants and the dye processes—these make up the very essence of Japanese concepts of color.

1. Ueda 1977, s.v. "iro," defines the original meaning of the word as "the feelings of the heart as they appear in the face" and suggests that the most basic interpretation is sexual passion. (Another meaning is a charming face that inspires love.) The *Man'yōshū* (Collection of a thousand leaves), an eighth-century poetry anthology, contains a poem regarding the betrayal of emotion through color:

iro ni idete
koiba hitomite
shirinu beshi
kokoro no uchi no
komori tsumaho mo.

Were the color to appear,
people seeing my love
would surely know:
I must hide it
deep in my heart.

A poem that uses red as a metaphor for amorous feelings relates:

kurenai no
fukasome no kinu
shita ni kite
ue ni tori kiba
koto nasamu ka mo

This gown dyed deep crimson
I wear beneath.
Were I to exchange it
with the top robe,
how the gossip would flow.

See Kojima, Kinoshita, and Satake 1971–75, 3:218–19 (book 11, no. 2566), 2:258 (book 7, no. 1313). A later example is the lament of Lady Rokujo in the Nō play *Nonomiya* (Shrine in the fields; late fourteenth–early fifteenth century; see cat. no. 102) that her desire (color), like burning coals, is seen from the outside: "iro wa hoka ni mietsu ran." See Koyama, Satō, and Satō 1973–75, 1:284.

2. A poem in the *Man'yōshū* (book 10, no. 1993) expresses the correspondence between love (or charm) and the color red by cleverly playing on the characteristics of the safflower, a plant whose petals produce a red dye despite their yellow appearance. The poem states:

yosonomi ni
mitsutsu koi namu
kurenai no
suetsumu hana no
iro ni idezu to mo

Only from afar
should this love of mine be seen.
Like the red of
the plucked petals [of safflower],
the color [love] does not appear on
     the surface.

See Kojima, Kinoshita, and Satake 1971–75, 3:86.

3. Although pronounced differently, *beni* and *kurenai* are written with the same Chinese character. A third reading is *kō*; it appears as the first character in the combination *kōbai* (dark pink). For simplicity the author has referred to all the names collectively as beni-red, shades produced when dyeing with benibana. To the Japanese these shades belong to a totally distinct category from vermillion (*aka*, *shū*, or *hi*), which is derived from earth pigments, although in English both colors are combined under the category red.

The benibana plant (safflower; *Carthamus tinctorius*) is a thistle that grows more than three feet tall. Its flowers, first pale yellow, appear in July and deepen with exposure to the sun. Finally a small point of red forms at the base of each pinlike petal. Once the red appears, the petals, which contain both yellow and red dyes, are plucked and dried for storage or fermented to make a concentrated dye. Only the latter color seems to have been commonly used in the past. The yellow dye is first washed away in running water; the red is then extracted by steeping the petals in an alkaline solution such as the lye from tree ash. For a more detailed discussion of the dye process see Bethe 1984, 71–73. See also Yamazaki 1974 and Yoshioka 1974. For a description of the cultivation and harvesting of the flower as well as many other aspects of benibana dyeing see Endo 1978.

4. Reds have either a purplish or orange overcast. The dye from safflower leans toward the purple (scarlet) when all the yellow has been extracted; if some of the yellow remains, however, it produces a warm shade of yellow-red (crimson). Shively 1965, in translating Saikaku, uses the latter term, while Dalby 1988 uses the former one. The semantic problems lie in the ambiguity of English color terms; in Japanese the color beni correlates with all of the shades produced by benibana.

5. Discussions of the magical power of colors can be found in Maeda U. 1975, 9, 17, and Maeda Y. 1960. See also Nagasaki S. 1977, 15–23.

6. For medicinal uses of benibana see Keys 1976, 223–24, and Tanaka 1973.

7. In the concluding verse of a long poem admonishing a friend for having taken a mistress and extolling the virtues of his proper wife (*Man'yōshū* [book 18, no. 4109]), Ōtomo Yakamochi comments:

kurenai wa
utsurou mono zo
tsurubami no
narenishi kinu ni
nao shikame ya mo

Beni-red [symbol of the mistress] fades.
But acorn gray [symbol of the wife] of the accustomed gown
is incomparable.

See Kojima, Kinoshita, and Satake 1971–75, 4:271–72.

8. The color name for purple is synonymous with the name of the dye plant: murasaki. The inner bark of the roots produces the dye. The roots themselves are often referred to by their medicinal name: *shikon* (written with the characters for purple and root). The *Man'yōshū* (book 14, no. 3500) uses the image of the extreme length of the gromwell roots as a metaphor for long love:

murasakigusa wa
ne o ka mo ouru
hito noko no
uraganashike o
ne o oenaku ni.

The roots of murasaki
grow endlessly long.
Beside his beloved daughter
I yearn
to sleep as long.

See Kojima, Kinoshita, and Satake 1971–75, 3:487.

The adjective *yukari* became associated with the color purple by the eleventh century, appearing in the *Genji monogatari* (Tale of Genji): "iro mo hata natsushiki yukari ni mo kato tsubeshi" (Even the color [of wisteria] is somehow companionable and inviting). The word appeared repeatedly in literature from that time on. See Murasaki 1979, 525.

9. De Bary, Chan, and Watson 1960, 199. A fuller discussion of gogyō and its relation to colors appears in Nagasaki S. 1977, 106–12.

10. See Maeda Y. 1960, 129–41, especially 137 (a chart summarizing the changes in ranking during the Nara period). See also Nagasaki S. 1977, 85–98.

11. See Nagasaki S. 1987 for a good study of layered combinations. In addition to presenting fine color plates of the combinations, he gives in full the texts of Heian-, Muromachi-, and Edo-period writings on the subject. For a thorough discussion of literary references to colors in the Heian period see Ihara 1982. See also Dalby 1988.

12. See Shively 1965. For a discussion in terms of textiles see Minnich 1963, 189–318, and Nagasaki S. 1990, 208–12. See also Ebata 1982, 80–84.

13. Endo 1978, 186.

14. Dalby 1988, 11–12.

15. Miura 1975 provides a chart summarizing the regulations on the use of purple and beni-red.

16. Sanemori, a lower-ranking Heike warrior, had to get special permission in the Heian period to wear red brocade. See Kitagawa and Tsuchida 1975, 414. The subject is dramatized in the Nō play *Sanemori*. See Nippon Gakujutsu Shinkōkai 1955, 51–53.

17. Itō 1985, 20.

18. Kirihata 1983b, 154.

19. Shively 1965, 124, 154.

20. A mordant is a liquid used to fix a dye to a cloth by strengthening the chemical bonding. Most mordants are derived from metals, although vinegar is sometimes employed. Lye, the most common mordant used in Japan since ancient times, was produced by burning straw or wood and passing water through the ashes (the water picks up the chemicals in the burnt ash). By the Nara period the Japanese knew that the best colors were produced when the lye from specific trees was used in conjunction with certain dyes. For example, lye from camellia ash (rich in alum) was used for purple. According to Shimura Fukumi, a modern dyer and Living National Treasure, the ashes of the tree whose bark produces the dye color generally produce the most attractive shade. The other common mordant used from antiquity was iron. Found naturally in certain waters and muds, it darkened the dye. (Mud dyeing still prevails on the island of Kumejima in Okinawa.) The metallic solutions used by dyers today include alum and tin (both of which brighten a color) as well as copper, lime, and chrome. All but the last were used in the Edo period.

21. See Boxer 1930, 184–95, for a list of imported goods. Both sappanwood and tin appear repeatedly among the shipments from Southeast Asia.

22. Murakami also states that dark purple would make the ninja more invisible at night than true black. Arguing from the fact that they were instructed to drink water only after they had passed it through their "red" gloves, he posits that the color was really suō mordanted with iron taken from *ohaguro* (tooth blackener), for both suō and ohaguro had disinfectant properties. See Murakami 1987, 202–4.

23. The edict must have been directed at experimental methods of surface decoration as well. See Shively 1965, 126.

24. Nagasaki S. 1990, 208.

25. Shively 1965, 128, quotes the *Tokugawa jikki* (True record of Tokugawa) and an account by Mitsui Takafusa (1684–1748) from *Chōnin kaōkenroku* (A record of observations on merchants; c. 1728). An additional reference appears in *Kyūshōran* (Matters of pleasure and fun; 1830), compiled by Kitamura Shinsetsu. See Nagasaki S. 1990, 195.

26. Noma K. 1960, 197–98.

27. See note 7 for a reference to gray in the Nara period.

28. For a discussion of the shifts in economic and social structure during the Edo period see Hauser essay and Nakane, Ōishi, and Totman 1990.

29. Nagasaki S. 1990, 199.

30. For discussions of actors' colors see Ebata 1982, 86–89, Nagasaki S. 1990, 201–8, and Noguchi 1982.

31. According to another story, the color was first used by Kikunojō (fl. 1750–72) in 1763 when he performed Osugi in *Eika Soga* (The glorious Soga). See Nagasaki S. 1990, 203.

32. Nagasaki S. 1990, 207.

33. Ibid., 208.

34. This is the author's supposition, based on the fact that imitation beni-red was common and vigilance over actors could be stringent.

35. Imada 1973, 33. Dewa is present-day Yamagata Prefecture.

36. See Hauser 1977. A sense of the complexity of specialization in the weaving industry (that carries on to the present day) can be seen in Haak 1973. Gary Leupp, in a lecture entitled "The Weavers of Nishijin: Wage-Workers in Tokugawa Cities" (Japan Foundation, Kyoto, February 1991), discussed the Tokugawa-period Nishijin guilds.

37. Hauser 1974b, 118. For a good discussion of the changing rural scene and village dynamics in the eighteenth century see Satō 1990, especially 71–75.

38. The fermentation process in making benimochi is described and illustrated in Endo 1978, 73–75, 85–87, 113–16. The Meiji woodblock print *Beni ichiran* (Beni at a glance), a part of *Oshiegusa* (Production notebook), illustrates and describes all of the steps in processing beni, from the original cultivation of the plant to its final use as a dye.

39. Imada 1973, 31–36. See also Bethe 1984, 71–72. In addition to the illustrations in the aforementioned *Beni ichiran* and figs. 33a,b and 34, a number of Edo-period books related to safflower dyeing can be found in the Ryōshō Library in Osaka: one by known authors (Yasukuro and Ozeki 1782) and two by unknown authors (*Benibana senshoku hō* [Methods of dyeing with safflower] and *Benibana seihōsho* [Methods of producing benibana]).

40. Imada 1973, 31–33.

41. Takubo 1976, 159.

42. A brief but well-illustrated description of the method of making beni pigment appears in Senshoku no bi 1983, 104.

43. Takubo 1976, 159.

44. For illustrations of itajime see Senshoku no bi 1983, 98; for a description of the process see Yoshioka 1973.

45. Kuki 1930, 19.

46. For this discussion of iki colors I am indebted to Nagasaki S. 1990, 213.

47. See Takubo 1976, 157, 159–60, for a comparison of the aesthetics of beni in the Heian and Edo periods.

48. See Matsumoto 1984.

Clothed in Words:
Calligraphic Designs on Kosode

On her left sleeve was a hand-painted likeness of the Yoshida monk, along with this passage: "To sit alone under a lamp, and read old books . . ." Assuredly, this was a woman of exquisite taste. ❧ —*Ihara Saikaku*, Kōshoku gonin onna *(Five women who loved love), 1686*[1]

The incorporation of words in kosode designs of the Edo period was in keeping with the rich tradition in Japan of utilizing written language in the visual and decorative arts. To fully appreciate kosode with words, it must be remembered that they were animated by living individuals. The natural charms of the woman described by Saikaku were heightened by the subtle elegance of her robe. This garment, so enlivened, amplified her virtues and attractiveness to the surrounding world. ❧ In contrast with the more sedate clothing described in Saikaku's novel, *Kosode with Hawks, Maple Trees, Waterfalls, Checks, and Characters* (cat. no. 146) presents a more upbeat, syncopated use of language. As will be discussed later in this essay, the characters and motifs have been ingeniously rendered so that they can be read on two levels. The naive viewer would see only a display of striking decorative images; the cognoscente would respond to a collection of playful baiting phrases. Whether demonstrating "exquisite taste" or engaging in streetwise repartee, language on kosode was used to enhance one's persona. Garments emblazoned with words literally wrapped the wearer in a cloak of language that announced the sensibilities, desires, and values of the owner. ❧ Textile artists drew ideas from such sources as calligraphy, painting, classical literature, Nō plays, and auspicious symbolism to represent a variety of subjects. Through such devices as wordplay, visual puns, and rebuses, designs incorporating characters exemplify the pictorial-literary basis of the imagery on many Edo-period kosode. ❧ ❧ WRITING SYSTEMS AND CALLIGRAPHY ❧ The history of written language in Japan began with the introduction of Chinese script (*kanji*) sometime before the fourth century.[2] The Japanese, not having devised a writing system of their own, eagerly embraced that of the Chinese. For the next few centuries Chinese writings on history, philosophy, and Buddhist doctrines were used for the study of kanji as well as grammar and vocabulary. Such scholarly and religious activity was motivated by a desire to emulate the more advanced continental civilization. ❧ Kanji are ideographic characters that were developed to convey particular meanings. Many are pictographic in origin; others represent abstract ideas or specific sounds. When the Japanese eventually saw a need to write the sounds of their own language, they utilized certain kanji to designate particular Japanese syl-

CATALOGUE NO. 127
Kosode on Screen (detail)
Left: Kosode fragment with fence, larch flowers (kara-matsu), and characters
First quarter eighteenth century
Right: Kosode fragment with bamboo fence and characters
First half eighteenth century
National Museum of Japanese History, Nomura Collection

CATALOGUE NO. 138
*Kosode with Chrysanthemums,
Water, and Characters*
Late seventeenth–early eighteenth
century
Kyoto National Museum

lables. In the ninth century two native syllabaries (*kana*) began to evolve from these phonogramic kanji (*man'yōgana*). The resulting writing forms became known as *katakana* and *hiragana*. The former, a more angular script, was used largely to clarify the proper reading of kanji, while the latter, more cursive in style, was used primarily for secular texts, especially poetry. Scholarly, religious, and official documents continued to be written in Chinese. Ultimately a combination of kanji and kana was used to write the Japanese language. All three writing systems—kanji (see cat. no. 138), katakana (see cat. no. 129), and hiragana (see cat. no. 136)— appear as decorative elements on Edo-period kosode.

CATALOGUE NO. 129
*Kosode with Vertical Bands of Sedge
Hats, Fans, and Characters*
Mid-eighteenth century
Okajima Collection

Following the example of the Chinese, the Japanese explored the aesthetic possibilities of writing kanji. By extending this exploration to their own writing systems, especially hiragana, the Japanese elevated their otherwise functional scripts to the level of calligraphy.[3] The smooth, flowing lines of hiragana became the perfect vehicle for expressing the spare and elegantly efficient qualities of the Japanese poetic form. While the composition and recitation of poetry were considered direct expressions of one's intelligence and sensibilities and were essential skills for highly educated Heian courtiers, artfully brushed calligraphy on well-chosen paper was, more than the words themselves, the ultimate indication of one's breeding, sensitivity, and character.[4]

The connection between the brushstrokes of calligraphy and the brushstrokes of painting brought the two art forms together naturally. Poems written on paintings are well documented; artistic writing can also be found on lacquerware, ceramics, folding screens, and sliding doors. The broad and simply tailored expanse of such Japanese garments as the kosode was yet another format for calligraphic expression.

EARLY USES OF CALLIGRAPHY ON CLOTHING

According to accounts from several mid-Heian-period literary sources words were utilized on formal costumes of the Heian court.[5] The language applied to such garments was often directly related to the poetic aesthetic of the aristocracy. A passage from the "Ne-awase" (Root-matching contest) chapter of *Eiga monogatari* describes one such robe:

> The ladies-in-waiting were wearing robes with light purple lining showing through the gossamer, beaten robes of lustrous light green, double-layered mantles of yellow figured silk, jackets of purple, and their light green trains had pictures drawn on them, done in embroidery, mother-of-pearl and edging and what not, and on one the poem "My Heart Goes Out" *[kokoro no yukite]* was written in small silver fragments in a dazzling way, and the figure of a cherry tree in bloom with its petals falling was painted as an uta-e [poem-picture].[6]

Few textiles or garments from the Heian period and succeeding Kamakura and Muromachi periods survive. Assessing the use of words on clothing during this time is therefore difficult. While those of the subsequent Momoyama period reveal no clear trend of utilizing language on clothing, there are numerous examples of such kosode from the Edo period. The earliest dates from between the Kan'ei and Meireki eras (fig. 38).[7] On this robe there are two tie-dyed characters: the kanji for mountain, 山 (*yama*), extends over the upper right shoulder and sleeve; a simplified form of the kanji meaning "to pass over/go over," 越 (*ko[su]*), rests on the

Kosode with Abstract Wave Pattern
(Seigaiha), *Pine Trees, Clouds,*
Flowers, and Characters
Seventeenth century
Tie-dyeing (kanoko and nuishime
shibori) on blue, brown, and white
parti-colored (somewake) figured
silk satin (rinzu)
53 ⅛ × 49 ¼ in. (135.0 × 125.0 cm)
Tōyama Memorial Museum,
Saitama Prefecture

ちぎりきなかたみにそでをしぼりつつすゑのまつ山なみこさじとは

left back. The characters are combined with an abstract wave pattern (*seigaiha*) and pictorial motifs of pine trees, clouds, and flowers. In the corpus of classical Japanese poetry, these characters appear together in numerous poems, complicating the process of determining exactly which one is being alluded to on this kosode. Even when the two kanji and the abstract and pictorial motifs are read jointly, only an educated guess as to the source of the design can be made. Indeed the Japanese of the Edo period may not at first have recognized the source of these characters. This word game would have provided a sophisticated amusement to a viewer who would be compelled to recall or research the literary origins. Both Kirihata Ken and Nagasaki Iwao suggest that this kosode may allude to a poem from the *Goshūi wakashū* (Later collection of gleanings of Japanese poetry), an eleventh-century imperial anthology. The poem reads:

chigiriki na	We'd pledged a love unchanging,
katami ni sode o	like the pine-clad mountain of Sue,
shiboritsutsu	never dampened by the waves,
Sue no matsuyama	but now I wring these waves of tears
nami kosaji to wa	from sodden sleeves: remembrances of you.[8]

Ascertaining the social class of the original owner of this kosode is problematic; by the beginning of the Edo period knowledge of classical literature had spread to both the military elite and affluent townsmen (see Hauser essay). The samurai and chōnin found characters incorporated into clothing designs to be a natural extension of their literary and pictorial interests.

CLASS EXPRESSIONS: KARIGANEYA AND "ON-HIINAKATA"

The graphic and thematic possibilities of integrating words into kosode designs were actively explored by textile designers during the third quarter of the seventeenth century, the height of the

Kanbun style. This style was characterized by a strong contrast between positive and negative space (see Nagasaki essay). A pattern that curved from the upper left shoulder across to the right shoulder and then down toward the lower left hem was typical (see Appendix A, cat. nos. 9, 12).[9]

Although there are few extant kosode with characters from this period, valuable research materials in the form of kosode order books (hinagata-chō) and kosode pattern books (hinagata-bon) give clear evidence of this phenomenon. Significant amongst these documents are the hinagata-chō of Kariganeya and the earliest of hinagata-bon, *On-hiinakata*.

Many graphically innovative Kanbun kosode designs utilizing characters can be found in the kosode order books produced in the early 1660s by Kariganeya, a Kyoto textile shop notable because of its special artistic lineage. Women of the aristocracy and the highest levels of the military elite patronized the store through several generations.[10]

Kariganeya designs often emphasized the playful manipulation of characters for the sake of design, as can be seen in the following examples. In one sketch (fig. 39) the character for tree, 木 (*ki*), is cleverly rendered as a blossoming cherry tree. The bough extending horizontally from sleeve to sleeve and vertical trunk with two downward sweeping branches form a giant pictogram. Although the kanji means tree and has its graphic roots in the image of a tree, its representational qualities are greatly enhanced by the foliage and exaggerated scale. In another design (fig. 40), the character for cool, 凉 (*suzu[shii]*), overlaps the edge of a cypress-slat fan *(hi-ōgi)* drawn on the upper part of the kosode. The fan wafts the strokes of the kanji like ribbons in a cool breeze. The final stroke forms the edge of yet another fan in motion. As in the first example, the form and context of the kanji are manipulated to create a picture. Here the gestalt suggests "coolness," although the kanji in this case does not depict the image of or mean "breeze." In a third example (fig. 41), the character for thousand, 千 (*chi*), is reproduced eight times, increasing in height diagonally across the back of the kosode.[11] The character for age or generation, 世 (*yo*), spreads across the shoulder. Combined, these two kanji read *chiyo*

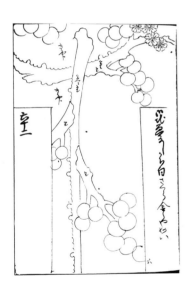

FIGURE 39
Page from a Kariganeya hinagata-chō (*On'e-chō*), 1661
Osaka Municipal Museum of Art

FIGURE 40
Page from a Kariganeya hinagata-chō (*On'e-chō*), 1663
Osaka Municipal Museum of Art

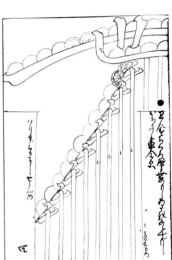

FIGURE 41
Page from a Kariganeya hinagata-chō, c. 1664
Osaka Municipal Museum of Art

(a thousand ages). The concept of generational longevity is extended beyond a simple reading of language, being graphically and literally dramatized by the ever-lengthening vertical strokes and repetition of *chi*.

These three examples of Kariganeya designs illustrate the extent to which the expressively modified forms of kanji were able to carry the design of a kosode by using written characters as actual building blocks of a picture whose ultimate meaning was larger than the significance of the component characters. For these images to be animated by a living wearer must have given further resonance to the tone and/or feeling evoked by the design.

In comparison with Kariganeya designs, those with characters illustrated in *On-hiinakata* (Design patterns; 1666 and 1667)[12] tended to put more emphasis on the extended meaning of the characters than on their immediate visual impact, creating a complex pictorial-linguistic network of associations. *On-hiinakata* were printed books, indicating a broad-based clientele, probably wealthy chōnin. The woodblock-printed designs are often less fluid and integrated than the hand-drawn ink illustrations from the Kariganeya hinagata-chō. This may have to do in part with the technically restrictive woodblock printing process, where the illustration chiseled into a block of wood (by a separate craftsman) is one step removed from the designer's initial drawing. But what the *On-hiinakata* designs seem to lack in fluidity is compensated for in their portrayal of more intellectually challenging themes.[13]

One such design (fig. 42) depicts the character for bush warbler, 鶯 (*uguisu*), intertwined with a blossoming plum branch. The Japanese viewer would have read this design on at least two levels. First, the seasonal reference was conveyed by the flowering plum, which blooms above the receding winter snow, and the bush warbler, whose song signals the advent of spring. Second, these subjects were literary and artistic metaphors for particular themes. The plum and bush warbler motif, for example, can be related to the "Hatsune" (First warbler) chapter of the *Genji monogatari* (Tale of Genji) and became associated with marital happiness.[14]

This type of substitution of word for image, drawing on the pictorial origins or inherent abstract qualities of certain characters, is a conceptual device seen on several kosode in the exhibition. In one work (cat. no. 128) the character for bird, 鳥 (*tori*), is arrayed across the garment in several different calligraphic styles. In another (cat. no. 131) the kanji for bush warbler is seen again. Both examples are in the Kanbun format, which, in its leaning toward broad and stylized designs, was well suited to the exchange of word for image. This device also occurred in painting.

FIGURE 42
Page from *On-hiinakata*, 1667

CATALOGUE NO. 128
Kosode on Screen
Kosode fragment with characters
in medallions and a basketwork
pattern
Early eighteenth century
National Museum of Japanese
History, Nomura Collection

A work from the early seventeenth century (fig. 43) is an especially interesting, albeit unusual, example of a bird and flower painting (*kachōga*), in which the ideogram for sparrow replaces the pictorial representation of the bird.

Another *On-hiinakata* design (fig. 44) superimposes the kanji for old, 老 (*o[i]*), on a repetitive pattern of pine needles, which are arranged to form a curved line exemplary of the Kanbun style. This can be read as *o[i]matsu* (old pine; an auspicious motif symbolizing longevity) and possibly alludes to a Nō play of the same name.[15]

Perhaps the most famous example of wordplay on clothing came not from the samurai or respectable chōnin, however, but from the *machi yakko* (town rogues). A genre painting from the first half of the seventeenth century (fig. 45) shows one such individual wearing a garment decorated with a picture of a *kama* (sickle), *wa* (circle), and the hiragana syllable *nu* (ぬ). This rebus reads *kamawanu*, which literally means "who cares." The witty design and resultant saying capture the nonchalant attitude of the rogues. In the late Edo period the kamawanu motif was glamorized by the kabuki actor Ichikawa Danjūrō VII (1791–1859) when he played Gorō in *Shōfuda-tsuki kongen kusazuribiki* (A certifiable, fundamental pull on the coattails; first performed in

FIGURE 44
Page from *On-hiinakata*, 1667

FIGURE 43
Shōkadō Shōjō (1584–1639)
Bamboo and the Character for Sparrow
Early seventeenth century
Hanging scroll; ink on paper
37 1/8 × 9 13/16 in. (94.3 × 24.9 cm)
Shin'enkan Collection, Los Angeles County Museum of Art,
L.83.50.106

CATALOGUE NO. 131
Kosode with Drying Fishing Nets and Characters
Third quarter seventeenth century
Kuriyama Kōbō Co., Ltd.

FIGURE 45
Shijōgawara yūraku-zu
(Entertainment along the banks of the Kamo River at Shijō) (detail)
First half seventeenth century
Pair of two-panel screens; ink and color on paper
Each: 65 11/16 × 67 11/16 in.
(166.9 × 172.0 cm)
Seikadō Bunko Art Museum, Tokyo
Important Cultural Property

1814). The motif, which was placed on a *juban* (undergarment), was dramatically revealed to the audience as Gorō exclaimed, "Tomete tomaranu . . . kamawanu" (Stop me if you can—you can't . . . who cares).[16] Danjūrō may have drawn inspiration for wearing the motif from his ancestor Komo no Jūzō, himself a machi yakko.[17] The kamawanu motif became Danjūrō's trademark; other kabuki actors adopted similar rebus designs. Fans who wanted to emulate their favorite actors decorated their own clothing with adaptations of such patterns.

CHIRASHIGAKI, MOJI MARUZUKUSHI MON'YŌ, AND OTHER SCATTERED WRITING FORMS

Chirashigaki (scattered writing), a compositional format of calligraphy that used written characters arranged asymmetrically, was popular in the Nara and Heian periods.[18] During the late sixteenth and early seventeenth centuries this elegant, aristocratic manner of writing was revived by artists in the Kyoto area. The placement of poetic language on an early-Edo-period kosode (cat. no. 135) is reminiscent of that style. Princess Saigū no Nyōgo (929–85)[19] was the author of the poem, which reads:

koto no ne ni	When winds blow down from off the peak
mine no matsukaze	and through the pines into the koto's strain,
kayounari	where does the music start?
izure no o yori	Is it on the mountain ridge
shirabesomekemu	or on the zither bridge?[20]

At first the characters appear to be randomly scattered over the surface of the kosode. Upon examination, however, the underlying Kanbun curve can be recognized. The tie-dyed and embroidered characters capture the brushstrokes of calligraphy. In addition, variations in the size and thickness of the kanji emulate the writing style of Hon'ami Kōetsu (1558–1637), a master of calligraphy and chirashigaki designs.

The colorful diagonal stripes of the kosode appear as a decorative background, but additional meaning can be attached to them because of a pun in the poem.[21] The particle *o* is homonymous with the words for string and ridge; in combination with the koto and mountain imagery, the stripes here could be either zither strings or the slope of a mountainside.[22]

Design patterns dominated by a scattering of circular forms containing characters are known as *moji maruzukushi mon'yō* and were fashionable for kosode from the Keian, Manji, and Kanbun eras.[23] In one example illustrated in *On-hiinakata* (see fig. 46), the kanji 大 (*dai* [large, long]) and 小 (*shō* [small, short]) alternate in a Kanbun-style layout. The characters symbolically represent

琴のねに峯の松風かよふなりいづれのをよりしらべそめけむ

CATALOGUE NO. 135
Kosode with Diagonal Stripes and Characters
Last quarter seventeenth century
Tokyo National Museum

FIGURE 46
Page from *On-hiinakata*, 1667

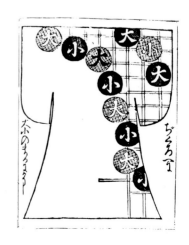

166

lunar calendar months: the former, months with thirty days; the latter, months with twenty-nine days.[24]

An additional moji maruzukushi mon'yō design is illustrated in an early seventeenth-century painting of bathhouse girls (yuna; fig. 47). One young woman is wearing a red-and-white tie-dyed kosode with large circular motifs enclosing the ideogram 沐 (moku-[suru] [to wash or bathe]). Like a walking signboard, this bold design brazenly advertises her profession.[25]

Scattered writing of another type can be seen in many of the bijinga created by such artists as Kaigetsudō Ando (active 1680–1717) and his followers. A stately beauty in a painting (fig. 48) attributed to Baiyūken Katsunobu (fl. 1716–35) is enveloped in a robe on which the enlarged kanji 戀 (koi [love]) and 聽 (ki[ku] [to listen]) are superimposed on a text written in kana.[26] The smaller words, largely indecipherable, are painted in a loose, cursive style typically seen in this genre. Given that there are no known extant eighteenth-century kosode with this type of writing design, it is hard to know if the Kaigetsudō artists were painting from actual subjects wearing such robes or from their own fantasies. Such writing designs, in order to be produced on cloth,

FIGURE 48
Baiyūken Katsunobu (fl. 1716–35)
Standing Woman
Early eighteenth century
Hanging scroll; ink and color on
paper
34 7/8 × 16 1/2 in. (88.6 × 41.9 cm)
Asian Art Museum of San
Francisco, The Avery Brundage
Collection, B60 D119

probably would have been reserved with a paste before the fabric
was dyed, leaving white characters against a shaded background.
It is interesting to note that while the faces of the women painted
by the Kaigetsudō school are all but indistinguishable, their
exquisitely detailed robes give the viewer an impression of the
individual taste and personality of each woman.

CATALOGUE NO. 29
*Kosode with Pine, Bamboo, Plum,
Waterfall, Rocks, and Characters*
Mid-eighteenth century
Marubeni Corporation

わが君は千世にやちよにさざれいしのいはほとなりてこけのむすまで

The mid-Edo period saw the distinctive, unadorned Kanbun-style background begin to give way to designs that covered more surface area of the kosode. Characters included in such designs were typically embroidered in silk and gold metallic thread, adding color, sheen, and texture to designs that were increasingly pictorial and rendered in yūzen dyeing (see Kirihata essay). Common sources for both words and images were auspicious and seasonal poems from such well-known anthologies as the *Kokin wakashū* and *Wakan rōeishū*.[27] Words from a variant of a famous poem found in each volume embellish *Kosode with Pine, Bamboo, Plum, Waterfall, Rocks, and Characters* (cat. no. 29). The poem reads:

waga kimi wa	My sovereign lord,
chiyo ni yachiyo ni	goes on a thousand years,
sazareishi no	eight thousand years,
iwao to narite	until the little pebbles grow to boulders
koke no musu made	and moss covers them.[28]

The felicitous theme of the poem[29] is handsomely illustrated by images of pine, bamboo, and plum, which symbolize, respectively, longevity, resilience, and regeneration.

Numerous extant examples of kosode from the eighteenth century point to the popularity of the *tachi-ki* (standing tree) motif (see cat. nos. 57, 140). This design is considered by some textile scholars to be influenced by flowering-tree patterns seen on imported Indo-European chintzes (*sarasa*).[30] The treelike structure of both the kanji for tree (see page 161) and the kosode itself, as it is often displayed with arms outstretched, only added to the strength of the design. Indeed the torso and branching arms of the person wearing the kosode became yet another component in a continuum of language to picture to garment to body.

Characters are often scattered amidst the foliage or flowers of tachi-ki kosode. Dispersed across the back of *Kosode with Double-Blossom Cherry Tree and Characters* (cat. no. 141) are the first three kanji of a Chinese poem by the Heian-period poet Minamoto Eimei (d. 939; also known as Minamoto no Fusaakira). His couplet, which appears in the spring section of the *Wakan rōeishū*, reads in Japanese:

始識春風機上巧

非唯織色織芬芳

hajimete shinnu, haru no kaze no kishō ni takumi naru koto o

tada iro o oru nomi ni arazu, funhō o mo oru

Now for the first time, I know the skill of the spring wind on the loom.

It weaves not only with colors alone, but with fragrances as well.[31]

The character for spring, 春 (*haru*), embroidered in red-orange silk on the left back, reiterates the seasonal reference made by both the poem and the cherry tree with its stylized blossoms. The manner in which this character has been integrated into the pic-

CATALOGUE NO. 141
Kosode with Double-Blossom
Cherry Tree and Characters
First half eighteenth century
Kanebo, Ltd.

FIGURE 49
Cosmetic Box with Design of Plum
Blossoms, Moon, and Characters
(detail)
Muromachi period, fifteenth
century
Black lacquer and gold maki-e
on wood
5 9/16 × 11 7/8 × 9 3/16 in.
(14.1 × 30.2 × 23.3 cm)
Tokyo National Museum

ture, intertwined with the branches of the tree, closely resembles a lacquerware design from the Muromachi period (see fig. 49).

Another tachi-ki garment, *Kosode with Maple Trees and Characters* (cat. no. 134), can be related to a pattern from *Shikishi on-hinagata* (Paper square designs; 1689; fig. 50) because of a well-known poem to which both designs may allude. The poem reads:

CATALOGUE NO. 134
Kosode with Maple Trees and Characters
Second half eighteenth century
Tabata Collection

okuyama ni	Autumn is saddest
momiji fumiwake	when one hears the call of the stag,
naku shika no	crying as he pads
koe kiku toki zo	through crimson leaves
aki wa kanashiki	in the deep mountains.[32]

Whereas the hinagata-bon design presents a picture of deer standing in maple leaves,[33] the kosode shows the kanji for deer, 鹿 (*shika*), rendered in several different calligraphic styles, scattered around the meandering trunk of a maple tree.

おく山に紅葉ふみわけなく鹿のこゑきく時ぞ秋は悲しき

FIGURE 50

Page from *Shikishi on-hinagata,* 1689

In *Kosode with Cherry Blossoms, Bamboo Fence, and Characters* (cat. no. 139) the tree is represented only by blooming cherry branches. When the garment was worn, the blossom-laden boughs would hang from the wearer's shoulders, the human trunk becoming the tree trunk. The kanji indicate places in Japan known for their cherry trees.[34] The presence of the flower-laced bamboo fence can possibly be explained when the names of these locales are examined. Two of them (霞関 ; *Kasumi[ga]seki*, on the back, and 白川関 ; *Shirakawa[no]seki*, on the front) end with the Japanese word for barrier (関 [*seki*]).

The division between the upper and lower parts of this kosode's decoration was a stylistic response to the widening of the obi, which began in the Genroku era. The aforementioned *Kosode*

with Hawks, Maple Trees, Waterfalls, Checks, and Characters (cat. no. 146) also shows this division. The main pictorial elements of this work lie on the lower half of the garment. Hawks, complete with falconry tassels, are flying in a landscape. The kosode's upper half is a dazzling pattern of checks accented by embroidered pairs of kanji in the areas generally reserved for family crests (*mon*).[35] These read from left to right across the back: 若鷹 (*waka-taka* [young hawk]), 舞鷹 (*mai-taka* [dancing hawk]), and 紅鷹 (*kō-taka* [red hawk]). On the front they read: 紫鷹 (*shi-taka* [purple hawk]) and 黄鷹 (*ki-taka* [yellow hawk]). By a simple shifting of syllable groupings and the resultant change in phonetic emphasis, Maruyama Nobuhiko has proposed the following alternative meanings: *wakatta ka* (Do you understand?), *maitta ka* (Have you had enough?), *kōta ka* (Did you buy it?), *shita ka* (Did you do it?), and *kiita ka* (Did you hear it?).[36] In the Edo period *taka* (hawk) could have the connotation of *yotaka* (night-hawk, meaning prostitute). It is unlikely that a common street-

CATALOGUE NO. 146
Kosode with Hawks, Maple Trees, Waterfalls, Checks, and Characters
Mid-eighteenth century
Kanebo, Ltd.

walker could have afforded such a high-quality kosode, but the suggestive wordplay indicates just such a wearer. Speculation about possible owners, ranging from a courtesan to even a male patron of this "nighthawk," makes this garment a most intriguing work.

AN ARTFUL BALANCE

The enthusiasm with which Japanese artists incorporated inventive forms and uses of writing in calligraphy was extended to other art forms, including ceramics, lacquer, painting, and textiles. Textile designers of the Edo period, utilizing calligraphic, pictorial, and literary innovations of the day, created kosode designs that had their own highly refined language of style and signification.

As incomplete as the information is about the specific dynamics of Edo society, these garments provide a window on the character of Edo culture. We can appreciate the interplay between language and image, the conceptual and technical innovations, the attraction of the written word and the beauty of the word written, and finally, the creative drive that is liberally mixed with a sense of *asobi* (playfulness).[37] This symmetry is beautifully expressed in the *Kosode with Pine, Bamboo, Plum, Fans, and Characters* (cat. no. 145). The kanji represented are taken from a Chinese poem by Xu Hun (fl. 832) in the pine section of the *Wakan rōeishū*. The couplet reads in Japanese:

青
山
有
雪
譜
松
性

碧
落
無
雲
稱
鶴
心

seizan ni yuki atte, matsu no sei o soranzu

hekiraku ni kumo nakushite, tsuru no kokoro ni kanaeri

Snow upon the green mountains professes the pine's constancy.
The cloudlessness of the blue vault gratifies the crane's desire.[38]

At first glance the upper and lower halves of the kosode appear to be radically divided. The parallel construction of the poem is well expressed in the kosode design, however, and an artful balance is achieved between the two contrasting zones. There is some obvious congruity between the fans in the upper half and the fan-shaped vegetation in the lower half, as well as a certain parity between the areas in terms of graphic complexity and density. Just as the images of the poem contrast—the white snow on green mountains (tangible) with the blue of cloudlessness (intangible); the "pine's constancy" (permanence) with the "crane's desire" (transience)—so the kosode imagery shows a unity based on many polarities: earth and sky, organic and man-made, naturalistic and stylized, volumetric and flat, pictorial and linguistic. The final polarity is at the heart of the use of calligraphic designs on clothing. On any level of understanding, this striking kosode would have invited a closer "reading" of the wearer.

NOTES

1. Saikaku 1956, 119–20.

2. Habein 1984, 7–8. Habein states that Chinese script, in the form of inscriptions on articles such as swords and mirrors from China or Korea, may have been introduced into Japan sometime before the fourth century. The earliest surviving inscriptions found in Japan (on swords and a mirror) date to the fifth and sixth centuries. Literary references to such objects date to the seventh century.

3. For additional information regarding Japanese language, writing systems, and calligraphy see Rosenfield, Cranston, and Cranston 1973 and Shimizu and Rosenfield 1984.

4. Morris 1986, 195–96.

5. *Murasaki Shikibu nikki* (Diary of Murasaki Shikibu, c. 1010) and *Eiga monogatari* (A tale of flowering fortunes) are two literary sources that mention the use of language on costume. See Kirihata 1980, 307–8.

6. Mostow 1988, 119. The incorporation of poetry in a picture design can be referred to as *uta-e*, *ashide*, or both. The poem is from Japan's first imperial anthology, the tenth-century *Kokin wakashū* (no. 358). It reads:

yamatakami
kumoi ni miyuru
sakurabana
kokoro no yukite
oranu hi zo naki

Cherry blossoms
in the lofty clouds
that cloak the mountain peak!
Never a day goes by, but
my heart goes out to pluck them.

See Kadokawa Shoten 1983, 17. Note: All poems in this essay have been translated by Thomas Blenman Hare, associate professor of Asian languages and comparative literature at Stanford University.

7. Only the back section of this kosode, which is in the collection of the Tōyama Memorial Museum in Saitama Prefecture, survives. It appears that this fragment was at one time made into an altar cloth (uchishiki). See Imanaga 1983b, 70–71, pl. 43.

8. Kirihata 1980, 310, and Nagasaki I. 1987, 152. For the poem, see Kadokawa Shoten 1983, 128 (*Goshūi wakashū*, no. 770).

9. Stinchecum 1984, 51.

10. Five Kariganeya kosode order books exist today in Japanese collections: three in the Osaka Municipal Museum of Art, two at the Kawashima Textile Museum in Kyoto. This discussion is limited to those belonging to the former, where 20 percent of the designs include characters. See Chizawa 1970, 27. The Osaka order books, initially compiled into two bound notebooks (dated 1661 and 1663) were, at some point, reorganized into three bound volumes. The third volume, undated (c. 1664) and untitled, was formed from pages thought to be unrelated to the other two. The earlier volumes are known as *On'e-chō* (or *Ongachō*). See Maruyama 1986, 196, and Nishimoto 1982, 41.

Ogata Dōhaku (d. 1604), the founder of Kariganeya, was married to the sister of the renowned calligrapher and designer Hon'ami Kōetsu (1558–1637). Dōhaku's grandson Ogata Sōken (1621?–87), was a serious student of calligraphy and the head of Kariganeya during the time the kosode hinagata-chō under discussion were produced. Sōken was the father of two influential Edo-period artists: Ogata Kōrin (1658–1716), a painter and decorative arts designer, and Ogata Kenzan (1663–1743), a calligrapher and ceramicist.

Kariganeya was patronized by women of both the military elite and the aristocracy. Perhaps the most distinguished client was Tokugawa Hidetada's daughter Kazuko (later Tōfukumon'in), who became the consort of emperor Go-Mizuno-o (r. 1611–29). The kosode designs ordered by her household can be found in the order books now in the Osaka Municipal Museum of Art. See Stinchecum 1984, 53, and Wilson 1991, 40–45.

11. The repetition of *chi* is significant for two reasons. *Yachi* (eight thousand) is a common way of expressing "many/multiple." *Yachiyo* (eight thousand ages), which appears in numerous poems, often refers to the idealized eternal reign of the emperor.

12. See Nagasaki essay. Forty-four of the two hundred designs in *On-hiinakata* include characters. See Kawakami 1982, 33.

13. Tsukamoto 1982, 7.

14. See Museum of Fine Arts 1990, 138, pl. 52.

15. Kirihata 1980, 311, and Maruyama 1986, 223, note 18.

16. See Shaver 1990, 224–25, and Gunji 1970, 95–96. The *Kabuki jiten* (Kabuki encyclopedia), however, explains that the kamawanu motif was "created by Ichikawa Danjūrō VII when he performed Yoemon in 'Kasane' during the first half of the nineteenth century." See Leiter 1979, s.v. "kamawanu."

17. Komo no Jūzō was the father of Ishikawa Danjūrō I. See Sanseidō 1987, s.v. "hatamoto yakko, machi yakko."

18. Noma S. 1974, 126.

19. Princess Saigū no Nyōgo was one of the *Sanjūrokkasen* (Thirty-six poetic geniuses).

20. Kawaguchi and Shida 1979, 169 (*Wakan rōeishū*, no. 469). This poem is also found in the *Shūi wakashū* (Collection of gleanings of Japanese poems; no. 451), a mid-

Heian-period imperial anthology. See Kadokawa Shoten 1983, 74.

21. The author wishes to thank Professor Hare for this observation.

22. Kyoto National Museum 1980, 252, no. 52.

23. Kamijō 1981, s.v. "maruzukushi mon'yō."

24. Kawakami 1982, 33. For a discussion of the lunar calendar see Dunn 1987, 146, and Kodansha 1983, s.v. "calendar, dates, and time."

25. In the late sixteenth century, after years of war, many poverty-stricken girls from the provinces found work in the cities as attendants at public bathhouses. Their job was not only to wash the backs of their male clients but also to serve as prostitutes. A depiction similar to the one in the painting is found in *Rekisei josō kō* (History of women's fashions) by Santō Kyōzan (1769–1858). See Santō 1975, 159.

26. Kakudo 1991, 136, pl. 74.

27. The *Wakan rōeishū* is the first notable work to juxtapose Chinese and Japanese poems. This juxtaposition made it a perfect copybook for calligraphy practice, which may be a reason for it being one of the most quoted anthologies. Of the numerous examples of kosode with character designs in the collection of the Tokyo National Museum, most of the design sources are poems found in the *Wakan rōeishū*. See Hashimoto 1980b, 34.

28. See Kadokawa Shoten 1983, 17 (*Kokin wakashū*, no. 343), and Kawaguchi and Shida 1979, 250 (*Wakan rōeishū*, no. 776), for the original poem. Written by an anonymous poet, the first line of this poem was later changed from "waga kimi wa" (my sovereign lord) to "kimi ga yo wa" (the reign of our sovereign lord). The variation was adapted to music by Hayashi Hiromori (1821–86) and became the Japanese national anthem. See Kodansha 1983, s.v. "national anthem." Cat. no. 80 is also decorated with characters from this poem.

29. The Kariganeya illustration mentioned earlier (fig. 41) may also allude to this poem.

30. Kamiya 1971, 72, 74, figs. 124–25; Kyoto National Museum 1980, 241, no. 10. Other scholars, however, consider the tachi-ki motif to be in the tradition of the use of plant designs on kosode. Nagasaki Iwao, personal communication.

31. Kawaguchi and Shida 1979, 77 (*Wakan rōeishū*, no. 121).

32. See Kadokawa Shoten 1983, 14 (*Kokin wakashū*, no. 215). The Kirihata essay contains another translation of a part of this poem.

33. The characters depicted on the printed kosode design read *okuyama* (remote mountain).

34. Hashimoto 1980a, 19, no. 8.

35. *Date-mon* (fancy crests) were decorative patterns used in place of family crests; see Maruyama essay. *Tanzen hiinakata* (Tanzen patterns; 1704) illustrates numerous examples of date-mon located on the upper center back of a kosode. Each date-mon consists of kanji paired with such images as plants, flowers, boats, dolls, fans, or books.

36. See Maruyama Nobuhiko's commentary on pl. 3 in Kirihata and Maruyama 1988, 162. Certain of the readings are unorthodox combinations of Chinese and Japanese pronunciations. One of the interpretations, *kōta ka*, is from the Kansai dialect.

37. For an overview of the element of playfulness in Japanese art see Tsuji 1986.

38. Kawaguchi and Shida 1979, 157 (*Wakan rōeishū*, no. 422).

A Wearable Art:
The Relationship of Painting to Kosode Design

ROBERT T. SINGER

The Western distinction between the "fine arts" and the "decorative arts" is foreign to Japanese tradition, which has until recently maintained a more integrated approach to the arts. The earliest examples of Japanese art criticism, the fifteenth-century *Gyomotsu on'e mokuroku* and *Kundaikan sayūchōki*, are primarily connoisseurship manuals on the appreciation of Chinese paintings. The latter source, however, also explains how such artworks should be displayed in Japanese interiors and illustrates specific decorative objects, such as flower vases and incense burners, that should be shown with the paintings.[1] ❧ The ancient word for art in Japanese is *geijutsu*. The character *gei* is applicable to all art forms—visual, performing, and literary—and is the same as that in the word *geisha* (art person). Fine art (painting and sculpture) is translated as *bijutsu*; craft (decorative art or applied art), as *kōgei*. There is even the term *bijutsu kōgei* (literally, art craft), which refers to craft objects considered to reach the level of fine art. These latter terms have been used to make a distinction between art and craft only since the late nineteenth century, when Japan was exposed to Western aesthetic ideals.[2] This influence continues to affect the study of art history at Japanese universities, where more attention is paid to painting and sculpture than to ceramics, lacquer, metalwork, or textiles, a bias that only recently shows evidence of being corrected.[3] ❧ Perhaps the tea ceremony best exemplifies the unity of the arts in traditional Japan.[4] A guest entering a tearoom first kneels in front of the tokonoma, in which hangs a scroll bearing calligraphy, painting, or a combination of the two.[5] After examining the hanging scroll, the guest pays equal attention to the flower arrangement and its holder, which are placed in front of the scroll, as well as to the companion incense container. The tea utensils themselves, each considered to be worthy of the highest degree of appreciation, are of natural materials: clay for the tea bowl, bamboo for the tea whisk and water ladle, iron for the kettle, and lacquer for the tea caddy. At the end of the sequence of steps involved in the preparation of the whipped green tea by the host and the drinking of it by the guest, the latter examines the utensils, taking time to ask questions about each object's maker, provenance, and name (which is assigned by a tea master). The importance of tea ceremony practitioners in creating a demand for artworks that in the West would be regarded as mere craft objects cannot be overestimated. It is worth noting too that the art of the tea ceremony extends to garden design, architecture, and textiles, to the total environment in which this harmonious gathering of friends takes place.[6]

CATALOGUE NO. 64
Uchikake with Bamboo and Clouds
(detail)
First half nineteenth century
Kanebo, Ltd.

Additional insight into the relationship between art and craft in Edo-period Japan is provided by a look at the structure of the society. *Eshi* (professional painters) were considered craftsmen, third in the Tokugawa social hierarchy. *Shokunin-zukushi* (Sketches of craftsmen at work) includes illustrations of eshi, indicating their artisan status.[7] Amateur painters, by contrast, who painted for pleasure rather than to support themselves, were generally of a higher class, either aristocratic or samurai.

To illustrate how artists themselves were not concerned with a distinction between art and craft, three schools of art, Rimpa, Nanga, and Maruyama, can be examined. The Rimpa school was started in the early seventeenth century by Tawaraya Sōtatsu (fl. 1602–30) and Hon'ami Kōetsu (1558–1637), revived in the early eighteenth century by Ogata Kōrin (1658–1716), and given new life in the early nineteenth century by Sakai Hōitsu (1761–1828). Rimpa works are archetypically Japanese in their decorative quality, abstraction, and use of precious materials. Rimpa artists were equally skilled in painting and calligraphy and in designing lacquer and textiles—occasionally they even painted directly on kosode.

The Nanga school was begun in the early eighteenth century by three artists—Gion Nankai (1677–1751), Yanagisawa Kien (1704–58), and Sakaki Hyakusen (1697–1752)—who found inspiration in the recently imported works of Chinese literati painters. Nanga artists also painted directly on kosode.

The Maruyama school was founded in Kyoto in the late eighteenth century by Maruyama Ōkyo (1733–95). Works of this school combine traditional Japanese decorative sensibilities with realistic qualities based on Western-influenced perspective and shading and, on occasion, direct sketching from nature. While the members of the Maruyama school were best known for their paintings, some drew kosode designs.[8] As will be discussed, extant kosode can be linked directly to these designs.

KOSODE BY IDENTIFIABLE ARTISTS OR SCHOOLS

Certain of the kosode in the exhibition bear paintings that can be directly related to artists of the Rimpa, Nanga, and Maruyama schools through signatures, seals, or stylistic similarities. While few pre-Edo, painted (kaki-e) examples remain, a famous Muromachi work, the dōbuku in the Uesugi Collection,[9] proves that such objects were not unknown before the Edo period. Four other examples of this practice are documented between 1680 and 1700 in novels by Ihara Saikaku. Of particular note is an anecdote (provided at the beginning of this catalogue) from *Kōshoku ichidai otoko* (The life of an amorous man; 1682) about the courtesan Kaoru, who had the celebrated female painter Kano Yukinobu

(1643–82) paint an autumn scene on white satin for use as a kosode instead of as a hanging scroll.[10] This incident, whether true or not, is a perfect illustration of the interchangeability of art and textile design at the time.

Three robes in the exhibition (cat. nos. 71 left, 72, 123), although not kaki-e, clearly show Rimpa stylistic influence.[11] The first is distinctive for its patterned waves in simplified bands of blue and white, while the latter two are dominated by a meander-

CATALOGUE NO. 123
Uchikake with Stream and Irises
First half nineteenth century
Kanebo, Ltd.

ing river motif of stylized water lines, all hallmarks of this painting style. At least two kosode exist that are by identified Rimpa artists. The first (fig. 51), in the collection of the Tokyo National Museum, is by Ogata Kōrin, who painted it for the wife of a wealthy Edo merchant. A great number of designs attributed to his influence are seen in hinagata-bon of the eighteenth century.[12] The second (cat. no. 62), by Sakai Hōitsu, bears a magnificent painting of a plum tree. Hōitsu splayed the abbreviated form of the tree up the back of the robe and out to both shoulders. There is no better example in Japanese textile art of a painting design adapted to a wearable medium. That Hōitsu literally used the kosode as a painting surface in the traditional manner can be seen in his liberal use of the *tarashikomi*[13] technique to produce a rounded illusion in the trunk and branches of the tree. Hōitsu's painted signature in the form of a seal can be seen at the right front edge (see detail of cat. no. 62).

Two kosode in the exhibition (cat. nos. 61, 63) are by known Nanga artists. The first, by Matsumura Goshun (1752–1811), is a

CATALOGUE NO. 62 (detail)

rare example of a landscape transposed onto a kosode. As the wearer turned, or as a viewer walked around the wearer, the scene curved in space, with the mountains at the ends of the sleeves fading into the distance. The composition is a unique adaptation of the restricted, two-dimensional space of a hanging scroll to the expansive, three-dimensional format of a kosode. That Goshun considered this work to be equal to his more traditional works is indicated by his use of a conventional signature and seal (see detail of cat. no. 61).

The second Nanga school kosode is attributed to Gion Nankai. The design immediately brings to mind Chinese literati paintings, in which bamboo was a favored theme; Chinese modelbooks may

also have provided design inspiration. Compared with Nankai's traditional bamboo paintings, this example is freer in execution, perhaps reflecting its medium. The work was commissioned by the Izumi merchant Karakaneya Okitaka for a favored courtesan.[14] To literally wear on one's back an artwork by a celebrated painter must have been a status symbol of the highest order. That it exists today in excellent condition (as do most of the other kaki-e works in this exhibition) speaks of the great esteem in which this kosode was held.

The design of another kosode (cat. no. 67) may be identified with certainty as by an artist of the Maruyama school or as influenced by such an artist. Although dyed rather than painted, the consistent ground plane and highly realistic treatment of the ducks (based on careful observation of nature) reveal Maruyama school antecedents. It can also be related to extant hinagata-bon and sketches of this school.[15]

In addition to kosode by identifiable artists and schools, there are many that display the same thematic concerns as other art forms. Kosode with depictions of landscapes, famous places, genre subjects, and even painting formats themselves demonstrate that the arts of the Edo period drew inspiration from common sources.

LANDSCAPE AS A DESIGN MOTIF
IN JAPANESE TEXTILES

The depiction of landscape has been valued more highly in the art of East Asia than in that of the Western world, taking precedence over the portrayal of people or human activities.[16] First in China and later in Japan *sansuiga* (landscape painting) was imbued with a philosophy of reverence for nature. The foundation for landscape painting was laid in China by the fifth century; this and each succeeding development in the tradition were soon conveyed to Japan, where modifications resulted in a distinctly Japanese form of expression. Given the supreme importance of landscape painting as a subject matter, it is not surprising that it should appear on Japanese textiles from a very early date.

Among the oldest Japanese examples of landscape depicted on cloth are two bast-fiber pieces in the Shōsō-in collection.[17] These ink paintings, which probably composed part of a curtain or banner, presage the treatment of landscape in textile design of later centuries, specifically in their evenly dispersed repeated wave patterns and multiple points of view over an extended surface. While these are paintings on fabric rather than textile designs as such, they still contain elements that are seen much later in the adaptation of landscape to kosode design.

CATALOGUE NO. 67
Uchikake with Cherry Blossoms,
Water, Ducks, and Characters
First half nineteenth century
Bunka Gakuen Costume Museum

Surviving textiles from the succeeding Heian period are so rare that there exist no remaining costumes with landscapes. There is literary evidence, however. Several passages in the *Murasaki Shikibu nikki* (Diary of Murasaki Shikibu; c. 1010), for instance, mention embroidered designs depicting the mountains known as Koshioyama and Komatsubara in Kyoto. Other Heian texts may also be cited. What is most significant about each of these is that the landscape depicted is Japanese, not Chinese or idealized, and is based on specific waka.[18]

In the succeeding Muromachi period there is more literary evidence for the depiction of landscape on clothing, consisting of, for example, descriptions of costumes worn in imperial processions.[19] From the brief but brilliant Momoyama period there is a kosode fragment decorated with tsujigahana that bears a scene of mountains, trees, and small buildings.[20] This and other works reveal the beginnings of a trend toward the depiction of landscape for its own sake. This pattern may be seen in other media, such as painting and lacquer, in which design and pure visual effect take precedence over literary allusion.

In the Edo period the peak of landscape depiction as a motif in kosode design occurred during the Genroku and Kyōhō eras. This short period corresponded, not coincidentally, with the highest point in the development of the yūzen-dyeing technique (see Kirihata essay). For the first time artists were able to execute painterly panoramic views of natural scenes on kosode.[21]

FAMOUS PLACES

Meisho-e (depictions of celebrated places) have a venerable history in Japanese painting, extending at least as far back as the tenth century. From the frequency with which they are mentioned in Heian-period sources, including the "E-awase" (Picture competition) chapter in the *Genji monogatari* (Tale of Genji), they must have been extremely popular. In the intervening centuries between the Heian and Edo periods, the tradition of meisho-e continued, stronger when influence from Chinese culture was weak (Kamakura period), weaker when Chinese influence was strong (Muromachi period). With the advent of the Edo period, however, there was a sea change in the ability of people to travel. The intense interest in tourism coincided with technical developments to produce a proliferation of landscape designs illustrating famous places (see Kirihata essay). Wearing a garment with such scenes proclaimed that one had both the money and leisure to travel to distant locales.

As Kyoto was the cultural capital of Japan from the ninth century on, scenes of the city and its environs were often shown on kosode as well as lacquer, hanging scrolls, and folding screens. Such representations on the latter are called *rakuchū rakugai-zu* (Scenes in and around Kyoto).[22] These screens are decorated with highly ordered and detailed topographical illustrations of the Imperial Palace, major temples and shrines, aristocratic estates, and merchant shops. They are so accurate that they can be dated based on the presence or absence of certain structures. These screens document the rise of the merchant class, the return of prosperity after the rampant destruction suffered in the Ōnin War, and the shifting balance of political power at different times in the sixteenth century and early seventeenth century.

CATALOGUE NO. 111
Kosode with Views of Kyoto
Mid-eighteenth century
National Museum of Japanese
History, Nomura Collection

The majority of later (seventeenth-century) rakuchū rakugai-zu screens divide Kyoto along a north-south axis: the east of the city depicted on the right screen, the west on the left. The most important of these for textile purposes is a pair known as the Funaki screens.[23] The scene in the center of the right screen of the Funaki pair parallels that on a kosode in the exhibition (cat. no. 111).

At the top of the kosode is Kiyomizu Temple, immediately recognizable by its projecting platform supported by a system of wooden pillars. To the upper right is a smaller building known as Oku-no-in; below this are the three streams of water known as the Otowa Falls, considered one of the five finest sources of water in Kyoto. In the center of the composition rises the Yasaka Pagoda; the dominant element in the bottom of the scene is the Gojō Bridge over the Kamo River. Among extant rakuchū rakugai-zu, this emphasis on the bridge is unique to the Funaki screens. It is possible that the designer of the kosode saw these screens or a later version of them. In the Funaki screens and others like them, the temple, pagoda, and bridge line up in a diagonal relationship; in the kosode, however, with its vertical format, they are placed one on top of the other.

In the course of Edo-period painting a movement toward increasingly close-up views of particular scenes is noticeable. In a katabira (cat. no. 112), the aforementioned Kiyomizu Temple is the main motif. That this kosode dates from considerably later in the Edo period fits in with the tendency toward the expansion of one part of a larger scene into an overall design theme. In the

CATALOGUE NO. 112
Katabira with View of Kiyomizu Temple (detail)
First half nineteenth century
Tokyo National Museum

katabira the seasonal element of cherry blossoms, for which Kiyomizu is celebrated, is emphasized. Just as a hanging scroll of this scene would be displayed in a Japanese home in the spring, the garment would have been worn at this time. Befitting the function of the garment and its decorative aspect, the scale of the cherry trees is exaggerated.

Other kosode in the exhibition display views of Nonomiya Shrine (cat. no. 102), Sumiyoshi (cat. no. 104), Uji Bridge (cat. no. 106), and Lake Biwa[24] (cat. nos. 105, 107–8). These sights are all in the Kyoto or Osaka areas, in the western part of Japan.

CATALOGUE NO. 105
Kosode with "Eight Views of Ōmi"
Mid-eighteenth century
Kanebo, Ltd.

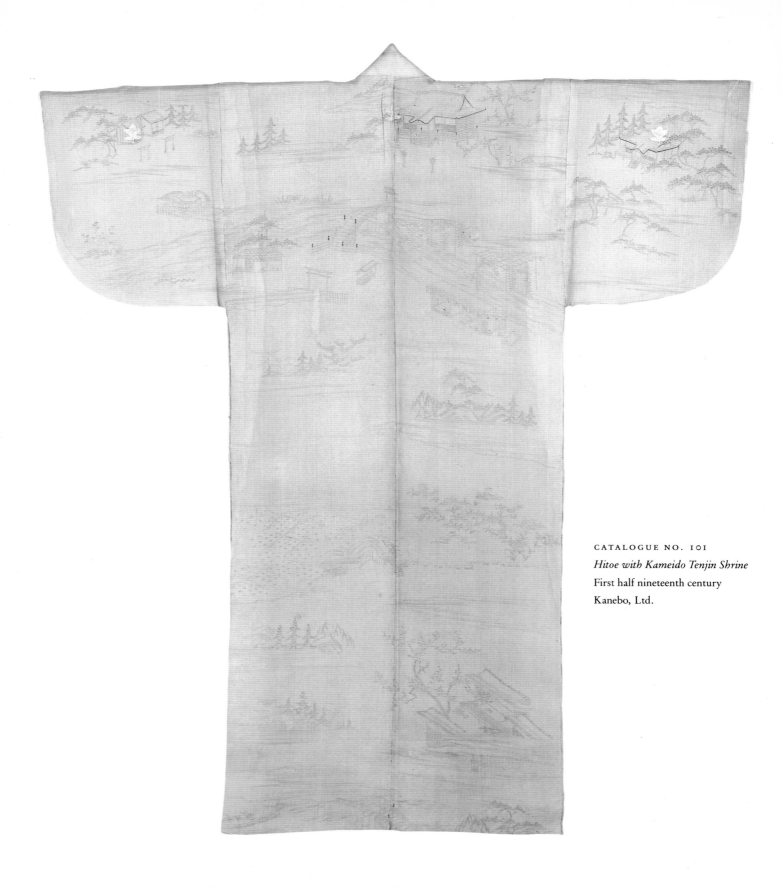

Representing the eastern side (Edo) are kosode decorated with views of Kameido Tenjin Shrine (cat. no. 101), the Sumida River (cat. no. 109), and Yoshiwara (cat. no. 110). Even an imaginary scene, that of Hōrai-san (the isle of the immortals, a symbol of eternal youth), is seen (cat. no. 75). A comparison with a hanging scroll showing a typical treatment of the same subject (fig. 52) by

Suzuki Kiitsu (1796–1858) reveals again how a landscape theme could be adapted to a wearable medium. In the kosode the central mass of Hōrai-san seen in Kiitsu's painting has been transformed into a panoramic view of smaller islands, some linked by bridges. As the wearer turned, the viewer of the kosode would have been guided through the paradisiacal scene.

GENRE SUBJECTS

Treatments of genre subjects became particularly common in the Edo period. The lowly origins of the merchant class and the move away from aristocratic concerns were partially responsible for this. Kosode examples include one decorated with agricultural scenes (cat. no. 37), which may be compared with a lacquer stationery box bearing a remarkably similar design (fig. 53). In both

CATALOGUE NO. 75
Kosode with Isle of the Immortals
(Hōrai-san)
Mid-eighteenth century
Tokyo National Museum

•

FIGURE 52
Suzuki Kiitsu (1796–1858)
Isle of the Immortals
Hanging scroll; gold paint on
indigo silk
42 3/16 × 14 in. (107.2 × 35.6 cm)
Los Angeles County Museum of
Art, gift of Kochukyo in honor of
the opening of the Pavilion for
Japanese Art, M.88.186

CATALOGUE NO. 37
*Kosode with Agricultural Scenes
of the Four Seasons*
First half nineteenth century
Tokyo National Museum

a two-dimensional painting subject was rearranged to function on a three-dimensional object. On the kosode the scene wraps around the garment; on the box the paths between the rice paddies continue down the front and the two sides. In a furisode (cat. no. 38) a tea-picking scene is handled in a much more symmetrical manner than would be the case in screen paintings of the same subject. A variation of a landscape scene is an image of drying fishing nets (cat. no. 60), a genre theme often seen in screen paintings.

Festival scenes are one of the most frequent genre subjects in Edo-period painting. One kosode (cat. no. 34) depicts a horse

FIGURE 53
Stationery Box (detail)
Seventeenth century
Lacquer on wood with
mother-of-pearl inlay
5 ½ × 16 × 13 in.
(14.0 × 40.6 × 33.0 cm)
Los Angeles County Museum of
Art, gift of the 1988 Collectors
Committee, M.88.83
•

CATALOGUE NO. 38
Furisode with Tea-picking Scenes
First half nineteenth century
Tokyo National Museum

CATALOGUE NO. 34
Kosode with Scene of Horse Racing
Mid-eighteenth century
Kyoto National Museum

race, perhaps that of the Wakamiya Festival of Kasuga Shrine in Nara. A pair of screens in the Nara Prefectural Museum of Art (fig. 54) includes a scene of that festival's crowded contest. In the kosode the designer cleverly focused on two riders, thereby intensifying the competitive essence of the scene. The flat, static checkerboard pattern serves as a foil for the swirling activity of the horses and multicolored maple leaves.[25] The precise design source for this kosode is found in a hinagata-bon of 1724 (*Tōryū moyō hinagata tsuru no koe* [Patterns of present-day fashion: The call of the crane pattern book]; fig. 55).

FIGURE 54
Kano Tan'yū (1602–74)
Kasuga Wakamiya Festival (detail)
Pair of six-panel screens; ink and color on paper
Each: 59 5/8 × 140 15/16 in.
(151.5 × 358.0 cm)
Nara Prefectural Museum of Art

Another example of a larger scene becoming the focal point of an entire composition is *Kosode with Banners* (cat. no. 33), in which festival banners are displayed at contrasting angles. No people are seen, but their presence is strongly suggested by the wild movement inherent in the position of the standards.

Even articles of clothing make their appearance on kosode. In three garments (cat. nos. 91–92, 129), sedge hats are rhythmically arranged, paralleling a similar but much earlier treatment of the same theme on a Shino dish (fig. 56). The abundance of hat designs in hinagata-bon of the Edo period testify to the popularity of this particular theme.

INCLUSION IN KOSODE DESIGN OF ACTUAL PAINTING FORMATS

There are a number of kosode in the exhibition that employ actual painting formats as decorative motifs. These garments depict hanging scrolls, folding screens, fans, *tanzaku* (narrow rectangular slips of paper), and *shikishi* (mounted squares of paper). This playful use of such subjects is a literal example of the influence of painting on kosode design. Examples include two kosode that picture hanging scrolls (cat. nos. 85, 99). In the first, a number of Chinese children are shown flying kites, playing games, etc. Two of them are admiring a hanging scroll. Replacing adults with youngsters in such mature pastimes as appreciating art is a theme seen in painting by the early Edo period.

FIGURE 55
Page from *Tōryū moyō hinagata tsuru no koe*, 1724

FIGURE 56
Footed Food Vessel (detail)
Momoyama period
Stoneware with iron underglaze
painting, Shino white glaze
2 9/16 × 6 1/4 in. (6.5 × 15.9 cm)
Los Angeles County Museum of
Art, promised gift of Julia and Leo
Krashen, L.90.15

CATALOGUE NO. 91
Kosode with Sedge Hats and Maple Leaves
Late seventeenth–early eighteenth century
Tokyo National Museum

In the second example, two scrolls are shown in front of a willow tree. This outdoor display is unusual, but a possible source for the idea may be a late-sixteenth-century screen in which a hanging scroll is being admired by three scholars (fig. 57). In the screen painting the scroll is supported by a stick held by an attendant; in the kosode the attendant and scholars have disappeared, their presence suggested only by the stick lying on the ground behind the scroll. This is an excellent example of a narrative element being abstracted and reduced to its essentials for decorative purposes. The informed viewer of the kosode would have understood the implicit reference to the original image. A more immediate source for this kosode's design is to be found in a hinagata-bon published in 1719 (see Nagasaki essay, fig. 22). Of particular

CATALOGUE NO. 85
Furisode with Japanese Bamboo Curtain and Chinese Children at Play (detail)
First half nineteenth century
Marubeni Corporation

interest in this kosode is the figure of a man riding a cloud. He is most likely Jurōjin, one of the seven gods of good fortune. He is shown, characteristic staff in hand, gazing at a deer, one of the animals (along with the crane) that often accompanies him. The contrast between the austere ink tones of the painting within a painting and the colorful hues lavished on the depiction of the silk border mounts is striking. To further emphasize the hanging scroll theme, the kosode designer scattered several scroll boxes on the ground but decorated them with brightly colored designs much more appropriate to a kosode than to actual scroll boxes. The kosode designer was inventive as well with the untied box cords, whose graceful curvilinear patterns befit their function as decorative elements on a woman's costume.

The folding screen, the other major painting format in Japanese art, is seen in two kosode (cat. nos. 98, 100). The first illustrates a number of single screens standing amid a field of grasses and flowers. The inclusion of scattered fans suggests a hot summer day and would remind the viewer of the Edo-period pastime of picnicking outdoors with screens arranged so as to attain a measure of privacy. That this is a katabira (summer garment) lends weight to this supposition. In the second, sections of three folding screens show illustrations of the fifty-three stages of the Tōkaidō, the Edo-period highway between Edo and Kyoto. These stations,

rest stops for food and lodging, are arranged in the order the traveler would encounter them along the way, and, just as in an actual screen painting, each is identified by a small label. This kosode showing screens is now itself part of a screen; although incomplete, it is possible that all fifty-three stages were originally included over the full expanse of the kosode.

It is interesting to note that both garments show screens displayed in what today would be considered a highly irregular way: instead of a zigzag configuration, each screen's panels are arranged almost willy-nilly. Since contemporary book illustrations also show screens displayed in this manner, it must be accepted that the present-day method was not the norm until comparatively

CATALOGUE NO. 98
Katabira with Folding Screens,
Plants, and Chinese Fans
Late eighteenth–early nineteenth
century
Kanebo, Ltd.

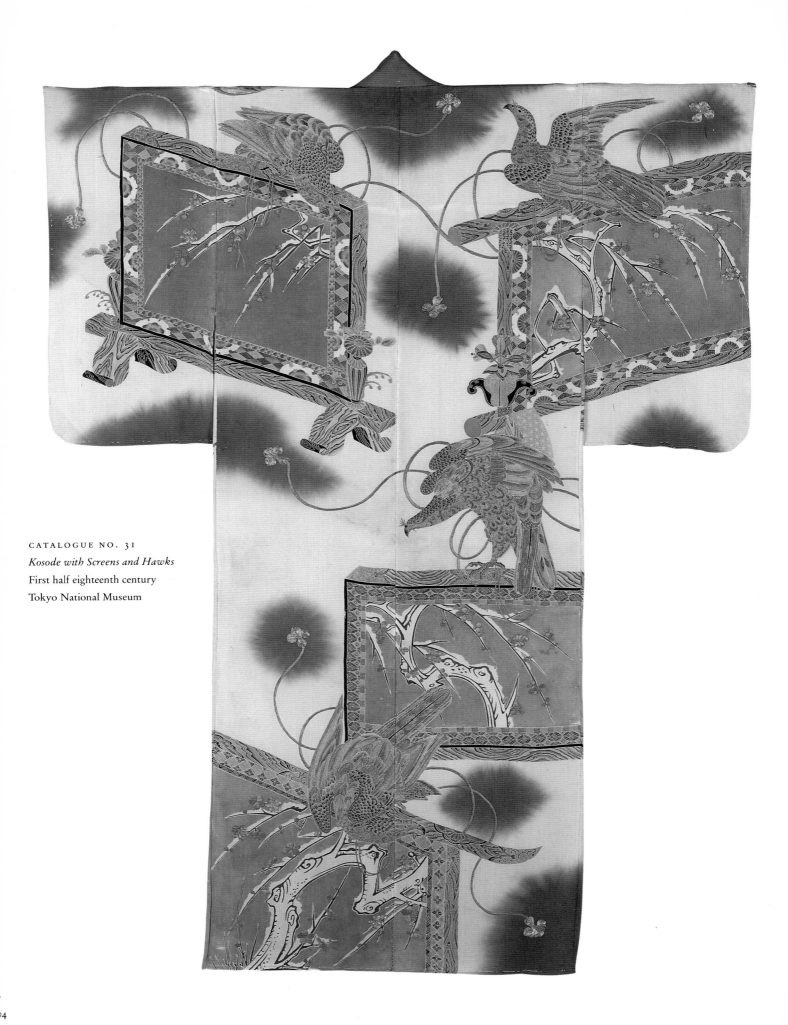

CATALOGUE NO. 31
Kosode with Screens and Hawks
First half eighteenth century
Tokyo National Museum

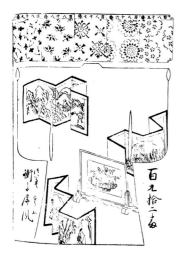

FIGURE 58

Page from *Tōryū shippō tokiwa hiinakata*, 1700

recently. That the inclusion of screens in kosode designs was not an isolated occurrence may be seen in the number of alternate designs seen in contemporary hinagata-bon (figs. 58–59).

A less common screen type is that with one panel supported by a pair of feet (*tsuitate*). Often providing privacy at the entrance to a temple or residence, this type of screen also prevents ill fortune from entering a building, based on the Chinese geomantic belief that malevolent spirits are unable to turn corners. In one of the most spectacular kosode in the exhibition (cat. no. 31), four screens of this sort are arranged across the surface. In a design tour de force, sections of a single plum tree are depicted on each screen, as if glimpsed through four windows. This is a startling adaptation of the single screen to the kosode format; one would normally expect a different tree to be shown on each screen. The portrayal of hawks is also striking. Edo-period folding screen paintings of hawks on wintry pine trees exist in substantial numbers, indicating their popularity among the samurai class, for whom hawks were a symbol of ferocity, and pines, of longevity. In this kosode the designer has lifted the hawks out of the picture frames and perched them not on pines, but on the fragmented plum tree. The plum was more auspicious and colorful, allowing the embroidery of snowy blossoms on the kosode surface. The decorative aspect is further enhanced by the brilliant colors used to delineate the silk brocades and wood frame surrounding each screen painting. Leaving aside the incredible technical skill of the yūzen-zome seen here, the design concept and adaptation from one format to another is breathtaking in its effectiveness. The probable source of this design is to be found in the winter section of *Yosei hinakata* (Patterns of lingering charm; 1692; fig. 60), in which appears a plum tree seen through windows of different sizes. The designer of this kosode brilliantly transformed the rectangles into tsuitate screens. A more pedestrian approach to the same subject, in which each tsuitate displays a different motif, is

FIGURE 59

Page from *Tōfū bijo hinagata*, 1715

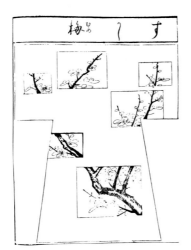

FIGURE 60

Page from *Yosei hinakata*, 1692

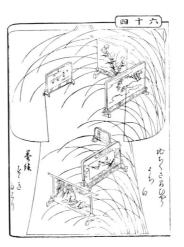

FIGURE 61

Page from *Hinagata kiku no i*, 1719

seen in *Hinagata kiku no i* (Printed patterns: The well of chrysanthemums; 1719; fig. 61).

Painted fans have a venerable history in Japan; the oldest extant examples date to the eleventh century. Indeed one of the founders of the Rimpa school, Tawaraya Sōtatsu, began as a fan painter. Three kosode in the exhibition (cat. nos. 65, 115–16) make use of painted fans as a primary design motif. In the first, indigo-ground fans alternate with white-ground fans, each painted with delicate renderings of flowers and birds. The fans are curved in space, unrealistically so, in order to form an immensely pleasing pattern of overlapping forms that seem to dance on a dark ground. In the second example, Chinese-style painted fans alternate with shikishi; both illustrate scenes from the *Genji monogatari*. In the

CATALOGUE NO. 65
Uchikake with Fans Decorated with
Plants and Flowers of the
Four Seasons
Late eighteenth–early nineteenth
century
Matsuzakaya Co., Ltd.

*Kosode with Vertical Stripes and
Fans, Snowflake Roundels, and
Pine-Bark Lozenges*
(Matsukawabishi) *Filled with Scenes
from Classical Literature* (detail)
Mid-eighteenth century
Tokyo National Museum

third kosode, round flat fans and open folding fans are intertwined with blossoming cherry trees.

When visiting a site famous for its blossoming plum or cherry trees, it was customary to write appropriate poems on tanzaku and to hang these slips from the trees. This custom suggests the unity of man and nature, the one celebrating the beauty of the other through poetry. In one kosode fragment (cat. no. 36)

CATALOGUE NO. 36

Kosode on Screen
Kosode fragment with cherry tree
and poem papers
First quarter eighteenth century
National Museum of Japanese
History, Nomura Collection

FIGURE 62
Willows and Cherry (detail)
Seventeenth century
Pair of six-panel screens; ink, color,
and gold on paper
Each: 61 ½ × 140 in.
(156.2 × 355.6 cm)
Courtesy of the Freer Gallery of
Art, Smithsonian Institution,
Washington, D.C., 1985.26;
1985.27

numerous poetry slips flutter from poles placed in a flowering cherry tree. A similar presentation, although far less crowded in keeping with the wide expanse offered by a folding screen, is seen in a work (fig. 62) in which actual tanzaku are affixed to the painting surface. The theme is supremely felicitous, heralding the advent of spring.

CONCLUSION

In a land where a work of art could be a tea bowl, an incense burner, or a flower arrangement, it is easy to understand how a garment could be treated with the same reverence as a painting. The Edo period was a time when established artists turned their attention to designing or decorating kosode. The paintings on fabric displayed in this exhibition demonstrate the exciting possibilities inherent in the combining of painting and textile design—in the creation of a wearable art.

NOTES

1. Alternative readings of the two titles are *Gyomotsu gyoga mokuroku* and *Kundaikan sōchōki*. A typical passage from the latter work reads: "When a set of four hanging scrolls is displayed, a flower vase or an incense burner should be placed in the center [of the tokonoma in front of the paintings]." See Wakimoto 1933, 39.

2. The word *bijutsu* was first used in its modern sense by Japanese commissioners to the Vienna World Exposition in 1873. See Moeran 1987, 28, and Chisolm 1963, 47–48. I am indebted to Joseph Newland for bringing these two references to my attention.

3. In the last decade increasing numbers of Japanese students have been allowed to specialize in ceramics, lacquer, and textiles and have found positions in universities and museums after completion of their graduate studies.

4. The term *tea ceremony* is abhorred by present-day tea practitioners because of its ritualistic implications. (Instead, *tea gathering* is preferred.) Since the term is so prevalent in Western sources, however, it will be used here.

5. Because the tokonoma is the only proper place to display art objects in a Japanese interior, the works take on a much greater importance than their counterparts in the West. The seasonal aspect of such artworks necessitates their constant rotation, making the tokonoma into a kind of continually renewed shrine to art.

6. See Lee 1963 and Hayashiya, Nakamura, and Hayashiya 1974.

7. One illustration shows painters in a workshop; another portrays a scroll mounter. The leaves, part of a set of forty-nine depicting different crafts, are from an album owned by the Tenri Library. See Amino and Ishida 1983, plates 46, 18.

8. Dōmyō 1990, 84.

9. See Itō 1985, 87, fig. 26.

10. Saikaku 1964, 185.

11. See Wilson 1990 for a discussion of the ways in which Rimpa design influenced the arts of lacquer, ceramics, and textiles.

12. For example, there are the *Hinagata Gionbayashi* (Gion grove designs; 1714) and *Tōfū bijo hinagata* (Contemporary beautiful women designs; 1715).

13. The tarashikomi technique employs the soft, blurred effect of pigment or ink dripped onto a wet ground to create an illusion of volume.

14. Nagasaki I. 1989, 165.

15. Dōmyō 1990.

16. For a discussion of the cultural and philosophical reasons for this phenomenon see Munakata 1991. Before the ninth century the depiction of man and his activities occupied the same central position in Chinese painting as it did in premodern Western art. From about the tenth century, however, the depiction of landscape became the dominant tradition in Chinese painting.

17. Reproduced in Gotō S. 1978, pl. 89, and Nara National Museum 1978, 31, pl. 28.

18. Kirihata 1988a, 50.

19. Ibid., 51.

20. Ibid. The fragment, in the Kanebō Collection, is illustrated in Itō 1985, 84, pl. 51.

21. There are also existing examples of hanging scrolls from the Edo period in which the pictures were yūzen dyed instead of painted, indicating the crossover popularity of the technique. See Nagasaki I. 1991.

22. The earliest extant pair, known as the Machida screens, are in the collection of the Tokyo National Museum and are datable to the 1520s. See Hayashiya and Murashige 1983.

23. The Funaki screens (Tokyo National Museum), named after a former owner, are datable to 1615–20 and are unique in that they depict a continuous panoramic scene across both screens. See Kawashima and Tsuji 1983.

24. A recent exhibition catalogue provides a useful survey of how the famous eight views of Lake Biwa and its environs (Ōmi) were employed as subject matter for paintings (hanging scrolls, screens, and handscrolls), textiles, lacquer, and woodblock prints. See Miyajima 1988. This imagery was derived from Chinese paintings of the "Eight Views of the Hsiao and Hsiang." See Maruyama essay, note 10.

25. This kosode was previously identified as a depiction of the horse race of the summer festival at Kamo Shrine in Kyoto. The maple leaves in the kosode, however, argue for a reidentification of the subject as the autumn Wakamiya Festival horse race in Nara. For a discussion and illustration of a sixteenth-century pair of horse race screens in the collection of Kasuga Shrine in Nara, see Izumi 1991. For a discussion and illustration of a pair of seventeenth-century screens depicting the Wakamiya Festival in the Shin'enkan Collection, see Singer 1984, 331. I am indebted to Professor Takeda Tsuneo for bringing the Izumi reference to my attention.

Fashion and the Floating World:
The Kosode in Art

MARUYAMA NOBUHIKO

In Japanese the term *fashion* is translated as *ryūkō* (to flow away), expressing the notion that all styles are transitory. Doubtless, change is the fate of all things, but in fashion, change itself is the object. The life of still-useful items is often cut short for the simple reason that they are outmoded. A comment from *Onna chōhōki* (Record of heavy jewels for women; 1692)[1] illustrates the ebb and flow of Edo-period fashion: "Even the appearance of the capital changes with time, with popular designs sometimes completely disappearing after five to eight years." A trend that lasts this long is by no means fleeting when thought of in the context of present-day styles, but the essence of the passage applies as much to today as to the Edo period. ❧ Until the middle of the seventeenth century, fashion innovation was largely set by the upper classes and imitated as much as possible by those below. A reversal of this trend occurred in the second half of the century, however, when dress became a popular art form, with new styles moving upward from the lower classes. What had been the exclusive preserve of the elite now became the domain of the chōnin. The Kyōhō-era *Mukashi mukashi monogatari* (Tales of olden days)[2] bemoans the fact that respectable women blindly followed the modes and manners of their social inferiors:

> The vogue for crested, plain, or striped kosode imitates the dress of prostitutes. In the past, women of society wore glittering kosode, such as those decorated with embroidery and thin gold leaf, and prostitutes [*yūjo*] wore plain or striped garments in order to distinguish them from other women. The same was true of obi— ordinary women of fashionable society wore narrow obi, and prostitutes' obi were very wide, so that one could tell which was which. But today women of the world imitate prostitutes and put on plain or striped kosode with wide obi. This is mere imitation and indicates no discernment whatsoever.

❧ Of special interest here is the fact that the clothing of prostitutes had become the object of emulation. Prostitutes were outcastes who lived a kind of rarefied existence in a world of artifice: the pleasure quarters. While possessing a degree of freedom from the constraints of a feudal system, such districts were subject to the same restrictions of sumptuary laws as the rest of society. Depending on a prostitute's classification, unwritten laws limited fabric choices, decorative methods, and manner of dress. Nevertheless, the licensed quarters remained without a doubt the place to try out the newest designs. ❧ Innovations in costume could also be explored on the kabuki stage. While the influence of the theater increased dramatically in the mid-eighteenth century, a number of fads named for popular kabuki actors had been

CATALOGUE NO. 198
Nishikawa Sukenobu (1671–1751)
Standing Beauty (detail)
First half eighteenth century
Entrusted to the Azabu Museum of
Arts and Crafts

recorded earlier in the *Honchō seji danki* (The ways of our world; 1735),[3] including *Kichiya musubi, Kodayū kanoko, Sawanojō bōshi,* and *Sen'ya-zome*.[4]

Paintings as Historical Documents

No better material exists for the study of the past than surviving objects. Although they may be imperfect in one way or another, such items remain the most eloquent witnesses to the era from which they come. In studying Edo-period fashion, extant kosode are among the most valuable resources. Their path to the present, like that of all clothing, was a perilous one; although vast quantities of kosode once existed, most perished through daily use. Those that have survived were owned by the elite or those associated with them. Such garments were not subject to the same amount of wear as commoners' clothing and were often carefully preserved (see introduction). Unfortunately, even among the survivors most have been altered, their provenance lost.[5]

Because they are bound by the above circumstances, it is impossible to reconstruct from extant kosode a comprehensive picture of Edo-period clothing, particularly the fashions of commoners, whose garments have all but disappeared. As a result, paintings depicting kosode become essential research tools that not only provide additional information but also convey aspects of fashion that cannot be inferred from isolated objects.

The usefulness of paintings as historical documents can be summarized in the following four points. First, they exist in large numbers. Although there is considerable variation in quality, their quantity alone makes them a significant subject for study. Second, paintings reveal the styles of ordinary chōnin, the clothing worn by people in the street. Third, in many cases the date of a particular painting can be inferred from its style or from the life dates of the artist; thus a detailed chronology of kosode development is more easily established from the graphic arts than from extant kosode. The fourth point is that paintings present an entire silhouette, showing how particular items of clothing were worn, something individual garments cannot convey.

Paintings (and prints) may permit us to supplement our study of extant garments, but we must keep in mind that no matter how realistically they depict kosode, they are ultimately secondary sources as historical material for textile and costume study. Consequently we must be wary of taking their content at face value. On this point we should pay attention to the words of late-Edo-period scholars regarding methods of historical investigation. Ise Sadatake (1717–84),[6] for example, in the "Koga wo shō to nasu"

(Old paintings as evidence) section of his *Ansai zuihitsu* (Writings of Ansai), asserts: "It is common practice to use old paintings as evidence when considering matters of the past. Because the artists of those times painted the appearance of things they saw with their own eyes, their paintings constitute evidence for later scholars for examining the past."

Sadatake, while recognizing the validity of using old paintings, calls attention to the following points. The artists of the past, first of all, were not aware of the possibility that their work might be used as historical evidence in later ages. They simply painted things as they saw them. Second, the artists often mixed pictorial fiction with reality. Third, if the artist persisted in painting every detail, the harmony of the whole would be lost; thus details were often simplified or eliminated. Sadatake concludes by emphasizing the importance of scrutinizing the content of the paintings in question: "We should believe old paintings and use them as historical evidence, but they contain things we should accept and things we ought to discard. Distinguishing between them depends on the mind of the scholar. If he puts his trust in everything they depict indiscriminately, maintaining that after all they are ancient pictures, his conclusions are certain to be erroneous."

Similar comments can be found in *Morisada mankō* (Observations of Morisada; 1837–53), by Kitagawa Morisada (b. 1810).[7] At the beginning of the ninth chapter, "Josei no funsō" (Women's costume), he notes: "In Edo, Kyoto, and Osaka, ukiyo-e artists are principally engaged in painting the portraits of kabuki actors. But after all, kabuki costumes are especially gorgeous, and in both construction and decorative technique differ considerably from ordinary clothing. Because kabuki costumes are so beautiful, however, even when artists are illustrating books or painting figures that do not represent actors, they frequently depict the figures in kabuki costume." What is important, as both Sadatake and Morisada note, is for the observer to combine a knowledge of artistic conventions and surviving objects with an attitude of careful scrutiny.

Twenty-six ukiyo-e paintings are displayed along with the kosode in the present exhibition. These paintings, pictures of the floating world, date from the mid-seventeenth century to the late eighteenth century. Derived from the genre paintings and bijinga popular from the late Momoyama period through the early Edo period, they are the best pictorial source material for the study of Edo-period fashion.

FICTION AND REALITY IN PAINTINGS OF FASHION

In discussing painted representations of dress, a distinction must be made between fiction and reality. This can be defined as whether or not something could exist and has nothing to do with the quality of the painting per se. In terms of kosode, paintings can either accurately or inaccurately capture the details of cut, construction, and decoration. This section will examine paintings that can be described as fictional or realistic or a combination of the two. Let us begin with paintings depicting fictional garments.

Yūraku bijin-zu (Amusements of beautiful women; cat. no. 180a,b) depicts women with languid expressions lounging in galleries surrounding a garden through which a small stream has been channeled. They are in various postures, one playing the samisen, another gazing at a spray of flowers, a third smoking a pipe, etc. All are portrayed with the same idiosyncratic physiognomy characterized by full cheeks and a prominent jaw. These are features typical of the abbreviated depiction of the human form, reduced to geometry, brought about by the formulaic representation of figures in paintings by Iwasa Matabei (1578–1650) and his school.[8]

Let us turn our attention first to the appearance of the beauty plucking the samisen. She wears a furisode of a novel design, the background divided into areas of black and white. On the black background, pinks and vine scrolls are embroidered in gold, red, and white thread, while the white area is scattered with roundels executed in light blue and white kanoko. The artist was extremely skillful in representing the characteristics of each textile technique reflected in the clothing. We can see, however, that he frankly discarded the conventions of realism in the composition of the whole. At first glance the artistic license taken by the painter in depicting the design of this furisode is not obvious. If the lines of the black-and-white material are followed, though, it is apparent that the upper part of the garment is composed of two different fabrics, while the lower half consists of one piece of cloth that has been dyed with two different background colors and is simply an example of black-and-white somewake. While it would be possible to construct and decorate a garment in this fashion, it would be far too time-consuming to be practical. The configuration of this furisode, therefore, is fictional. The painting is characterized by realistic detail and fictitious construction; part of its charm lies in this interweaving of fact and fantasy.

Next I would like to call attention to the standing woman holding a red string to which a small bird is tethered. The depiction of this figure is quite detailed, as seen in the representation of the form of the hair, dressed in the *hyōgomage* (Chinese knot) style, the hairline, the flat form of the obi, and the gold-leaf

CATALOGUE NO. 180a,b
Amusements of Beautiful Women
Early seventeenth century
Entrusted to the Azabu Museum of Arts and Crafts

decoration (surihaku). The artist, however, has let aesthetic considerations override verisimilitude. While the diagonal black-and-white somewake design is technically feasible, it would not drape in such a precise manner.

In general, paintings of the Matabei school portray the upper half of the costume with great attention to each detail of the sleeves, neckband, garment front, etc. In contrast, they abbreviate details that should appear on the lower half, such as the overlap of the skirt, indicating this part simply as undifferentiated volume. Although the depiction in question may be lacking in realism, this is not to deny the possibility that a kosode creating a similar visual impression once existed.

Two paintings, *Lovers with Attendant* (cat. no. 178) and *Woman Playing Samisen and Woman Writing Letter* (cat. no. 179), possibly part of a pair of six-panel screens or sliding doors, are also examples of the work of the Matabei school. One particular motif, the small, circular design seen on the hem of the kosode of the woman playing the samisen, cannot be traced to extant garments. Inspired by a design on a woven textile, it became a convention in paintings by the Matabei and other schools. An actual woven pattern became an imaginary kosode design; it was presented as real in paintings but was not in fact used on kosode.

Kitsuen bijin-zu (Beauty smoking a pipe; cat. no. 183) belongs to a group of genre paintings, the so-called Kanbun Beauties, painted around the mid-seventeenth century.[9] It portrays a courtesan relaxing and smoking a pipe. The stray hairs of her coiffure, the ink landscape suggesting the "Eight Views of the Hsiao and Hsiang"[10] painted on a folding screen, and the depiction of the patterned paper on the back of the screen are all realistic. The painter, however, was completely uninterested in three-dimensional representation. The most extreme example of this is in the flat treatment of the diamond-lattice pattern. This kind of stylization appears in hinagata-bon, but here the gold outlines are unusually thick. It is difficult to imagine what technique of textile decoration could possibly be indicated by the wavy lines placed within two of the blue diamonds. Even the cursory handling of the kanoko shibori within each lozenge shape serves to enhance the sense of unreality. Oddly enough, the painting's allure lies in the stylized arrangement of the kosode pattern, which demonstrates the painter's lack of understanding of the techniques of weaving and dyeing.

Kyosoku bijin-zu (Beauty reclining on an armrest; cat. no. 184) is another example of the Kanbun Beauties genre. The model was probably a popular courtesan of the day. *Yukiwa* (snow roundels) in various colors of kanoko shibori decorate her black uchikake, while the gold kosode bears a bold pattern of hemp-palm leaves

CATALOGUE NO. 179 (detail)

CATALOGUE NO. 178
Attributed to Iwasa Matabei
(1578–1650) or School of Matabei
Lovers with Attendant
Early seventeenth century
Frank Lloyd Wright Archives,
Frank Lloyd Wright Foundation

CATALOGUE NO. 179
Attributed to Iwasa Matabei
(1578–1650) or School of Matabei
Woman Playing Samisen and
Woman Writing Letter

Early seventeenth century
Frank Lloyd Wright Archives,
Frank Lloyd Wright Foundation

superimposed on a ground pattern of quatrefoils. In their representation, however, a number of distortions and stylizations are conspicuous. Both the hemp-palm leaves and the cloudlike forms that crowd the surface of the kosode are flat and lack a sense of reality. The application of gold was not based on an understanding of the use of gold thread or gold leaf on textiles. The shade of green in the painting is also inaccurate for kosode—it does not correspond to any known dye color of the period. The bold pattern in the Kanbun style reflects the general aesthetic of the time, but there is little reality in its representation.

The paintings that have been described to this point are all works of the early Edo period and stand, as it were, at the entrance to the world of ukiyo-e paintings. With the innovations introduced by Hishikawa Moronobu (c. 1618–94),[11] however, the foundations of ukiyo-e became solidified. Thereafter, refined and skillful representations of clothing that reflect a considerable knowledge of weaving and dyeing techniques gradually emerged. These not only appear natural but also possess a realism that directly brings to mind specific textile designs and the techniques for executing them.

CATALOGUE NO. 184
Beauty Reclining on an Armrest
Second half seventeenth century
Entrusted to the Azabu Museum of
Arts and Crafts

For example, let us look at *Tachi bijin-zu* (Standing beauty; cat. no. 185), which bears the inscription: "Nihon e Hishikawa Moronobu zu" (A Japanese painting: Picture by Hishikawa Moronobu). A couple of elements are still fictional or unclear in their technical accuracy. For example, the ground pattern of the red figured satin that appears in the furisode worn by this figure is one often used by artists of various schools and was probably not copied from an actual garment (similar to the motif mentioned earlier regarding cat. no. 179). It is also impossible to judge whether the clamshell motif (derived from *kai-awase* [a shell-matching game]) so beautifully distributed over the entire surface of the kosode is meant to represent a pattern executed using a paste resist or one created by means of shibori, with a paste resist applied afterward to the outlines to make them sharper. (For kosode in the exhibition decorated with a kai-awase motif, see cat. nos. 81–82). Each pattern decorating the shells is not just carefully drawn, however, but is indeed depicted marvelously, with attention to the decorative techniques that would have been used for each. The yellow ocher shells are ornamented with scenes that appear to be from the *Genji monogatari* (Tale of Genji), executed as ink drawings. Clearly the cloud and chrysanthemum patterns on the black shells are intended to represent multicolored embroidery. An outline stitch defines the cloud shapes, which are filled in with satin stitch, while the chrysanthemums are delineated in float stitch. Each embroidery stitch is acknowledged. In the light blue shells on the right shoulder and at the hem the chrysanthemums are represented as embroidery, while the clouds appear filled in with kanoko shibori. Turning to the tightly wrapped obi, patterned with yukiwa, it can be seen that even the figured twill weave has been painstakingly drawn. Moronobu was born into a family of craftsmen whose specialty was the lush embroidery and gold-leaf decoration (nuihaku) applied to kosode and Nō robes. In the strict attention to detail seen in his attitude toward painting, we cannot help but sense the depth and richness of his knowledge of textiles.

Bijin dokushō-zu (Beauty reading a book; cat. no. 186), by Moronobu's son Hishikawa Morofusa (fl. 1685–1703), shows a courtesan, alone except for a *kamuro* (a little girl brothel attendant). The woman, seated in front of a two-panel screen decorated with a painting of autumn flowers and grasses, is balancing a book on her knee. Morofusa painted bijinga during the Jōkyō and Genroku eras, but it is said that in the middle of his career he realized that he could not match the painterly skills of his great father and so put down his brush. In the skill and care with which he portrayed weaving and dyeing techniques, however, Morofusa was in

CATALOGUE NO. 185
Hishikawa Moronobu (c. 1618–94)
Standing Beauty
Late seventeenth century
Entrusted to the Azabu Museum of Arts and Crafts

220

no way inferior to Moronobu. In this painting the style of the patterns scattered on the black suhama areas of the katasuso should be noted. When examined closely, the pattern filling these areas clearly represents the decorative techniques of embroidery in the small red and yellow flowers and applied gold leaf in the tortoiseshell diaper and mist patterns. This closely resembles the fabrics of Keichō kosode.[12] Morofusa executed these details in the most realistic manner, just as if he had placed a fragment of old Keichō cloth by his side as he painted, displaying the depth of his erudition in the subjects of weaving and dyeing.

A work by Tamura Suiō (fl. c. 1680–1730), *Mitate Eguchi no kimi-zu* (A parody of Lady Eguchi; cat. no. 187), likewise faithfully depicts details of clothing.[13] The subject is taken from the Nō play *Eguchi*, which is based on the story of a woman born into this world as a prostitute who was able to reject attachment to the floating world of pleasure and who was reborn as Fugen, the Buddhist deity. In this painting Suiō depicted with extreme fidelity the cloth of the furisode worn by Eguchi, a red rinzu with a woven *sayagata* (key fret) and orchid pattern. Attention should

CATALOGUE NO. 186
Hishikawa Morofusa
(fl. 1685–1703)
Beauty Reading a Book
Late seventeenth–early eighteenth century
Entrusted to the Azabu Museum of Arts and Crafts

also be paid to the realistic representation of folds created by tucking the skirts of the kosode into the front of the obi. The artist's determination to accurately portray the ground pattern has resulted in an exaggeration of its size in proportion to the whole, but the balance has not been lost. There are many examples of paintings in which the artist has glossed over details, but paintings like this one, where the artist has exaggerated them, are extremely rare.

The furisode rendered in the painting *Tachi bijin-zu* (Standing beauty; cat. no. 191) is another example in which the artist has paid careful attention to characteristics of textile decoration. The

CATALOGUE NO. 191
Standing Beauty
Early eighteenth century
Entrusted to the Azabu Museum of
Arts and Crafts

design is a combination of popular Edo-period auspicious motifs: young pine trees and plum blossoms against abstract cloud forms. The fabric appears to be crimson chirimen; the cloud forms were executed in kanoko shibori. The rest of the pattern looks like embroidery. The kanoko dots are large, like white pills, and are depicted in a way that suggests that the outlines of the clouds were corrected after the shibori dyeing was executed. Some of the dots are imperfect as well, creating a most realistic impression. Various embroidery techniques are represented also: the petals of the plum blossoms appear to be satin stitch, while the long floats are anchored by couching stitches (*koma-nui*) that at the same time represent the stamens of the flowers. The trunk of the plum tree is depicted in the same way; the bark appears to be satin stitch held in place with white couching yarns. The area covered by the pine branches is broad; the pine needles seem to be portrayed in a divided satin stitch, which is appropriate for embroidering a flat surface. As in the treatment of the plum blossoms, the individual pine needles are shown in koma-nui. The new buds of the pine and certain parts of the branches appear as if embroidered with couched gold thread. This painting deserves special mention for its realistic depiction of decorative techniques.

ASPECTS OF FASHION SEEN IN PAINTINGS

Our discussion of whether or not specific paintings have accurately or inaccurately captured decorative techniques has lightly touched on various aspects of Edo-period fashion, including embroidery, the application of gold, and auspicious motifs. This section will focus on other elements of fashion seen in paintings: kaki-e, yūzen-zome, date-mon, *tsuma moyō*, and *tatejima*.

KAKI-E

Kaki-e refers to the technique of using a brush to paint on fabric with ink, pigment, or dye. To apply a design unerringly, without the bleeding of the ink or colors, requires a considerable degree of experience and skill. During the early modern period the technique was employed mainly for decorating the clothing of the upper classes. Fashionable during the Jōkyō and Genroku eras, kaki-e kosode are mentioned in the fiction of Ihara Saikaku. In *Wankyū issei monogatari* (A tale of Wankyū's life; 1685), for example, there is a comment about a kosode with kaki-e painted by Miyazaki Yūzen in sumi (ink). *Kōshoku sandai otoko* (Three

CATALOGUE NO. 191 (detail)

licentious gentlemen; 1686) describes a kosode decorated with a scene of a pine tree ripped in two by lightning as being "painted in color in the Yūzen style." *Saikaku oridome* (Saikaku's finish; 1694) includes a story about a profitable sale of a hand-painted kosode.

That Saikaku's statements are not fantasies is attested to by the depictions of such kosode in *Yūjo tachi sugata-zu* (Portrait of a standing courtesan; cat. no. 194) and *San bijin-zu* (Three beauties; cat. no. 182). The kaki-e kosode seen on the figure on the right in the latter work features a design of scattered fan papers, rectangles, or circles, within which scenes probably taken from the *Genji monogatari*, *Ise monogatari* (The tales of Ise), or similar sources are painted in sumi. It closely resembles a white satin kaki-e kosode in the exhibition that features a design of fans and decorated paper squares containing scenes from the *Genji monogatari* (cat. no. 115). This kosode, probably dating from the second half of the eighteenth century, is still an effective reflection of the resplendent zenith of kaki-e kosode art: the Genroku era.

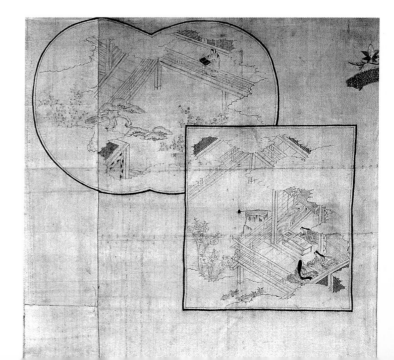

In the painting *Yosooi bijin-zu* (Woman getting dressed; cat. no. 201), by Chōbunsai Eishi (1756–1829),[14] the lower half of the kosode with the white ground is filled with the sinuous curves of a stream, branches of bush clover, and a scene of fulling cloth. Eishi depicted the design as having been created primarily by yūzen dyeing (see Kirihata essay). A small amount of embroidery is meant to be suggested for the bush clover and figures. The juxtaposition of bush clover and cloth fulling with a flowing stream or river alludes to the theme of the Six Tama Rivers. A kosode in the exhibition (cat. no. 72) is decorated with a similar motif.[15]

CATALOGUE NO. 201

Chōbunsai Eishi (1756–1829)

Woman Getting Dressed

Late eighteenth–early nineteenth century

Entrusted to the Azabu Museum of Arts and Crafts

Kō taki bijin-zu (Beauty preparing incense; cat. no. 199), by Kawamata Tsunemasa (fl. 1716–48),[16] portrays an elegant uchi-kake decorated with *misu* (bamboo blinds). Blinds of this type, hung within the rooms of the imperial palace and the homes of the nobility, shielded women of aristocratic birth from exposure to prying eyes. They were used as a decorative motif on kosode throughout the Edo period; a number of examples appear in the pages of printed kosode design books. For example, in *Shin hina-gata Kyō kosode* (New designs for kosode of the capital; 1770) there is an entry entitled *Misu ni yomogi* (Mugwort with bamboo blinds). Explanatory notes are appended that specify a brown ground with white, paste-resisted areas and yūzen details. The exhibition includes an example of a design of bamboo blinds reserved by means of paste resist (cat. no. 85) and one executed by other techniques (cat. no. 53).

With the increasing width of the obi, the asymmetrical and large-scale designs characteristic of Kanbun kosode were no longer viable. Kosode design came to be sharply divided into upper and lower halves. Symmetrical designs incorporating family crests became popular. Decorative patterns used in place of such crests are known as date-mon. They were placed on haori or kosode in the same spots as regular family crests (in the center of the back at the base of the neck and on the back and front of each sleeve; see cat. nos. 33, 146), but normal rules of use were not attached to them. Reputedly, date-mon were first used by prostitutes, actors, and pleasure-seekers who competed in showiness of dress, but the use of the term in the "Machi" (Town) section of *Shokoku on-hiinakata* (Patterns for many provinces; 1686) indicates that respectable chōnin were also wearing the fashion. In the Kyōhō-era painting *Ni bijin-zu* (Two beauties; cat. no. 188), by Furuyama Morotane (fl. c. 1716–44),[17] the seated figure wears a kosode decorated with crests in the form of flower-laden rafts, while the standing woman displays a robe with roundels containing ink paintings of rustic pavilions.

TSUMA MOYŌ

Tsuma moyō (skirt design) refers to a type of kosode composition in which the pattern extends from the lower end of the neckband to the hem and is clustered primarily along the front edges of the garment (see Appendix A). What is probably the oldest illustration of tsuma moyō appeared in *Shin hinakata* (New designs; 1690), but at that time it was just a passing fad. The full-blown fashion for skirt designs began around the Hōreki and Meiwa eras. As the use of skirt designs increased, what had originally been termed tsuma moyō gradually came to be called *Edo-zuma* (Edo skirts).

Two paintings in the exhibition display tsuma moyō. In Chō-bunsai Eishi's painting *Ni bijin-zu* (Two beauties; cat. no. 202) the standing figure holding a samisen wears a light violet kosode with a skirt pattern of orchids, while the seated figure holding a drum wears a light brown kosode decorated with bamboo grass and bellflowers. In *Hagi no Tamagawa* (The River Tama at Hagi; cat. no. 200), by Kubo Shunman (1757–1820),[18] the figure on the right wears a pale gray furisode with a hand-painted sumi design of orchids. This probably reflects the fashion of the Tenmei and Kansei eras. The kosode design composition based on a bilaterally symmetrical skirt design that emerged in the mid-Edo period changed in the late Edo period into one where the focus of the design was concentrated around the hem. Even in the case of a

CATALOGUE NO. 188
Furuyama Morotane
(fl. c. 1716–44)
Two Beauties
Early eighteenth century
Entrusted to the Azabu Museum of
Arts and Crafts

CATALOGUE NO. 202
Chōbunsai Eishi (1756–1829)
Two Beauties
Late eighteenth–early nineteenth
century
Entrusted to the Azabu Museum of
Arts and Crafts

Kubo Shunman (1757–1820)
The River Tama at Hagi
Late eighteenth–early nineteenth
century
Entrusted to the Azabu Museum of
Arts and Crafts

matron's formal kosode, for example, what had originally been an allover pattern was confined to seven inches from the hem (see cat. no. 60), then five (see cat. no. 59), and finally, by the end of the Edo period, to a band around the hem three inches wide. This tendency was even more marked in everyday clothing, in which the design was not merely restricted to a narrow strip along the hem but was banished from the outside of the garment altogether, appearing on the inside instead. Such designs, along with simplified patterns such as stripes and komon, became popular.

TATEJIMA

In the same painting by Shunman, the figure on the left wears a sheer black kosode with *tatejima* (vertical stripes). A chapter on demeanor ("Yōgi no bu") in *Miyako fūzoku kewai den* (Commentaries on customs and dressing in the capital; 1813)[19] explains how to choose clothing that enhances one's height: "Clothing should be cut on the narrow side, and the pattern should be something like flowers and grasses that spread upward rather than to the side. Stripes should be vertical, or, in the case of checks, the vertical element should be dominant. Checks with strong horizontal bars will increase the sense of breadth, and will not help create an illusion of height."

In the early Edo period the wearing of vertical stripes was rare, restricted mainly to prostitutes; horizontal stripes were the norm. By the mid-Edo period the use of tatejima gradually increased (see cat. no. 116). Vertical stripes almost completely replaced horizontal stripes by the late Edo period. Human figures are often represented in extremely attenuated forms in ukiyo-e paintings from the mid-Edo period onward. Clearly indicating a fashion sensibility that regarded a slender figure as beautiful, tatejima went hand in hand with a narrowing of the kosode's dimensions.[20]

CONCLUSION

The context provided by ukiyo-e paintings allows for a greater exploration of Edo-period fashion. Extant garments are our primary means of understanding the clothing styles of the Tokugawa period, but paintings flesh out what kosode alone cannot. Reflecting in their time an idealized life of pleasure, the paintings now provide material evidence as well as pleasure for the modern viewer.

NOTES

1. An educational manual for women, *Onna chōhōki* was written by Inamura Gaihaku.

2. An important source for the customs and fashions of the Edo period, this work by Takarazu Shuso was reprinted in the Tenpō era under the title *Yaso-ō mukashi monogatari* (Tales of an eighty-year-old man). In addition to the Kyōhō-era version, many later copies exist.

3. This encyclopedia, by Kikuoka Tenryō (1747–1815), details the origins of utensils and other objects of everyday use during the Edo period. Published in five volumes, the first is devoted to clothing.

4. Kichiya musubi, named for Uemura Kichiya, was a way of tying an obi. The ends of the knot were left to droop limply; a lead weight was inserted inside each corner of the stitched edges to make the ends hang as low as possible. This style was popular among young women. Before its adoption by Kichiya it was originally known as *tamazusa musubi* (folded-letter knot). Kodayū kanoko was a type of dyeing said to have been first used on the stage by the onnagata Itō Kodayū II (d. 1689) in the Jōkyō and Genroku eras. Sawanojō bōshi was a form of headgear made popular during the Genroku era by the premier onnagata of the day, Ogino Sawanojō (1656–1704). Weights were inserted into both sides of the head covering to prevent the ends from curling up; it was also known by such names as *omori zukin* (weighted head cloth) and *sagari bōshi* (drooping hat). Sen'ya-zome was a kind of boldly patterned purple shibori dyeing named after the actor Nakamura Sen'ya (fl. 1716–18), who popularized it.

5. Maruyama 1989, 5.

6. Sadatake was an antiquarian of the mid-Edo period. A resident of Edo and vassal of the shogun, his knowledge of the practices of the aristocracy and military elite was wide-ranging. In his studies of the customs of the samurai, in particular, he captured a picture of an historical period.

7. *Morisada mankō* was a journal in thirty volumes, with a four-volume supplement. Originally completed in 1853, additional volumes were added later. The author recorded and classified customs he had observed and included illustrations with his detailed explanations. An indispensable source for the study of customs of the early modern period, the work was reprinted in 1912 under the title *Ruijū kinsei fūzoku-shi* (Intended as a classification and collection of early modern customs).

8. Iwasa Matabei was a painter of the early Edo period. He was raised by the Iwasa family of Echizen and went to Edo at the invitation of the bakufu in his later years. He established a new style of painting, combining features of the Tosa and Kano schools. In addition to painting themes from Chinese and Japanese legends, Matabei developed a new style of genre painting. Some critics consider him the founding father of ukiyo-e.

9. *Kanbun bijin-zu* (pictures of Kanbun beauties) usually depict a single, standing figure of a woman and were so called because this subgenre was believed to have been especially popular during the Kanbun era.

10. The "Eight Views of the Hsiao and Hsiang" was a popular theme in Chinese and Japanese ink landscape paintings. The title refers to eight famous sights along the Hsiao and Hsiang Rivers in Hunan, China.

11. Hishikawa Moronobu was an artist of the early Edo period. He went to Edo during the Manji era and for more than thirty years was a prolific producer of paintings and woodblock prints, in particular woodblock illustrations for books. Drawing inspiration from Matabei's groundbreaking achievements, he refined the style and established the distinctive look (as defined by pose, line, and decoration) of mature ukiyo-e.

12. See Gluckman essay, note 41.

13. Tamura Suiō painted pictures of bijinga in a refined style reminiscent of Hishikawa Moronobu.

14. Chōbunsai Eishi was a competitor of Kitagawa Utamaro (1753–1806) and established a unique style of prints of bijinga. Toward the end of the Kansei era his focus shifted from woodblock prints to ukiyo-e paintings, on which he concentrated until his death.

15. Six different rivers in Japan had the same name: Tama. Poems about each of these appear in certain of the imperial poetry anthologies. Various combinations of motifs taken from these poems were known as the Six Tama Rivers. In cat. no. 72, for example, the combination of bush clover (*hagi*) and a stream may allude to Tama no Hagi, the River Tama at Hagi.

16. Little is known about Kawamata Tsunemasa, a painter who lived in Edo and specialized in bijinga.

17. The facts of Furuyama Morotane's career are uncertain. In addition to paintings of beautiful women, his extant works include a small number of woodblock prints.

18. Kubo Shunman studied with Kitao Shigemasa (1739–1820), a painter from the Kitao school, and lived in Edo. A multitalented man, Shunman exercised his skills in illustrating popular books such as *kibyoshi* (yellow-cover books) and *share-bon* (smart books) and designing nishiki-e, ukiyo-e paintings, and *surimono* (special-edition prints). He also wrote popular fiction and comic verse. Many of his ukiyo-e paintings from the Tenmei through the Kansei eras are fine works.

19. *Miyako fūzoku kewai den*, a commentary on customs and manners (with particular attention to dress and personal appearance), was written by Sayama Hanshichimaru and illustrated by Hayami Shungyosai.

20. See introduction, note 16.

Checklist of the Exhibition

NOTE: This outline is a guide to both the organization of the checklist and the exhibition. Checklist entries begin on page 240.

4. Ordinary objects

    A) Gabions

      cat. nos. 87–88

    B) Boats

      cat. nos. 89–90

    C) Hats

      cat. nos. 91–92

    D) Fans

      cat. nos. 93–94

    E) Doors

      cat. nos. 95–96

    F) Potted plants

      cat. no. 97

    G) Painting formats

      cat. nos. 98–100

5. Famous places

    A) Pilgrimage sites

      cat. nos. 101–2

    B) Scenic locales

      (1) Sumiyoshi

        cat. nos. 103–4

      (2) Uji Bridge and "Eight Views of Ōmi"

        cat. nos. 105–8

    C) Edo

      cat. nos. 109–10

    D) Kyoto

      cat. nos. 111–12

6. Literature

    A) Books

      cat. nos. 113–14

    B) The *Tale of Genji* and scenes alluding to classical literature

      cat. nos. 115–20

    C) The *Tales of Ise*

      cat. nos. 121–24

    D) Nō plays

      cat. nos. 125–26

NOTE: As seen in the chronology, the Edo period has conventionally been separated into three stylistic divisions—early, middle, and late—corresponding roughly to the seventeenth century, eighteenth century, and first half of the nineteenth century. Since there is no general agreement as to the exact commencement and termination of each division, these designations have not been used in the checklist. Instead, an attempt has been made to date each piece as specifically as possible within its proper century.

As there will be a rotation of most of the artworks halfway through the exhibition (owing to the fragility of the objects), the following symbols are used to indicate when particular pieces will be on display:

○ First rotation   ● Second rotation.

Pieces not marked will not be rotated. Page numbers indicate where illustrations in the text may be found.

CATALOGUE NO. 1
Kosode on Screen
Left: Kosode fragment with scattered floral motifs
Momoyama period, late sixteenth–early seventeenth century
Tsujigahana style; tie-dyeing (nuishime and bōshi shibori) on purple plain-weave silk (nerinuki)
Right: Kosode fragment with horizontal bands of squares and of camellias and wisteria
Momoyama period, late sixteenth–early seventeenth century (dedicatory inscription Kanbun 3 [1663])
Tsujigahana style; tie-dyeing (nuishime and bōshi shibori) and ink painting (kaki-e) on white plain-weave silk (nerinuki)
75 × 68 1/4 in.
(190.5 × 173.4 cm)
National Museum of Japanese History, Nomura Collection
○
Page 76

CATALOGUE NO. 2
Kosode on Screen
Left: Kosode fragment with Chinese bellflowers and camellias
Momoyama period, late sixteenth–early seventeenth century
Tsujigahana style; tie-dyeing (nuishime, bōshi, and kanoko shibori) on red-brown and white parti-colored (somewake) plain-weave silk (nerinuki)
Right: Kosode fragment with flowers and clouds
First quarter seventeenth century
Keichō-Kan'ei style; tie-dyeing (kanoko shibori), silk thread embroidery, and traces of stenciled gold leaf (surihaku) on black plain-weave silk (nerinuki)
74 7/8 × 68 1/4 in.
(190.2 × 173.4 cm)
National Museum of Japanese History, Nomura Collection
●
Pages 77, 83 (detail)

CATALOGUE NO. 3
Kosode on Screen
Kosode fragment with mountains, snowflake roundels, wisteria, and plants of the four seasons
Early seventeenth century
Keichō-Kan'ei style; tie-dyeing (nuishime, bōshi, and kanoko shibori), silk thread embroidery, and traces of stenciled gold and silver leaf (surihaku) on red, black, white, and light blue parti-colored (somewake) figured silk satin (rinzu)
74 3/4 × 67 7/8 in.
(189.9 × 172.4 cm)
National Museum of Japanese History, Nomura Collection
○
Page 84

CATALOGUE NO. 4
Kosode on Screen
Left: Kosode fragment with grapevines and lozenges
Momoyama period, late sixteenth–early seventeenth century
Tsujigahana style; tie-dyeing (nuishime and kanoko shibori) and ink painting (kaki-e) on white plain-weave silk (nerinuki)
Right: Kosode fragment with mountains, waves, roundels, fan papers, and flowers
Early seventeenth century
Keichō-Kan'ei style; tie-dyeing (nuishime, bōshi, and kanoko shibori), silk thread embroidery, and traces of stenciled gold leaf (surihaku) on black figured silk satin (rinzu)
75 × 68 in.
(190.5 × 172.7 cm)
National Museum of Japanese History, Nomura Collection
●
Pages 64 (detail), 78

CATALOGUE NO. 5

Kosode with Abstract Shapes, Birds, Plants, and Flowers

Early seventeenth century

Keichō-Kan'ei style; tie-dyeing (nuishime, bōshi, and kanoko shibori), silk thread embroidery, and stenciled gold leaf (surihaku) on red, brown, and white parti-colored (somewake) figured silk satin (rinzu)

54 ¹³/₁₆ × 45 ¹/₄ in.

(139.2 × 115.0 cm)

Tabata Collection

Important Cultural Property

○

Page 85

CATALOGUE NO. 6

Kosode on Screen

Kosode fragment with leaves, fans, and plants

Second quarter seventeenth century

Keichō-Kan'ei style; tie-dyeing (bōshi, nuishime, and kanoko shibori), silk and metallic thread embroidery, and stenciled gold leaf (surihaku) on red, black, and white parti-colored (somewake) figured silk satin (rinzu)

68 ⁷/₈ × 68 ⁷/₈ in.

(174.9 × 174.9 cm)

National Museum of Japanese History, Nomura Collection

●

Pages 86, 87 (detail)

CATALOGUE NO. 7

Kosode with Waterfall, Chrysanthemums, and Footed Tray

Mid-seventeenth century

Tie-dyeing (kanoko and nuishime shibori), traces of gold leaf (surihaku), ink painting (kaki-e), and silk thread embroidery on white figured silk satin (rinzu)

62 ³/₈ × 47 ³/₈ in.

(158.4 × 120.3 cm)

National Museum of Japanese History, Nomura Collection

○

Page 89

CATALOGUE NO. 8

Kosode with Noshi and Flowering Plants

First half seventeenth century

Tie-dyeing (nuishime shibori), silk and metallic thread embroidery, and traces of stenciled gold leaf (surihaku) on white and brown parti-colored (somewake) figured silk satin (rinzu)

57 ³/₄ × 52 in.

(146.7 × 132.1 cm)

Kanebo, Ltd.

●

Page 88

CATALOGUE NO. 9

Kosode with Flower-filled Maple Leaves

Third quarter seventeenth century

Tie-dyeing (kanoko shibori) and silk and metallic thread embroidery on red-brown figured silk satin (rinzu)

58 ¹/₈ × 48 ³/₈ in.

(147.6 × 122.9 cm)

National Museum of Japanese History, Nomura Collection

○

CATALOGUE NO. 9

CATALOGUE NO. 10

CATALOGUE NO. 10
Kosode with Oversized Grass Blades
Mid-seventeenth century
Tie-dyeing (kanoko shibori), silk
and metallic thread embroidery, and
stenciled gold leaf (surihaku) on
black figured silk satin (rinzu)
59 1/8 × 49 5/8 in.
(150.2 × 126.0 cm)
National Museum of Japanese
History, Nomura Collection
●

CATALOGUE NO. 11
Katabira with Chrysanthemums
Third quarter seventeenth century
Tie-dyeing (kanoko, bōshi, and
nuishime shibori) and silk and
metallic thread embroidery on
brown plain-weave ramie (asa)
61 5/8 × 48 5/8 in.
(156.5 × 123.5 cm)
Kyoto National Museum
○

Page 91

CATALOGUE NO. 12
*Kosode with Chrysanthemums
and Water*
Third quarter seventeenth century
Tie-dyeing (kanoko and nuishime
shibori) on white silk satin (shusu)
63 × 52 5/8 in.
(160.0 × 133.7 cm)
Nara Prefectural Museum of Art
●

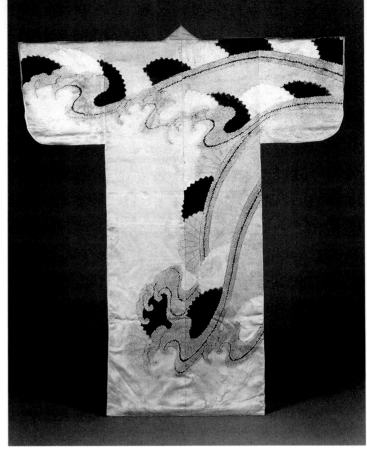

CATALOGUE NO. 12

CATALOGUE NO. 13
Kosode with Floral Roundels
Late seventeenth century
Tie-dyeing (kanoko shibori) and
silk and metallic thread embroidery
on yellow, blue, and red parti-
colored (somewake) figured silk
satin (rinzu)
60 1/2 × 51 3/8 in.
(153.7 × 130.5 cm)
Tokyo National Museum
○

CATALOGUE NO. 13

CATALOGUE NO. 14
Kosode with Drumheads, Wisteria, and Rocks
Late seventeenth century
Tie-dyeing (kanoko shibori) and
silk and metallic thread embroidery
on white figured silk satin (rinzu)
62 × 50¾ in.
(157.5 × 128.9 cm)
Tokyo National Museum

CATALOGUE NO. 15
*Kosode with Flowering Plum Tree,
Bamboo, and Snowflake Roundels*
Late seventeenth–early eighteenth
century
Tie-dyeing (kanoko and bōshi
shibori) and silk and metallic thread
embroidery on purple figured silk
satin (rinzu)
59 × 50 in.
(149.9 × 127.0 cm)
National Museum of Japanese
History, Nomura Collection
○

CATALOGUE NO. 16
Kosode with Flowers, Rafts, and Water
First quarter eighteenth century
Tie-dyeing (kanoko shibori) and silk and metallic thread embroidery on white figured silk satin (rinzu)
60 × 47 in.
(152.4 × 119.4 cm)
National Museum of Japanese History, Nomura Collection

CATALOGUE NO. 17
Kosode with Chrysanthemum Leaves and Flowers, Waterfall, and Characters
First quarter eighteenth century
Tie-dyeing (nuishime and kanoko shibori), stenciled imitation tie-dyeing (kata kanoko), silk and metallic thread embroidery, and ink on white figured silk satin (rinzu)
61 1/8 × 50 1/2 in.
(155.3 × 128.3 cm)
National Museum of Japanese History, Nomura Collection

Kosode with Water, Larch Flowers
(Kara-matsu), *and Wisteria*
First half eighteenth century
Tie-dyeing (kanoko shibori), stenciled imitation tie-dyeing (kata
kanoko), silk and metallic thread
embroidery, and ink on white
figured silk satin (rinzu)
62 ¼ × 47 ½ in.
(158.1 × 120.7 cm)
Tokyo National Museum

•

CATALOGUE NO. 19
*Katabira with Screens and
Paulownia Tree*
First half eighteenth century
Paste-resist dyeing (noribōsen),
stenciled imitation tie-dyeing
(kata kanoko), and silk and
metallic thread embroidery on
black plain-weave ramie (asa)
62 × 48 ¾ in.
(157.5 × 123.8 cm)
Nara Prefectural Museum of Art

○

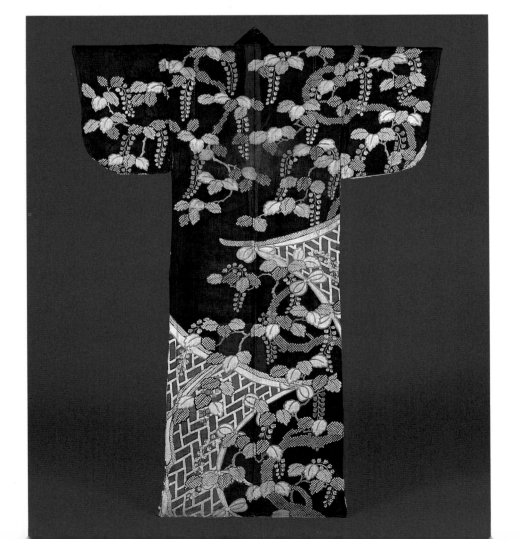

CATALOGUE NO. 20

CATALOGUE NO. 22
Kosode with Flowering Camellia Trees and Fence
First half eighteenth century
Stenciled imitation tie-dyeing (kata kanoko), applied indigo (ai-zuri), and silk and metallic thread embroidery on white figured silk satin (rinzu)
62 ½ × 47 ½ in.
(158.8 × 120.7 cm)
National Museum of Japanese History, Nomura Collection

●

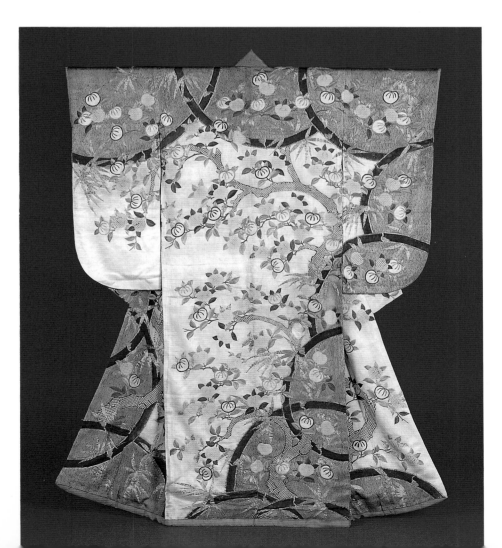

CATALOGUE NO. 23
Furisode with Mandarin Orange Trees and Interlocking Bamboo Circles
Early eighteenth century
Tie-dyeing (mokume and nuishime shibori), stenciled imitation tie-dyeing (kata kanoko), applied indigo (ai-zuri), and silk and metallic thread embroidery on white silk satin (shusu)
64 ½ × 52 in.
(163.8 × 132.1 cm)
Kanebo, Ltd.

○

CATALOGUE NO. 24

CATALOGUE NO. 24
*Kosode with Chrysanthemums,
Net Pattern, and Characters*
Early eighteenth century
Tie-dyeing (kanoko shibori), stenciled imitation tie-dyeing (kata
kanoko), and silk and metallic
thread embroidery on white
figured silk satin (rinzu)
63 ⅛ × 55 in.
(160.3 × 139.7 cm)
Tokyo National Museum
●

CATALOGUE NO. 25
*Hitoe with Bamboo, Plum, Rafts,
and Characters*
First quarter eighteenth century
Paste-resist dyeing (yūzen) and silk
and metallic thread embroidery on
white silk crepe (chirimen)
62 ¼ × 53 in.
(158.1 × 134.6 cm)
Tōyama Memorial Museum
○
Page 140

CATALOGUE NO. 26
*Kosode with Plum Tree and
Architectural Motif*
Late seventeenth–early eighteenth
century
Paste-resist dyeing (yūzen), stenciled imitation tie-dyeing (kata
kanoko), and silk and metallic
thread embroidery on light purple
silk crepe (chirimen)
57 ¾ × 48 ¼ in.
(146.7 × 122.6 cm)
Kanebo, Ltd.
●
Page 102

CATALOGUE NO. 27
*Katabira with Lattice, Flowering
Plum Tree, Chrysanthemums, and
Bush Clover* (Hagi)
First half eighteenth century
Paste-resist dyeing (yūzen) and silk
and metallic thread embroidery on
white plain-weave ramie (asa)
65 × 47 ½ in.
(165.1 × 120.7 cm)
Matsuzakaya Co., Ltd.
○
Page 141

CATALOGUE NO. 28

CATALOGUE NO. 33

CATALOGUE NO. 32
Kosode with Fence, Maple Branches,
and Plum Blossoms
Mid-eighteenth century
Paste-resist dyeing (yūzen), dip-
dyeing (tsuke-zome), and silk and
metallic thread embroidery on
white silk crepe (chirimen)
59 ¼ × 50 in. (150.5 × 127.0 cm)
National Museum of Japanese
History, Nomura Collection

•

252   Page 124

CATALOGUE NO. 33
Kosode with Banners
Mid-eighteenth century
Paste-resist dyeing (yūzen), clamp-
resist dyeing (itajime), and silk and
metallic thread embroidery on pale
yellow plain-weave silk (hira-ginu)
62 × 48 ½ in.
(157.5 × 123.2 cm)
Matsuzakaya Co., Ltd.

○

CATALOGUE NO. 34
Kosode with Scene of Horse Racing
Mid-eighteenth century
Paste-resist dyeing (yūzen) and silk
and metallic thread embroidery on
light beige silk crepe (chirimen)
51 ½ × 51 ⅞ in.
(130.8 × 131.8 cm)
Kyoto National Museum

•

Pages 3 (detail), 22 (detail), 198

CATALOGUE NO. 35
Kosode with Wisteria, Shoji, and
Pine Needles
Second quarter eighteenth century
Paste-resist dyeing (shiro-age) and
silk and metallic thread embroidery
on blue silk crepe (chirimen)
57 ⅜ × 50 in.
(145.7 × 127.0 cm)
National Museum of Japanese
History, Nomura Collection

○

Page 101

CATALOGUE NO. 36

Kosode on Screen
Kosode fragment with cherry tree
and poem papers
First quarter eighteenth century
(dedicatory inscription Kyōhō 9
[1724])
Paste-resist dyeing (yūzen),
appliqué, and silk and metallic
thread embroidery on yellow ocher
silk crepe (chirimen)
67 3/8 × 74 3/4 in.
(171.1 × 189.9 cm)
National Museum of Japanese
History, Nomura Collection
●

Page 207

CATALOGUE NO. 37

*Kosode with Agricultural Scenes of
the Four Seasons*
First half nineteenth century
Paste-resist dyeing (yūzen) on light
brown figured silk satin (rinzu)
64 1/8 × 46 5/8 in.
(162.9 × 118.4 cm)
Tokyo National Museum
○

Pages 51 (detail), 196

CATALOGUE NO. 38

Furisode with Tea-picking Scenes
First half nineteenth century
Paste-resist dyeing (yūzen) on light
blue-gray plain-weave silk (habutae)
61 5/8 × 51 1/2 in.
(156.5 × 130.8 cm)
Tokyo National Museum
●

Pages 127 (detail), 197

CATALOGUE NO. 39

*Kosode with Horizontal Bands,
Dutch Rush, Flowers, and Rabbits*
Early nineteenth century
Paste-resist dyeing (yūzen) and silk
and metallic thread embroidery on
white and red silk crepe (chirimen)
64 × 51 1/2 in.
(162.6 × 130.8 cm)
Kyoto National Museum
○

Page 138

CATALOGUE NO. 40

Kosode with Chrysanthemums
Early nineteenth century
Tie-dyeing (nuishime shibori) and
paste-resist dyeing (yūzen) on
yellow twill-figured plain-weave
silk (saya)
65 1/4 × 48 5/8 in.
(165.7 × 123.5 cm)
National Museum of Japanese
History, Nomura Collection
●

CATALOGUE NO. 40

CATALOGUE NO. 41
*Katabira with Rustic Pavilion,
Waterfall, Gabions, and Flowering
Plants*
Second half eighteenth century
Paste-resist and indigo dyeing
(chaya-zome) on yellow plain-
weave ramie (asa)
63 7/8 × 47 1/2 in.
(162.2 × 120.7 cm)
Kanebo, Ltd.

○

CATALOGUE NO. 42
*Katabira with Rustic Pavilions,
Rocks, and Streams*
Second half eighteenth century
Paste-resist and indigo dyeing
(chaya-zome) and silk and metallic
thread embroidery on white plain-
weave ramie (asa)
63 3/8 × 49 5/8 in.
(161.0 × 126.0 cm)
Tokyo National Museum

●

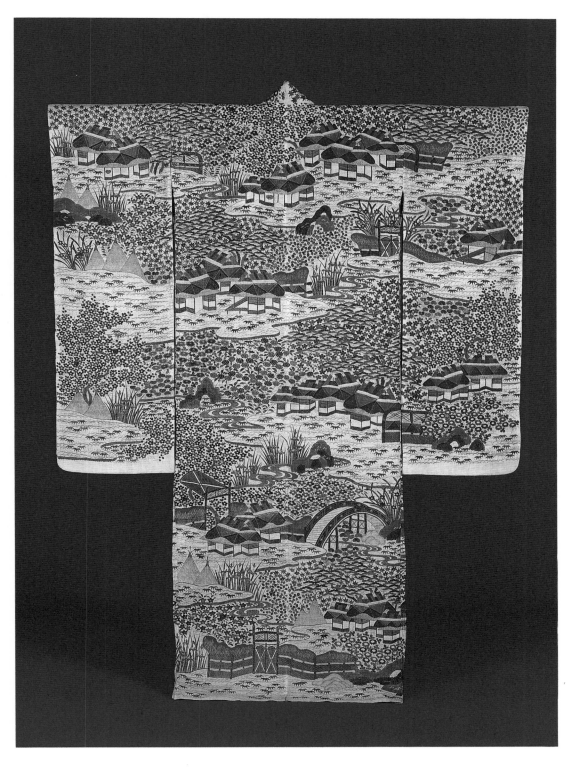

*Katabira with Rustic Landscape and
Seasonal Plants*
Second half eighteenth century
Paste-resist and indigo dyeing
(chaya-zome), silk and metallic
thread embroidery, and pigment
on white plain-weave ramie (asa)
65 ¼ × 50 ⅝ in.
(165.7 × 128.6 cm)
National Museum of Japanese
History, Nomura Collection

○

CATALOGUE NO. 44
*Katabira with Curtains, Large
Drum, and Seasonal Plants*
Late eighteenth century
Paste-resist and indigo dyeing
(chaya-zome) on white plain-weave
ramie (asa)
69 ⅝ × 52 ¼ in.
(176.8 × 132.7 cm)
Tokyo National Museum

●

CATALOGUE NO. 45
*Katabira with Birds, Pine Branches,
Ivy, Flowers, Gabions, and Water*
First half nineteenth century
Paste-resist and indigo dyeing
(chaya-zome) and silk and metallic
thread embroidery on white plain-
weave ramie (asa)
57 ⅞ × 48 in.
(147.0 × 121.9 cm)
Kuriyama Kōbō Co., Ltd.

○

CATALOGUE NO. 46
*Katabira with Chrysanthemums,
Bamboo, and Clouds*
First half nineteenth century
Paste-resist dyeing (yūzen) and silk
and metallic thread embroidery on
white plain-weave ramie (asa)
55 ⅛ × 43 ⅛ in.
(140.0 × 109.5 cm)
Tōyama Memorial Museum

●

Page 35

CATALOGUE NO. 47
*Uchikake with Wisteria, Floral
Bouquets, and Fans Alternating
with Fret Patterns* (Sayagata)
First half nineteenth century
Stenciled imitation tie-dyeing (kata
kanoko) and silk and metallic
thread embroidery on white figured
silk satin (rinzu)
67 ¼ × 50 ½ in.
(170.8 × 128.3 cm)
Tokyo National Museum

○

CATALOGUE NO. 48
*Uchikake with Floral Bouquets
Alternating with Serpentine-Line
Patterns* (Tatewaku)
First half nineteenth century
Stenciled imitation tie-dyeing (kata
kanoko) and silk and metallic
thread embroidery on white figured
silk satin (rinzu)
67 ⅞ × 50 in.
(172.4 × 127.0 cm)
Tokyo National Museum

●

CATALOGUE NO. 49

Katabira with Landscape with Pavilion, Gate, Rope Curtain, and Nobleman's Cart
First half nineteenth century
Paste-resist dyeing (yūzen), stenciled imitation tie-dyeing (kata kanoko), and silk and metallic thread embroidery on white plain-weave ramie (asa)

69 ⅜ × 49 in.
(176.2 × 124.5 cm)
Tokyo National Museum
○

CATALOGUE NO. 50
*Katabira with Flowering Plants,
Curtains, Fan, and Rustic Pavilion*
Late eighteenth–early nineteenth
century
Paste-resist dyeing (yūzen) and silk
and metallic thread embroidery on
white plain-weave ramie (asa)
67 ⅛ × 50 in.
(170.5 × 127.0 cm)
Tokyo National Museum

●

CATALOGUE NO. 51
Katabira with Rustic Landscape
First half nineteenth century
Paste-resist dyeing (shiro-age) and
silk and metallic thread embroidery
on blue plain-weave ramie (asa)
70 ⅛ × 49 ⅜ in.
(178.1 × 125.4 cm)
Los Angeles County Museum of
Art, gift of the 1992 Collectors
Committee, AC1992.42

CATALOGUE NO. 52
Koshimaki with Pine, Bamboo,
Plum, and Tortoiseshell Pattern
Early nineteenth century
Silk and metallic thread embroidery
on brown plain-weave silk
(nerinuki)
65 × 49 in.
(165.1 × 124.5 cm)
The Newark Museum, Herman and
Paul Jaehne Collection, gift of
Herman and Paul Jaehne, 1941

CATALOGUE NO. 53
Uchikake with Bamboo Curtains
and Plum Trees
First half nineteenth century
Brush-dyeing (hiki-zome) and silk
and metallic thread embroidery on
white figured silk satin (rinzu)
70 × 49¾ in.
(177.8 × 126.4 cm)
Bunka Gakuen Costume Museum

○

Page 70

CATALOGUE NO. 54
Furisode with Palace Curtains,
Clouds, and Fans
Mid-nineteenth century
Appliqué, tie-dyeing (kanoko and
nuishime shibori), paste-resist
dyeing (yūzen), and silk and
metallic thread embroidery on red
figured silk satin (rinzu)
70⅝ × 49½ in.
(179.4 × 125.7 cm)
National Museum of Japanese
History, Nomura Collection

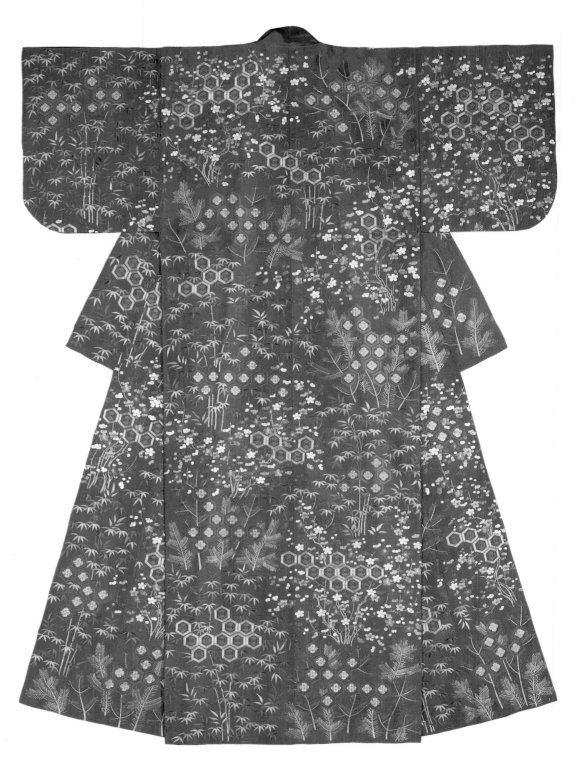

CATALOGUE NO. 52

CATALOGUE NO. 54

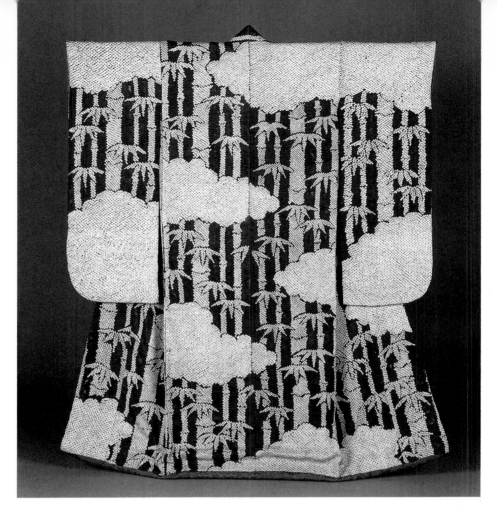

CATALOGUE NO. 55

CATALOGUE NO. 64

CATALOGUE NO. 68

CATALOGUE NO. 67

*Uchikake with Cherry Blossoms,
Water, Ducks, and Characters*
First half nineteenth century
Tie-dyeing (kanoko shibori) and
silk and metallic thread embroidery
on red figured silk satin (rinzu)
69 5/8 × 48 in.
(176.8 × 121.9 cm)
Bunka Gakuen Costume Museum
○
Pages 28 (detail), 189

CATALOGUE NO. 68

*Kosode with Cherry Tree and
Bamboo Gabions*
Early eighteenth century
Paste-resist dyeing (yūzen),
stenciled imitation tie-dyeing (kata
kanoko), silk and metallic thread
embroidery, and pigment on blue
silk crepe (chirimen)
63 1/4 × 49 1/2 in.
(160.7 × 125.7 cm)
Kanebo, Ltd.
●

CATALOGUE NO. 69

Kosode with Banana Plants in Rain
Late eighteenth–early nineteenth
century
Paste-resist dyeing (yūzen) and silk
and metallic thread embroidery on
light beige silk crepe (chirimen)
67 1/2 × 48 1/8 in.
(171.5 × 122.2 cm)
Suntory Museum of Art
○

CATALOGUE NO. 70
Kosode with Thistles and Butterflies
First half eighteenth century
Tie-dyeing (mokume shibori) and
silk and metallic thread embroidery
on white silk crepe (chirimen)
59 × 50½ in.
(149.9 × 128.3 cm)
Tōyama Memorial Museum

●

CATALOGUE NO. 71
Kosode on Screen
Left: Kosode fragment with water,
maple leaves, and autumn grasses
Mid-eighteenth century
Paste-resist dyeing (yūzen) and tie-
dyeing (nuishime shibori) on red
and white parti-colored (somewake)
silk crepe (chirimen)
Right: Kosode fragment with
autumn flowers and plovers
First half eighteenth century
(dedicatory inscription Genbun 5
[1740])
Paste-resist dyeing (yūzen) and tie-
dyeing (nuishime, kanoko, and
bōshi shibori) on white, purple, and
light gray parti-colored (somewake)
silk crepe (chirimen)
67½ × 74⅝ in.
(171.5 × 189.5 cm)
National Museum of Japanese
History, Nomura Collection

○

Page 121

CATALOGUE NO. 72
*Furisode with Stream and Bush
Clover* (Hagi)
First half nineteenth century
Tie-dyeing (kanoko shibori), paste-
resist dyeing (yūzen), and silk and
metallic thread embroidery on
white figured silk satin (rinzu)
63⅝ × 51¾ in.
(161.6 × 131.4 cm)
Kanebo, Ltd.

●

Page 121

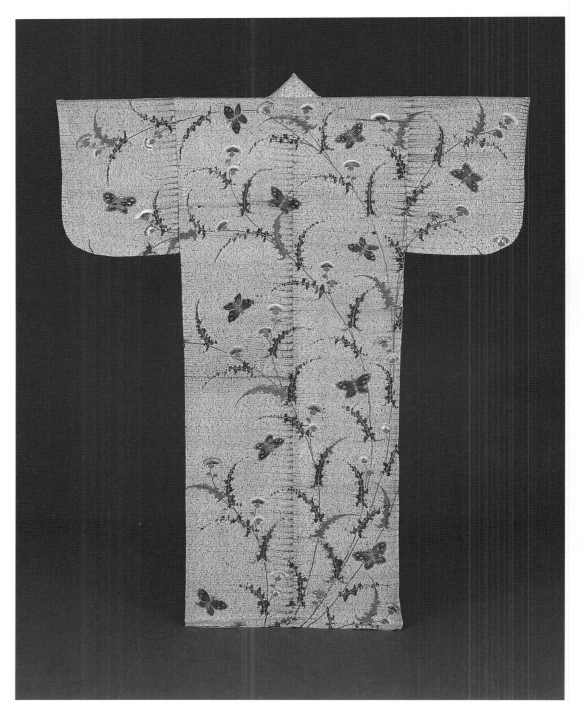

CATALOGUE NO. 70

CATALOGUE NO. 73
*Kosode with Snow-covered
Chrysanthemum Tendrils
and Butterflies*
Second half eighteenth century
Paste-resist dyeing (shiro-age) and
silk and metallic thread embroidery
on black silk crepe (chirimen)
62 ³/₄ × 47 ³/₈ in.
(159.5 × 120.4 cm)
Tabata Collection

○

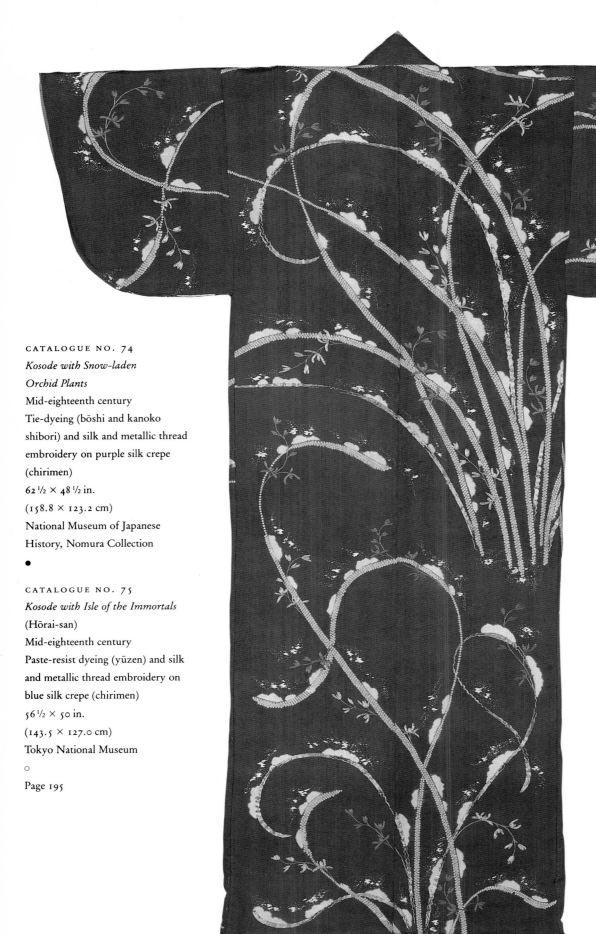

CATALOGUE NO. 74
*Kosode with Snow-laden
Orchid Plants*
Mid-eighteenth century
Tie-dyeing (bōshi and kanoko
shibori) and silk and metallic thread
embroidery on purple silk crepe
(chirimen)
62 ½ × 48 ½ in.
(158.8 × 123.2 cm)
National Museum of Japanese
History, Nomura Collection

●

CATALOGUE NO. 75
Kosode with Isle of the Immortals
(Hōrai-san)
Mid-eighteenth century
Paste-resist dyeing (yūzen) and silk
and metallic thread embroidery on
blue silk crepe (chirimen)
56 ½ × 50 in.
(143.5 × 127.0 cm)
Tokyo National Museum
○
Page 195

CATALOGUE NO. 76
Katabira with Isle of the Immortals
(Hōrai-san)
First half nineteenth century
Paste-resist dyeing (yūzen),
stenciled imitation tie-dyeing (kata
kanoko), silk and metallic thread
embroidery, ink, and pigment on
white plain-weave ramie (asa)
62 ⅛ × 48 ⅞ in.
(157.8 × 124.1 cm)
Kanebo, Ltd.

●

Page 39

CATALOGUE NO. 77
*Kosode with Plum, Bamboo-filled
Pine-Bark Lozenges* (Matsukawabishi), *and Characters*
Early eighteenth century
Stenciled imitation tie-dyeing (kata
kanoko), applied indigo (ai-zuri),
and silk and metallic thread
embroidery on white figured silk
satin (rinzu)
52 ⅝ × 47 ¾ in.
(133.7 × 121.2 cm)
Tabata Collection
○

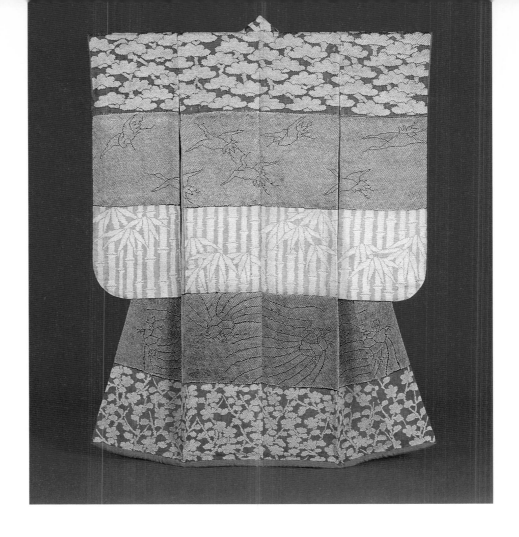

CATALOGUE NO. 78
*Furisode with Pine, Crane,
Bamboo, Tortoise, and Plum*
First half nineteenth century
Tie-dyeing (sō-kanoko shibori) on
purple, blue, yellow, black, and red
parti-colored (somewake) figured
silk satin (rinzu)
64 ¾ × 50 ½ in.
(164.5 × 128.3 cm)
Kanebo, Ltd.

•

CATALOGUE NO. 79
*Furisode with Paulownia Tree
and Phoenixes*
Late eighteenth–early nineteenth
century
Tie-dyeing (bōshi and kanoko
shibori) and silk and metallic thread
embroidery on red-orange figured
silk satin (rinzu)
66 ½ × 49 ½ in.
(168.9 × 125.7 cm)
Los Angeles County Museum of
Art, gift of Miss Bella Mabury,
M.39.2.6

CATALOGUE NO. 80

*Kosode with Snow-covered
Mandarin Orange Trees and
Characters*

Late eighteenth century

Paste-resist dyeing (yūzen),
stenciled imitation tie-dyeing (kata
kanoko), and silk and metallic
thread embroidery on light blue
silk crepe (chirimen)

65 × 50 in.

(165.1 × 127.0 cm)

Los Angeles County Museum of
Art, gift of Miss Bella Mabury,
M.39.2.8

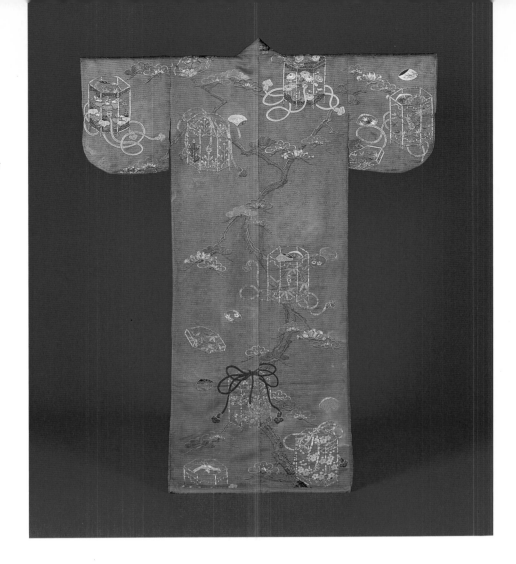

CATALOGUE NO. 81
*Kosode with Pine Tree and Shell
Game Containers*
Second half eighteenth century
Silk and metallic thread embroidery
on red figured silk satin (rinzu)
60 ¼ × 47 ¾ in.
(153.0 × 121.3 cm)
Tokyo National Museum

○

Page 132 (detail)

CATALOGUE NO. 82
*Kosode with Mandarin Orange
Trees and Shell Game Containers*
Second half eighteenth century
Tie-dyeing (nuishime shibori),
paste-resist dyeing (yūzen),
stenciled imitation tie-dyeing (kata
kanoko), silk and metallic thread
embroidery, and touches of gold
leaf (surihaku) on white and red-
orange parti-colored (somewake)
figured silk satin (rinzu)
61 ⅞ × 49 ⅛ in.
(157.2 × 124.8 cm)
Kanebo, Ltd.

●

CATALOGUE NO. 83
Kosode with Rolls of Silk and Pines
Late eighteenth–early nineteenth
century
Tie-dyeing (kanoko and nuishime
shibori) and silk and metallic thread
embroidery on white figured silk
satin (rinzu)
60 × 50⅛ in.
(152.4 × 127.3 cm)
Kanebo, Ltd.
○
Page 38

CATALOGUE NO. 84
Furisode with Rolls of Silk
First half nineteenth century
Tie-dyeing (kanoko and nuishime
shibori) and silk and metallic thread
embroidery on white figured silk
satin (rinzu)
59¼ × 49¼ in.
(150.5 × 125.1 cm)
Kanebo, Ltd.
●

CATALOGUE NO. 84

CATALOGUE NO. 85
*Furisode with Japanese Bamboo
Curtain and Chinese Children
at Play*
First half nineteenth century
Paste-resist dyeing (yūzen) and silk
and metallic thread embroidery on
white figured silk satin (rinzu)
64¾ × 48¼ in.
(164.5 × 122.6 cm)
Marubeni Corporation
○
Pages 201 (detail), 229

CATALOGUE NO. 86
*Kosode with Japanese Palace
Curtains, Cypress-Slat Fan, and
Chinese Crown, Clouds, and
Peonies*
First half nineteenth century
Paste-resist dyeing (yūzen) and silk
and metallic thread embroidery on
blue silk crepe (chirimen)
64⅝ × 50¾ in.
(164.1 × 128.9 cm)
Tokyo National Museum
●

CATALOGUE NO. 86

CATALOGUE NO. 87
Kosode with Bamboo, Water, and Gabions
Mid-eighteenth century
Paste-resist dyeing (shiro-age),
stenciled imitation tie-dyeing (kata
kanoko), and silk and metallic
thread embroidery on light blue silk
crepe (chirimen)
57 × 49 ⅝ in.
(144.8 × 126.0 cm)
Tabata Collection
○

CATALOGUE NO. 88
*Katabira with Gabions, Cherry
Blossoms, and Characters*
First half eighteenth century
Tie-dyeing (kanoko and bōshi
shibori) and silk and metallic thread
embroidery on black plain-weave
ramie (asa)
56 × 47 ⅜ in.
(142.2 × 120.3 cm)
National Museum of Japanese
History, Nomura Collection
●

CATALOGUE NO. 89
*Katabira with Boats, Wisteria,
and Bamboo Fence*
First half eighteenth century
Tie-dyeing (kanoko and bōshi
shibori), stenciled imitation tie-
dyeing (kata kanoko), and silk and
metallic thread embroidery on
white plain-weave ramie (asa)
60 × 45 in.
(152.4 × 114.3 cm)
National Museum of Japanese
History, Nomura Collection
○

CATALOGUE NO. 90

Kosode with Boats, Water, and Plum Blossoms

Early eighteenth century

Stenciled imitation tie-dyeing (kata kanoko) and silk and metallic thread embroidery on white figured silk satin (rinzu)

61 ³⁄₈ × 52 ¹⁄₄ in.

(155.9 × 132.7 cm)

National Museum of Japanese History, Nomura Collection

●

CATALOGUE NO. 91

Kosode with Sedge Hats and Maple Leaves

Late seventeenth–early eighteenth century

Tie-dyeing (kanoko shibori) and silk and metallic thread embroidery on white figured silk satin (rinzu)

58 ⁵⁄₈ × 53 ¹⁄₂ in.

(148.9 × 135.9 cm)

Tokyo National Museum

○

Page 200

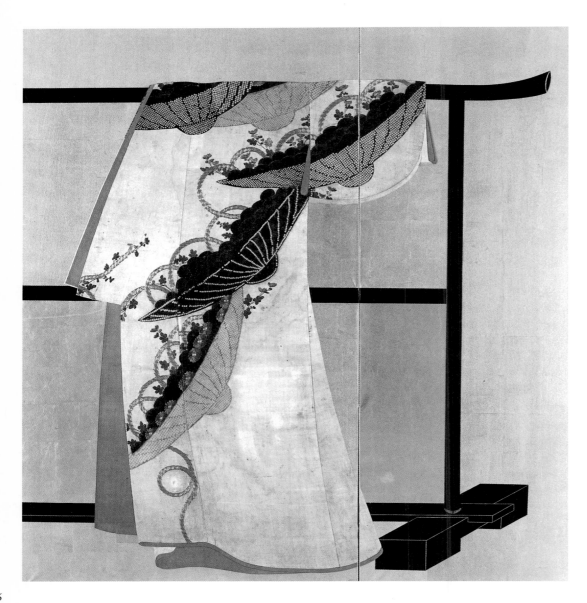

CATALOGUE NO. 90

CATALOGUE NO. 92

Kosode on Screen

Kosode fragment with flower-filled sedge hats

Third quarter seventeenth century

Tie-dyeing (kanoko and bōshi shibori), silk and metallic thread embroidery, and stenciled gold leaf (surihaku) on white silk satin (shusu)

67 ¹⁄₂ × 75 in.

(171.5 × 190.5 cm)

National Museum of Japanese History, Nomura Collection

●

CATALOGUE NO. 93

Kosode on Screen

Kosode fragment with fans and
circles enclosing characters
Late seventeenth–early eighteenth
century
Tie-dyeing (kanoko shibori) and
silk and metallic thread embroidery
on white silk satin (nume)
68 × 75 in.
(172.7 × 190.5 cm)
National Museum of Japanese
History, Nomura Collection
○
Page 7 (detail)

CATALOGUE NO. 94

Kosode with Fans and
Chrysanthemums
Early eighteenth century
Tie-dyeing (kanoko shibori) and
silk and metallic thread embroidery
on white figured silk satin (rinzu)
65 ½ × 53 ⅝ in.
(166.4 × 136.2 cm)
Marubeni Corporation

●

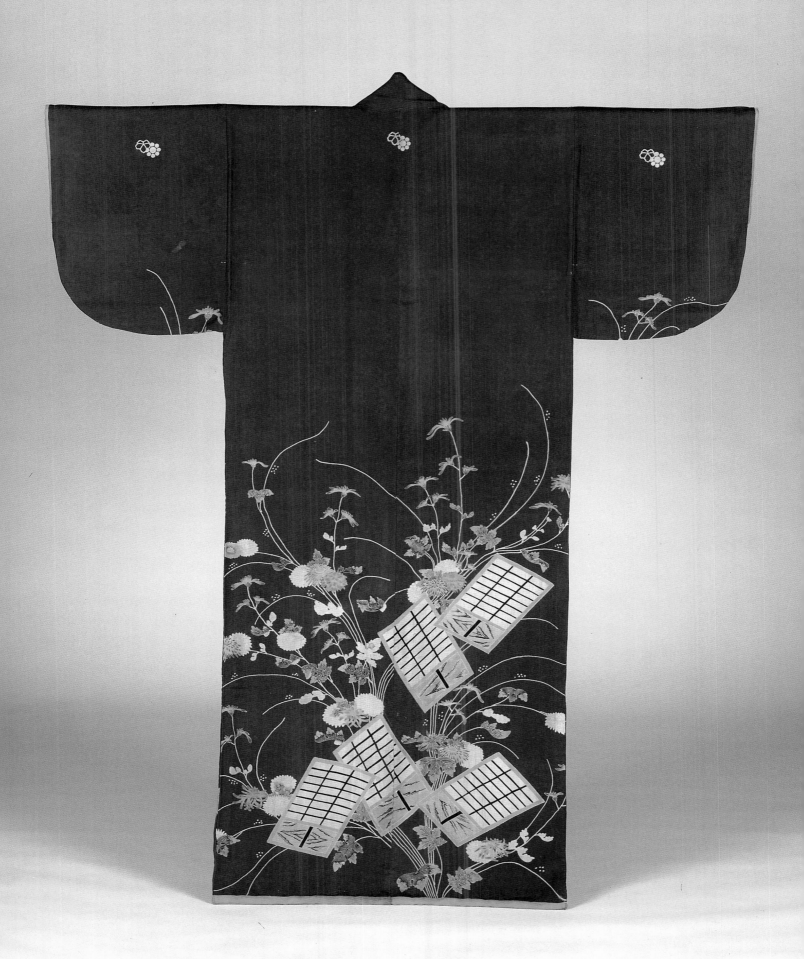

CATALOGUE NO. 95
*Kosode with Chrysanthemums and
Scattered Shoji*
Second half eighteenth century
Paste-resist dyeing (yūzen) and silk
and metallic thread embroidery on
blue-gray plain-weave silk (habutae)
57 3/8 × 51 in.
(145.7 × 129.5 cm)
Kyoto Senshoku Kaikan

○

CATALOGUE NO. 96
*Katabira with Plum Tree and
Overhung Doors* (Tsukiage-do)
Mid-eighteenth century
Tie-dyeing (kanoko and nuishime
shibori), ink, and silk and metallic
thread embroidery on white plain-
weave ramie
62 1/8 × 47 3/8 in.
(157.8 × 120.3 cm)
National Museum of Japanese
History, Nomura Collection

●

CATALOGUE NO. 96

CATALOGUE NO. 95

CATALOGUE NO. 97
Katabira with Potted Plants
Late eighteenth–early nineteenth
century
Paste-resist and indigo dyeing
(chaya-zome) on white plain-weave
ramie (asa)
58 1/2 × 48 in.
(148.6 × 121.9 cm)
Marubeni Corporation

○

CATALOGUE NO. 98
*Katabira with Folding Screens,
Plants, and Chinese Fans*
Late eighteenth–early nineteenth
century
Paste-resist and indigo dyeing
(chaya-zome) on white plain-weave
ramie (asa)
64 × 50 1/4 in.
(162.6 × 127.6 cm)
Kanebo, Ltd.

●

Page 203

CATALOGUE NO. 97

CATALOGUE NO. 99
*Kosode with Hanging Scrolls,
Camellias, and Willow Trees*
First quarter eighteenth century
Paste-resist dyeing (yūzen) and ink
painting (kaki-e) on brown plain-
weave silk (hira-ginu)
59 ¼ × 51 ¼ in.
(150.5 × 130.2 cm)
Tokyo National Museum
○
Pages 100, 202 (detail)

CATALOGUE NO. 100
Kosode on Screen
Kosode fragment with folding
screens depicting the fifty-three
stages of the Tōkaidō
Second half eighteenth century
Paste-resist dyeing (yūzen) on blue-
gray silk crepe (chirimen)
67 ¼ × 75 in.
(170.8 × 190.5 cm)
National Museum of Japanese
History, Nomura Collection
●
Page 61 (detail)

CATALOGUE NO. 101
Hitoe with Kameido Tenjin Shrine
First half nineteenth century
Ink and color (kaki-e) on pale
yellow silk crepe (chijimi)
51 ½ × 48 in.
(130.8 × 121.9 cm)
Kanebo, Ltd.
○
Page 194

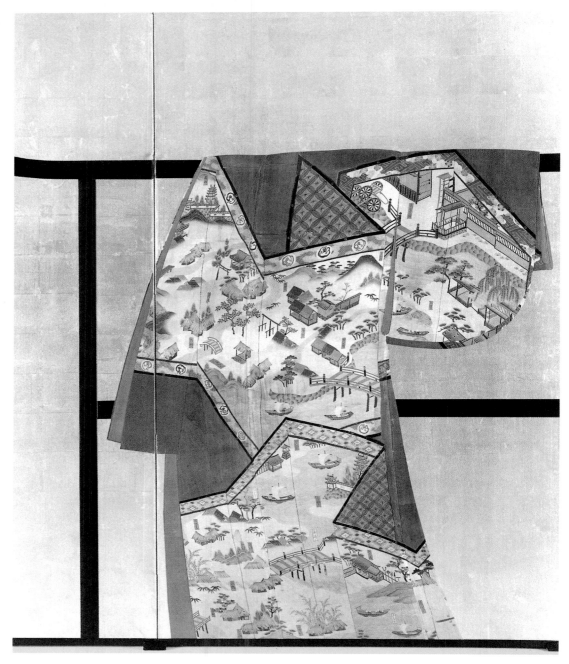

CATALOGUE NO. 100

CATALOGUE NO. 102

CATALOGUE NO. 102
Katabira with Nonomiya Shrine
Early nineteenth century
Paste-resist dyeing (yūzen) on white
plain-weave ramie (asa)
63 ¼ × 45 ½ in.
(160.7 × 115.6 cm)
Kyoto National Museum

●

CATALOGUE NO. 103
Katabira with View of Sumiyoshi
First half nineteenth century
Paste-resist dyeing (yūzen) and silk
and metallic thread embroidery on
white plain-weave ramie (asa)
63 × 48 ½ in.
(160.0 × 123.2 cm)
Tokyo National Museum

○

Page 128

CATALOGUE NO. 104
Kosode with View of Sumiyoshi
Late eighteenth–early nineteenth
century
Paste-resist dyeing (yūzen) and silk
and metallic thread embroidery on
beige silk crepe (chirimen)
62 ½ × 54 ½ in.
(158.8 × 138.4 cm)
Tokyo National Museum

●

CATALOGUE NO. 104

CATALOGUE NO. 106

CATALOGUE NO. 105
*Kosode with "Eight Views
of Ōmi"*
Mid-eighteenth century
Paste-resist dyeing (yūzen), dip-
dyeing (tsuke-zome), and silk and
metallic thread embroidery on
white silk crepe (chirimen)
59 ¼ × 48 in.
(150.5 × 121.9 cm)
Kanebo, Ltd.
○
Page 193

CATALOGUE NO. 106
Kosode with View of Uji Bridge
First half nineteenth century
Paste-resist dyeing (shiro-age) and
silk and metallic thread embroidery
on blue silk crepe (chirimen)
64 ½ × 49 ¼ in.
(163.8 × 125.1 cm)
Tokyo National Museum
●

CATALOGUE NO. 107
*Katabira with "Eight Views
of Ōmi"*
Late eighteenth–early nineteenth
century
Paste-resist dyeing (yūzen) and silk
and metallic thread embroidery on
white plain-weave ramie (asa)
60 ⅛ × 47 ⅝ in.
(152.7 × 121.0 cm)
Tabata Collection
○
Page 129

CATALOGUE NO. 108

Kosode on Screen

Kosode fragment with "Eight
Views of Ōmi"

Second half eighteenth century

Ink painting (kaki-e) and dip-
dyeing (tsuke-zome) on white silk
crepe (chirimen)

68 × 75 in.

(172.7 × 190.5 cm)

National Museum of Japanese
History, Nomura Collection

●

CATALOGUE NO. 109

Juban with Scenes of Edo

Mid-nineteenth century

Cotton thread embroidery on gray
plain-weave cotton

57 × 49 ½ in.

(144.8 × 125.7 cm)

National Museum of Japanese

History, Nomura Collection

○

Pages 42 (detail), 50

CATALOGUE NO. 110

*Kosode with Views of Yoshiwara
Pleasure Quarters*

Second half eighteenth century

Paste-resist dyeing (yūzen) and silk
and metallic thread embroidery on
brown silk crepe (chirimen)

65 × 52 ½ in.

(165.1 × 133.4 cm)

Kanebo, Ltd.

●

Page 57 (detail)

CATALOGUE NO. 111

Kosode with Views of Kyoto

Mid-eighteenth century

Paste-resist dyeing (yūzen) and silk
and metallic thread embroidery on
white silk crepe (chirimen)

59 ¼ × 51 ½ in.

(150.5 × 130.8 cm)

National Museum of Japanese
History, Nomura Collection

○

Page 191

CATALOGUE NO. 112

*Katabira with View of Kiyomizu
Temple*

First half nineteenth century

Paste-resist dyeing (shiro-age),
stenciled imitation tie-dyeing (kata
kanoko), and silk and metallic
thread embroidery on light blue
plain-weave ramie (asa)

68 ½ × 48 in.

(174.0 × 121.9 cm)

Tokyo National Museum

●

Page 192 (detail)

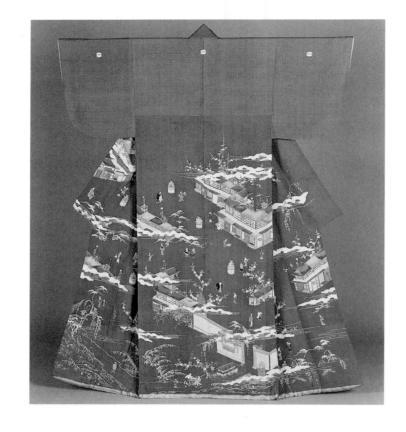

CATALOGUE NO. 113

Kosode with Books

First half nineteenth century

Tie-dyeing (nuishime and kanoko shibori) and silk and metallic thread embroidery on white figured silk satin (rinzu)

66 ½ × 48 ¼ in.

(168.9 × 122.6 cm)

National Museum of Japanese History, Nomura Collection

○

Page 94 (detail)

CATALOGUE NO. 114

Kosode with Books and Characters

Second half eighteenth century

Tie-dyeing (kanoko and nuishime shibori) and silk and metallic thread embroidery on white silk satin (nume)

62 × 45 ¾ in.

(157.5 × 116.2 cm)

National Museum of Japanese History, Nomura Collection

●

CATALOGUE NO. 115

Kosode on Screen

Kosode fragment with scenes
from the *Genji monogatari*
(Tale of Genji)
Second half eighteenth century
Ink painting (kaki-e) on white silk
satin (nume)
68 ¼ × 75 in.
(173.4 × 190.5 cm)
National Museum of Japanese
History, Nomura Collection
○
Page 226 (detail)

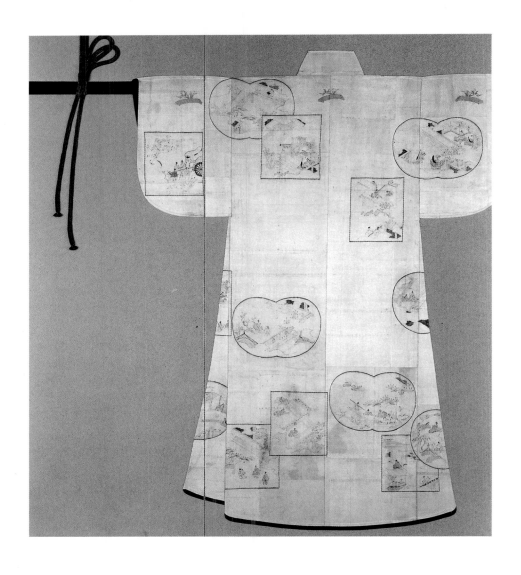

CATALOGUE NO. 116

CATALOGUE NO. 116
*Kosode with Vertical Stripes and
Fans, Snowflake Roundels, and
Pine-Bark Lozenges
(Matsukawabishi) Filled with Scenes
from Classical Literature*
Mid-eighteenth century
Paste-resist dyeing (yūzen) and silk
and metallic thread embroidery on
light yellow silk crepe (chirimen)
57 ½ × 50 ⅞ in.
(146.1 × 129.2 cm)
Tokyo National Museum
●

Page 207 (detail)

CATALOGUE NO. 117
*Kosode with Streams, Flowering
Plants, Pavilions, and Insect Cages*
First half nineteenth century
Paste-resist dyeing (shiro-age) and
silk and metallic thread embroidery
on purple and light green parti-
colored (somewake) silk crepe
(chirimen)
65 ⅜ × 48 ¼ in.
(166.1 × 122.6 cm)
Tokyo National Museum
○

CATALOGUE NO. 117

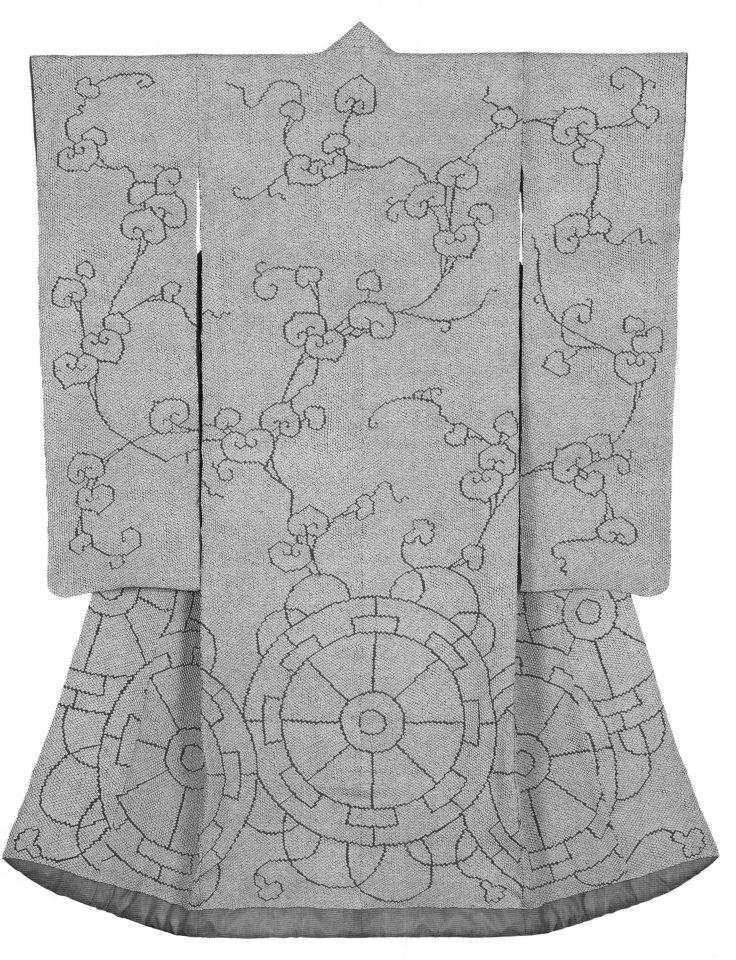

CATALOGUE NO. 118

CATALOGUE NO. 118

Furisode with Oxcart Wheels (Genji-guruma) and Wild Ginger
First half nineteenth century
Tie-dyeing (sō-kanoko shibori)
on red figured silk satin (rinzu)
68 × 49 3/8 in.
(172.7 × 125.4 cm)
Marubeni Corporation

●

CATALOGUE NO. 119

Furisode with Symbols from an Incense Identification Game (Genji-kō) and Flowering Vines
First half nineteenth century
Paste-resist dyeing (yūzen) and brush-dyeing (hiki-zome) on blue and gray silk crepe (chirimen)
61 1/4 × 50 in.
(155.6 × 127.0 cm)
National Museum of Japanese History, Nomura Collection

○

Page 149

CATALOGUE NO. 120

Furisode with Symbols from an Incense Identification Game (Genji-kō) and Flowering Plants
Third quarter nineteenth century
Paste-resist dyeing (yūzen) on blue-gray silk crepe (chirimen)
59 5/8 × 48 1/4 in.
(151.4 × 122.6 cm)
Tokyo National Museum

●

Pages 26 (detail), 150

CATALOGUE NO. 121

Kosode with Plank Bridges (Yatsuhashi), Irises, and Butterflies
First half nineteenth century
Silk and metallic thread embroidery on purple figured silk satin (rinzu)
66 × 49 in. (167.6 × 124.5 cm)
Los Angeles County Museum of Art, gift of Miss Bella Mabury, M.39.2.9

○

Front cover and page 118

CATALOGUE NO. 122

Furisode with Plank Bridges (Yatsuhashi), Irises, and Swallows
Late eighteenth–early nineteenth century
Paste-resist dyeing (yūzen) and silk and metallic thread embroidery on yellow-green silk crepe (chirimen)
72 1/2 × 49 1/2 in. (184.2 × 125.7 cm)
Los Angeles County Museum of Art, gift of Mrs. Philip A. Colman in memory of Philip A. Colman, M.90.8

●

Page 119

CATALOGUE NO. 123

Uchikake with Stream and Irises
First half nineteenth century
Tie-dyeing (kanoko and nuishime shibori), paste-resist dyeing (yūzen), and silk thread embroidery on white figured silk satin (rinzu)
69 11/16 × 49 5/8 in.
(177.0 × 126.0 cm)
Kanebo, Ltd.

○

Page 183

CATALOGUE NO. 124

Kosode with Stream, Plank Bridges, Water Plantains, and Plum Blossoms
First half eighteenth century
Tie-dyeing (kanoko shibori), brush-dyeing (hiki-zome), and silk and metallic thread embroidery on white silk crepe (chirimen)
62 1/8 × 46 1/2 in. (157.8 × 118.1 cm)
Kanebo, Ltd.

●

CATALOGUE NO. 124

CATALOGUE NO. 125

CATALOGUE NO. 126

CATALOGUE NO. 127

Kosode on Screen

Left: Kosode fragment with fence,
larch flowers (kara-matsu), and
characters

First quarter eighteenth century

Tie-dyeing (nuishime shibori), silk
and metallic thread embroidery, and
appliqué (metallic yarn
supplementary weft on twill-weave
silk ground) on green and white
parti-colored (somewake) figured
silk satin (rinzu)

Right: Kosode fragment with
bamboo fence and characters

First half eighteenth century

Tie-dyeing (kanoko and nuishime
shibori) and paste-resist dyeing
(noribōsen) on red and cream parti-
colored (somewake) silk crepe
(chirimen)

68 ⅛ × 75 in.

(173.0 × 190.5 cm)

National Museum of Japanese
History, Nomura Collection

○

Page 154 (detail)

CATALOGUE NO. 130

CATALOGUE NO. 132
Kosode on Screen
Kosode fragment with flowering
plum branches and character
for pine
Last quarter seventeenth century
(dedicatory inscription Shōtoku 6
[1716])
Tie-dyeing (kanoko shibori), silk
and metallic thread embroidery, and
traces of gold leaf (surihaku) on
black figured silk satin (rinzu)
68 × 74 3/4 in.
(172.7 × 189.9 cm)
National Museum of Japanese
History, Nomura Collection

●

CATALOGUE NO. 133
Kosode with Musical Instruments,
Chrysanthemums, and Characters
Early eighteenth century
Tie-dyeing (kanoko shibori) and
silk and metallic thread embroidery
on white silk satin (shusu)
60 3/4 × 51 in.
(154.3 × 129.5 cm)
Kanebo, Ltd.

○

CATALOGUE NO. 134
Kosode with Maple Trees and
Characters
Second half eighteenth century
Paste-resist dyeing (yūzen),
stenciled imitation tie-dyeing (kata
kanoko), and silk and metallic
thread embroidery on white twill-
figured plain-weave silk (saya)
57 7/8 × 48 5/8 in.
(147.0 × 123.6 cm)
Tabata Collection

●

Page 173

CATALOGUE NO. 135
Kosode with Diagonal Stripes and
Characters
Last quarter seventeenth century
Tie-dyeing (kanoko and nuishime
shibori) and silk and metallic thread
embroidery on white
figured silk satin (rinzu)
61 3/8 × 53 3/4 in.
(155.9 × 136.5 cm)
Tokyo National Museum

○

Page 167

CATALOGUE NO. 133

CATALOGUE NO. 140

CATALOGUE NO. 142

CATALOGUE NO. 142

*Katabira with Mandarin Orange
Tree, Rocks, Waves, and Characters*

Second half eighteenth century

Paste-resist dyeing (yūzen),
stenciled imitation tie-dyeing (kata
kanoko), and silk and metallic
thread embroidery on white plain-
weave ramie (asa)

63 ½ × 51 ⅛ in.

(161.3 × 129.9 cm)

Tokyo National Museum

●

CATALOGUE NO. 143

*Katabira with Pine Trees, Waves,
and Characters*

Second quarter eighteenth century

Stenciled imitation tie-dyeing (kata
kanoko), paste-resist dyeing
(noribōsen), and silk and metallic
thread embroidery on white plain-
weave ramie (asa)

62 × 48 ¼ in. (157.5 × 122.6 cm)

Tōyama Memorial Museum

○

CATALOGUE NO. 144

*Uchikake with Wild Ginger,
Chevron-filled Clouds, and
Characters*

Late eighteenth–early nineteenth
century

Paste-resist dyeing (yūzen) and silk
and metallic thread embroidery on
white figured silk satin (rinzu)

60 ⅛ × 49 ¾ in. (152.7 × 126.4 cm)

Kanebo, Ltd.

●

Page 69

CATALOGUE NO. 145

*Kosode with Pine, Bamboo, Plum,
Fans, and Characters*

Mid-eighteenth century

Paste-resist dyeing (yūzen), tie-
dyeing (shibori), and silk and
metallic thread embroidery on light
blue, white, and purple parti-
colored (somewake) twill-figured
plain-weave silk (saya)

59 ⁹⁄₁₆ × 51 ½ in. (151.3 × 130.8 cm)

Tabata Collection

○

Page 176

CATALOGUE NO. 146

*Kosode with Hawks, Maple Trees,
Waterfalls, Checks, and Characters*

Mid-eighteenth century

Paste-resist dyeing (yūzen) and silk
and metallic thread embroidery on
beige silk crepe (chirimen)

56 ½ × 50 ⅞ in. (143.5 × 129.2 cm)

Kanebo, Ltd.

●

Page 175

CATALOGUE NO. 143

CATALOGUE NO. 148 (detail)

CATALOGUE NO. 147
Obi with Snowflake Roundels,
Spring Plants, and Characters
Third quarter seventeenth century
Tie-dyeing (kanoko and nuishime
shibori) and ink painting (kaki-e)
on white figured silk satin (rinzu)
5 ¼ × 111 ¹³/₁₆ in. (13.4 × 284.0 cm)
Sendai City Museum
Important Cultural Property
○
Page 79 (detail)

CATALOGUE NO. 148
Obi with Flowering Plum Branches
and Tablets
Third quarter seventeenth century
Paste resist (shiro-age), tie-dyeing
(kanoko shibori), and stenciled
imitation tie-dyeing (kata kanoko)
on blue figured silk satin (rinzu)
5 ⅛ × 108 ⅝ in. (13.0 × 276.0 cm)
Sendai City Museum
Important Cultural Property
●

CATALOGUE NO. 147 (detail)

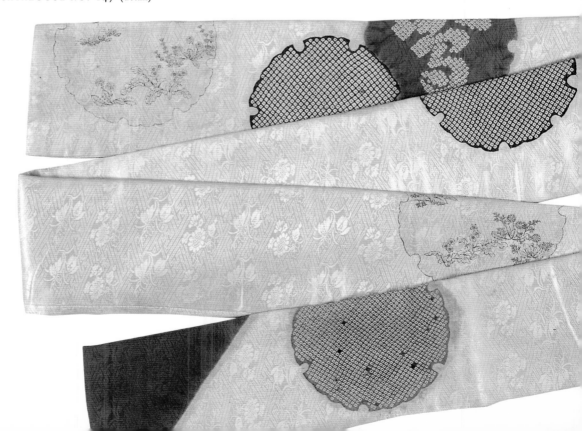

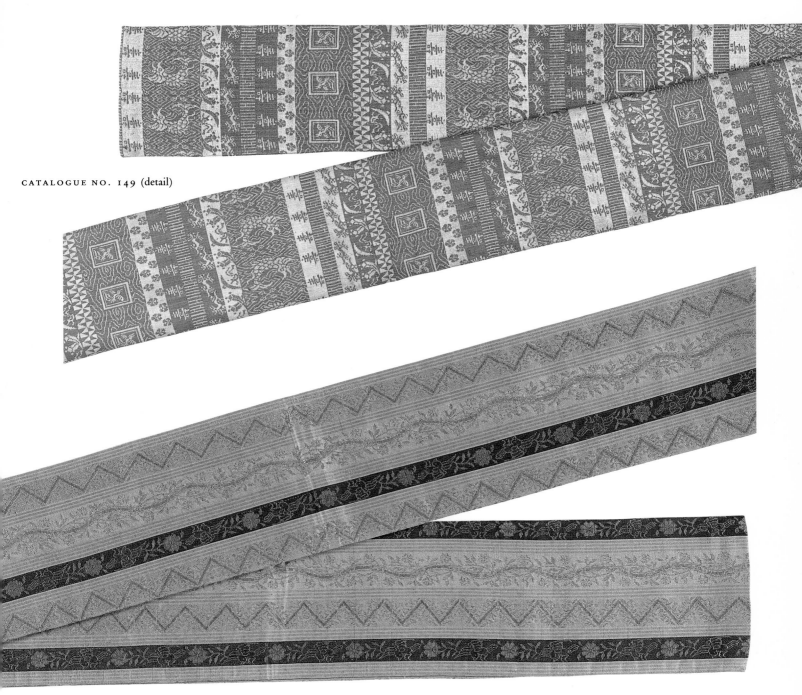

CATALOGUE NO. 149 (detail)

CATALOGUE NO. 150 (detail)

CATALOGUE NO. 149

*Obi with Bands of Geometric
Patterns and Auspicious Motifs*

Third quarter seventeenth century

Compound weave silk (fūtsū-ori)

4 1/8 × 122 in.

(10.5 × 310.0 cm)

Sendai City Museum

Important Cultural Property

○

Page 32 (detail)

CATALOGUE NO. 150

*Obi with Bands of Floral Meanders
and Birds*

Third quarter seventeenth century

Silk and metallic yarn
supplementary weft on silk satin
ground (mōru-ori)

4 1/2 × 106 11/16 in.

(11.5 × 271.0 cm)

Sendai City Museum

Important Cultural Property

●

CATALOGUE NO. 152
(detail)

CATALOGUE NO. 151 (detail)

CATALOGUE NO. 153 (detail)

CATALOGUE NO. 154 (detail)

CATALOGUE NO. 151
Obi with Cherry Blossoms
and Rafts
Early eighteenth century
Silk and metallic thread embroidery,
tie-dyeing (nuishime shibori), and
stenciled imitation tie-dyeing (kata
kanoko) on white figured silk satin
(rinzu)
6 ¹¹/₁₆ × 125 ⅝ in.
(17.0 × 319.0 cm)
Nara Prefectural Museum of Art

○

CATALOGUE NO. 152
Obi with Paulownia, Phoenix, and
Floral Roundels
Late eighteenth–early nineteenth
century
Paste-resist dyeing (yūzen) and tie-
dyeing (nuishime shibori) on
purple, red, and white parti-colored
(somewake) silk crepe (chirimen)
7 ¹³/₁₆ × 138 ³/₁₆ in.
(19.8 × 351.0 cm)
Nara Prefectural Museum of Art

●

CATALOGUE NO. 153
Obi with Flower Rafts and Waves
Late eighteenth century
Silk and metallic thread embroidery
on light green silk satin (shusu)
9 ½ × 148 in.
(24.1 × 375.9 cm)
Bunka Gakuen Costume Museum

○

CATALOGUE NO. 154
Obi with Birds, Waves, Plants,
and Anchors
Late eighteenth century
Paste-resist dyeing (yūzen),
stenciled imitation tie-dyeing (kata
kanoko), and silk and metallic
thread embroidery on green silk
crepe (chirimen)
9 ⅝ × 155 ½ in.
(24.4 × 395.0 cm)
Kyoto National Museum

●

CATALOGUE NO. 155 (detail)

CATALOGUE NO. 155
Obi with Carp, Duckweed, and Waves
Late eighteenth–early nineteenth century
Silk and metallic thread embroidery on green silk satin (shusu)
10¾ × 154 in.
(27.3 × 391.2 cm)
Marubeni Corporation
○
Page 4 (detail)

CATALOGUE NO. 156
Obi with Scattered Double Cherry Blossoms, Oxcart Wheels (Genji-guruma), and Lozenges
Late eighteenth century
Silk and metallic thread embroidery on light green silk satin (shusu)
11½ × 146 in.
(29.2 × 370.8 cm)
Bunka Gakuen Costume Museum
●

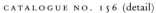

CATALOGUE NO. 156 (detail)

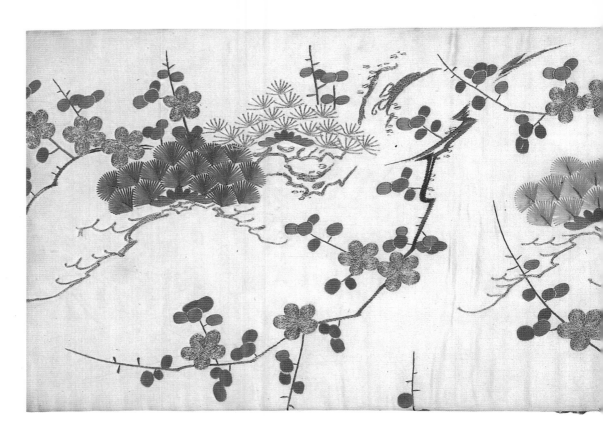

CATALOGUE NO. 157 (detail)

CATALOGUE NO. 157
*Obi with Pine, Bamboo, Plum,
Crane, and Tortoise*
Late eighteenth–early nineteenth
century
Silk and metallic thread embroidery
on white silk satin (shusu)
11½ × 155¾ in.
(29.2 × 395.6 cm)
Marubeni Corporation
○

CATALOGUE NO. 158
Obi with Lions and Peonies
Early nineteenth century
Silk and metallic thread embroidery
on light blue silk satin (shusu)
11⅝ × 150⅞ in.
(29.5 × 383.2 cm)
Kyoto National Museum
●

CATALOGUE NO. 158 (detail)

CATALOGUE NO. 159
Obi with Puppies, Snow,
Chrysanthemums, and Narcissus
First half nineteenth century
Silk and metallic thread embroidery
on red silk velvet
10 1/2 × 155 1/8 in.
(26.7 × 394.0 cm)
Tokyo National Museum
○

CATALOGUE NO. 160
Obi with Diamond Pattern and
Flowers
First half nineteenth century
Silk and metallic thread embroidery
on purple silk velvet
11 7/8 × 174 1/2 in.
(30.2 × 443.2 cm)
Tokyo National Museum
●

Page 33 (detail)

CATALOGUE NO. 159 (detail)

CATALOGUE NO. 160 (detail)

CATALOGUE NO. 161
Koshimaki Obi with Flower Carts,
Tree Peony, and Wisteria
Late eighteenth century
Silk and metallic yarn
supplementary weft on green and
white silk twill-weave satin ground
(nishiki)
3 ½ × 146 in.
(8.9 × 370.8 cm)
Tokyo National Museum

○

CATALOGUE NO. 162
Koshimaki Obi with Flowers
and Butterflies
Early nineteenth century
Silk and metallic yarn
supplementary weft on purple silk
twill-weave satin ground (nishiki)
3 ⅝ × 145 ½ in.
(9.2 × 369.6 cm)
Tokyo National Museum

●

CATALOGUE NO. 161

CATALOGUE NO. 162

CATALOGUE NO. 163

CATALOGUE NO. 164

CATALOGUE NO. 163
Kosode Fragment with Fan Roundels, Flowering Vines, and Wild Ginger Leaves
Momoyama period, late sixteenth–early seventeenth century
Tsujigahana style; tie-dyeing (kanoko shibori), silk thread embroidery, ink painting (kaki-e), and gold leaf (surihaku) on white plain-weave silk (nerinuki)
25 ³/₄ × 15 ¹/₄ in.
(65.4 × 38.7 cm)
Los Angeles County Museum of Art, gift of Miss Bella Mabury, M.39.2.304
Endsheets (detail) and page 82 (detail)

CATALOGUE NO. 164
Kosode Fragment with Mountains, Snowflake Roundels, Wisteria, and Plants of the Four Seasons
Note: Cat. nos. 3, 164, are fragments from the same kosode.
Early seventeenth century
Keichō-Kan'ei style; tie-dyeing (nuishime, bōshi, and kanoko shibori), silk thread embroidery, and traces of stenciled gold and silver leaf (surihaku) on red, black, white, and light blue parti-colored (somewake) figured silk satin (rinzu)
27 ¹/₈ × 11 ¹/₂ in. (68.9 × 29.2 cm)
Los Angeles County Museum of Art, Costume Council Fund, M.85.188
Page 87 (detail)

CATALOGUE NO. 165
Kosode Fragment with Tortoiseshell Pattern, Waves, and Cherry Blossoms
First half seventeenth century
Tie-dyeing (kanoko shibori), silk and metallic thread embroidery, and stenciled gold leaf (surihaku) on white figured silk satin (rinzu)
28 × 13 ¾ in.
(71.1 × 34.9 cm)
Los Angeles County Museum of Art, gift of Miss Bella Mabury, M.39.2.293

CATALOGUE NO. 166
Kosode Fragment with Decorated Shells
Second half seventeenth century
Tie-dyeing (nuishime shibori), silk and metallic thread embroidery, and stenciled imitation tie-dyeing (kata kanoko) on off-white silk satin (shusu)
25 ¼ × 13 ⅛ in.
(64.1 × 33.3 cm)
Los Angeles County Museum of Art, gift of Miss Bella Mabury, M.39.2.288

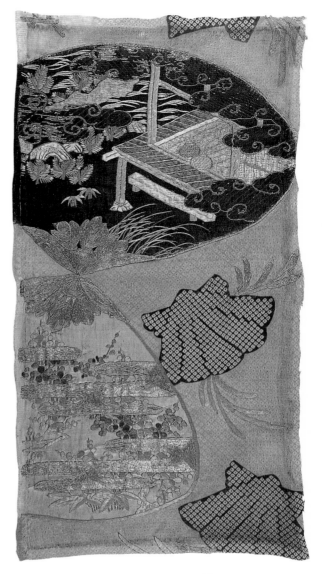

CATALOGUE NO. 165

CATALOGUE NO. 166

CATALOGUE NO. 167

CATALOGUE NO. 168

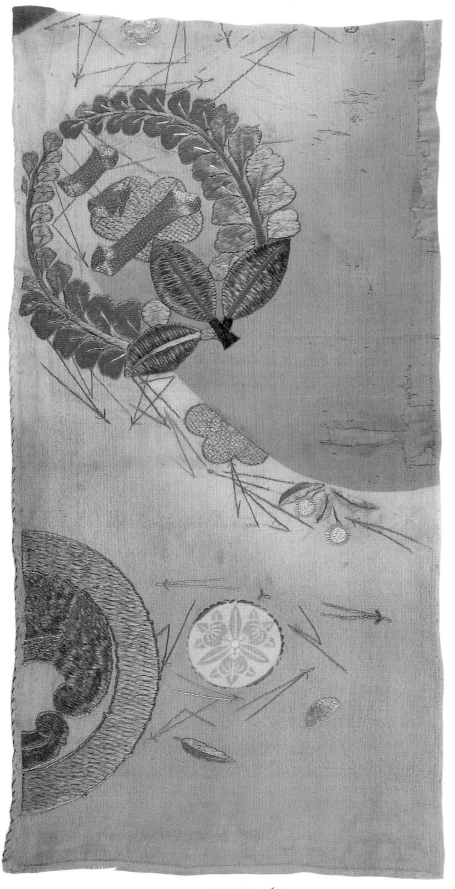

CATALOGUE NO. 169

Kosode Fragment with Chrysanthemums and Chevron Pattern
Late seventeenth century
Tie-dyeing (kanoko shibori) and silk and metallic thread embroidery on white silk satin (shusu)
33 ½ × 14 in.
(85.1 × 35.6 cm)
Los Angeles County Museum of Art, gift of Miss Bella Mabury, M.39.2.248

CATALOGUE NO. 168
Katabira Fragment with Camellias and Waterfall
Early eighteenth century
Paste-resist dyeing (noribōsen), tie-dyeing (kanoko shibori), and silk and metallic thread embroidery on black plain-weave ramie (asa)
33 × 12 ⅝ in.
(83.8 × 32.1 cm)
Los Angeles County Museum of Art, gift of Miss Bella Mabury, M.39.2.240

CATALOGUE NO. 169
Kosode Fragment with Pine Needles and Crests
First half eighteenth century
Brush-dyeing (hiki-zome), silk and metallic thread embroidery, and paste-resist dyeing (noribōsen) on shaded blue silk crepe (chirimen)
28 ¼ × 13 ¾ in.
(71.8 × 34.9 cm)
Los Angeles County Museum of Art, gift of Miss Bella Mabury, M.39.2.285

CATALOGUE NO. 170

CATALOGUE NO. 170
Kosode Fragment with
Chrysanthemums against a Bamboo
Fence
First half eighteenth century
Stenciled imitation tie-dyeing (kata
kanoko), silk and metallic thread
embroidery, and tie-dyeing
(nuishime shibori) on red figured
silk satin (rinzu)
33 ½ × 13 ¾ in. (85.1 × 34.9 cm)
Los Angeles County Museum of
Art, gift of Miss Bella Mabury,
M.39.2.237

CATALOGUE NO. 171
Kosode Fragment with Flowing
Water and Pickerel Weed (Mizu aoi)
First half eighteenth century
Stenciled imitation tie-dyeing (kata
kanoko) and silk and metallic
thread embroidery on white silk
crepe (chirimen)
34 × 11 in.
(86.4 × 27.9 cm)
Los Angeles County Museum of
Art, gift of Miss Bella Mabury,
M.39.2.249

CATALOGUE NO. 171

CATALOGUE NO. 172

Kosode Fragment with Bamboo, Pine, and Fan with Painted Scene

First half eighteenth century

Stenciled imitation tie-dyeing (kata kanoko), silk and metallic thread embroidery, and ink painting (kaki-e) on white figured silk satin (rinzu)

33 ¾ × 13 ¼ in.

(85.7 × 33.7 cm)

Los Angeles County Museum of Art, gift of Miss Bella Mabury, M.39.2.243

CATALOGUE NO. 173

Kosode Fragment with Bamboo, Chrysanthemum, and Emblems of Good Fortune (Takaramono)

Mid-eighteenth century

Silk and metallic thread embroidery on white figured silk satin (rinzu)

33 ¾ × 14 ³/₁₆ in.

(85.7 × 36.0 cm)

Los Angeles County Museum of Art, gift of Miss Bella Mabury, M.39.2.239

CATALOGUE NO. 174

CATALOGUE NO. 174

*Kosode Fragment with Waves,
Waterfall, and Cherry Blossoms*
Mid-eighteenth century
Silk and metallic thread embroidery
and appliqué on white figured silk
satin (rinzu)
30½ × 13¼ in.
(77.5 × 33.7 cm)
Los Angeles County Museum of
Art, gift of Miss Bella Mabury,
M.39.2.244

CATALOGUE NO. 175

*Kosode Fragment with Cranes in
Flight and Geometric Design of
Interlocking Circles* (Shippō)
Late eighteenth–early nineteenth
century
Tie-dyeing (sō-kanoko shibori) on
red figured silk satin (rinzu)
32¾ × 13⅞ in.
(83.2 × 35.2 cm)
Los Angeles County Museum of
Art, gift of Miss Bella Mabury,
M.39.2.256

CATALOGUE NO. 175

CATALOGUE NO. 176
*Kosode Fragment with
Chrysanthemums, Snow, and
Characters*
Late eighteenth–early nineteenth
century
Paste-resist dyeing (yūzen) and silk
and metallic thread embroidery on
blue silk crepe (chirimen)
33 × 14 ⅛ in.
(83.8 × 35.9 cm)
Los Angeles County Museum of
Art, gift of Miss Bella Mabury,
M.39.2.251

CATALOGUE NO. 177
*Kosode Fragment with Brushwood
Fence and Chrysanthemums*
Late eighteenth–early nineteenth
century
Tie-dyeing (kanoko shibori) and
silk and metallic thread embroidery
on black figured silk satin (rinzu)
31 ¾ × 13 ½ in.
(80.6 × 34.3 cm)
Los Angeles County Museum of
Art, gift of Miss Bella Mabury,
M.39.2.250

CATALOGUE NO. 177

CATALOGUE NO. 176

CATALOGUE NO. 178
Attributed to Iwasa Matabei
(1578–1650) or School of Matabei
Lovers with Attendant
Early seventeenth century
Ink, color, gold powder and leaf,
and silver leaf on paper
51 ½ × 22 ¼ in. (130.8 × 56.5 cm)
Frank Lloyd Wright Archives,
Frank Lloyd Wright Foundation
○
Page 217

CATALOGUE NO. 179
Attributed to Iwasa Matabei
(1578–1650) or School of Matabei
*Woman Playing Samisen and
Woman Writing Letter*
Early seventeenth century
Ink, color, gold powder and leaf,
and silver leaf on paper
51 × 22 ¼ in. (129.5 × 56.5 cm)
Frank Lloyd Wright Archives,
Frank Lloyd Wright
Foundation
●
Pages 216 (detail),
217

CATALOGUE NO. 180a,b
Amusements of Beautiful Women
Early seventeenth century
Hanging scrolls; ink and color on
paper
Each: 36 ⁹/₁₆ × 22 ¾ in.
(92.9 × 57.8 cm)
Entrusted to the Azabu Museum of
Arts and Crafts
Page 215

CATALOGUE NO. 181
Iwasa Matabei (1578–1650)
*Genre Scenes Cut into a Circular
Format*
Early seventeenth century
Hanging scroll; ink and color on
paper
Diam.: 19 ³/₁₆ in.
(48.7 cm)
Entrusted to the Azabu Museum of
Arts and Crafts
○

CATALOGUE NO. 182
Three Beauties
Second half seventeenth century
Hanging scroll; ink and color on
paper
14 ³/₁₆ × 21 ⁹/₁₆ in. (36.0 × 54.8 cm)
Entrusted to the Azabu Museum of
Arts and Crafts
●
Page 226

CATALOGUE NO. 183
Beauty Smoking a Pipe
Second half seventeenth century
Hanging scroll; ink and color
on paper
17 ¹⁵/₁₆ × 11 ¾ in. (45.6 × 29.9 cm)
Entrusted to the Azabu Museum of
Arts and Crafts
○
Page 218

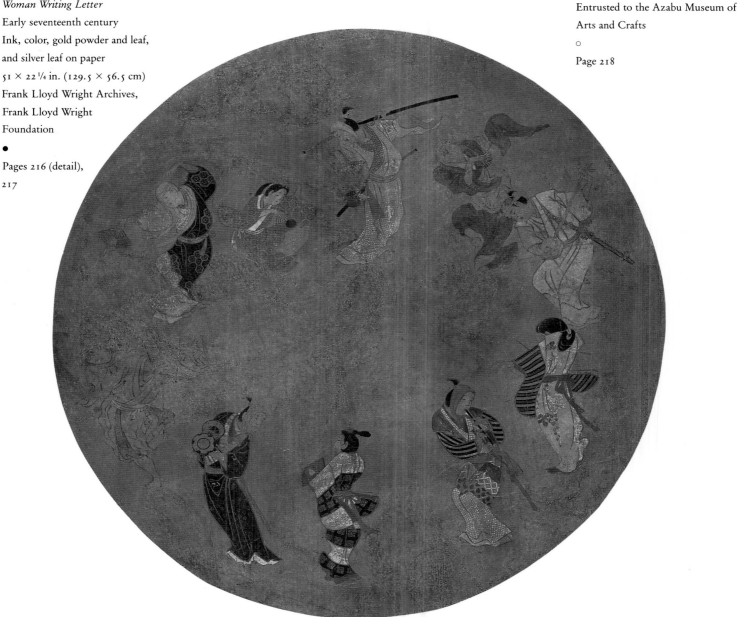

CATALOGUE NO. 181

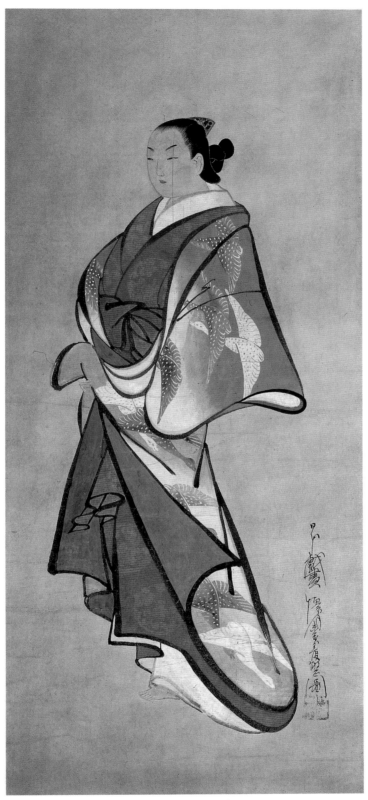

CATALOGUE NO. 189

CATALOGUE NO. 190
Kaigetsudō Doshu (fl. c. 1715)
Standing Beauty
Early eighteenth century
Hanging scroll; ink and color
on paper
41 3/8 × 17 3/4 in.
(105.1 × 45.0 cm)
Entrusted to the Azabu Museum of
Arts and Crafts

●

CATALOGUE NO. 191
Standing Beauty
Early eighteenth century
Hanging scroll; ink and color
on paper
38 3/4 × 16 1/8 in.
(98.4 × 41.0 cm)
Entrusted to the Azabu Museum of
Arts and Crafts

○

Pages 224, 225 (detail)

CATALOGUE NO. 192
Miyagawa Isshō (fl. 1751–63)
Procession of a Courtesan
Mid-eighteenth century
Hanging scroll; ink and color
on silk
35 7/16 × 14 9/16 in.
(90.0 × 37.0 cm)
Entrusted to the Azabu Museum of
Arts and Crafts

●

Page 31

CATALOGUE NO. 193
Nishikawa Terunobu (fl. 1716–35)
*Kabuki Actor Specializing in Female
Roles* (Onnagata)
Early eighteenth century
Hanging scroll; ink and color
on silk
41 3/8 × 15 in.
(105.0 × 38.0 cm)
Entrusted to the Azabu Museum of
Arts and Crafts

○

Page 31

CATALOGUE NO. 190

CATALOGUE NO. 194

Okumura Masanobu

(1686–1764)

Portrait of a Standing Courtesan

First half eighteenth century

Hanging scroll; ink and color

on silk

18 13/16 × 10 3/8 in.

(47.8 × 26.4 cm)

Entrusted to the Azabu Museum of

Arts and Crafts

●

元文戊午季夏上院

灑揮馬以應伏氏之雪
真庭娃曰心偽松亭やら

生圓通又入圓通
名ら是空へら色
万十惟人上畫工
金沙灘畔春風

又草堂門稿備筆

CATALOGUE NO. 197

常行畫

CATALOGUE NO. 195

Kawamata Tsuneyuki (c. 1676–
c. 1741)

*Teahouse Patronized by Young
Actors*

First half eighteenth century

Hanging scroll; ink and color
on paper

34 ½ × 10 ⅜ in.

(87.6 × 26.4 cm)

Entrusted to the Azabu Museum of
Arts and Crafts

○

CATALOGUE NO. 196

Kawamata Tsunemasa
(fl. 1716–48)

*Procession of a Courtesan in
the Snow*

First half eighteenth century

Hanging scroll; ink and color
on paper

15 ⁷/₁₆ × 19 in.

(39.2 × 48.2 cm)

Entrusted to the Azabu Museum of
Arts and Crafts

●

CATALOGUE NO. 197

Nishikawa Sukenobu (1671–1751)

Standing Beauty

1738

Hanging scroll; ink and color
on silk

40 ¾ × 14 ¾ in.

(103.6 × 37.4 cm)

Entrusted to the Azabu Museum of
Arts and Crafts

○

CATALOGUE NO. 198

Nishikawa Sukenobu (1671–1751)

Standing Beauty

First half eighteenth century

Hanging scroll; ink and color
on paper

34 ¾ × 13 ⁷/₁₆ in.

(88.2 × 34.2 cm)

Entrusted to the Azabu Museum of
Arts and Crafts

●

Page 210 (detail)

CATALOGUE NO. 198

CATALOGUE NO. 196

CATALOGUE NO. 201

Chōbunsai Eishi (1756–1829)

Woman Getting Dressed

Late eighteenth–early nineteenth
century

Hanging scroll; ink and color
on silk

37 1/16 × 13 3/4 in. (94.2 × 34.8 cm)

Entrusted to the Azabu Museum of
Arts and Crafts

○

Page 227

CATALOGUE NO. 202

Chōbunsai Eishi (1756–1829)

Two Beauties

Late eighteenth–early nineteenth
century

Hanging scroll; ink and color on
silk

32 3/8 × 12 7/8 in. (82.2 × 32.7 cm)

Entrusted to the Azabu Museum of
Arts and Crafts

●

Page 232

CATALOGUE NO. 203

Shin hinagata akebonozakura

1781

Woodblock-printed book; ink on
paper

10 1/8 × 7 in. (25.8 × 17.8 cm)

Tokyo National University of
Fine Art and Music

Page 98

CATALOGUE NO. 204

Gofuku moyō shokoku on-hinakata

1668

Woodblock-printed book; ink on
paper

9 1/16 × 6 7/16 in. (23.0 × 16.3 cm)

Tokyo National University of
Fine Art and Music

Page 98

CATALOGUE NO. 205

Shōtoku hinagata

1713

Woodblock-printed book; ink on
paper

8 1/2 × 6 1/4 in. (21.5 × 15.8 cm)

Tokyo National University of
Fine Art and Music

Page 98

CATALOGUE NO. 206

Hinagata kiku no i

1719

Woodblock-printed book; ink on
paper

10 1/8 × 7 3/16 in. (25.7 × 18.2 cm)

Tokyo National University of
Fine Art and Music

Page 98

CATALOGUE NO. 203

CATALOGUE NO. 204

CATALOGUE NO. 205

CATALOGUE NO. 206

Appendix A

NAGASAKI IWAO

NOTE: This appendix illustrates changes in design format from the mid-sixteenth century to the first half of the nineteenth century. The diagrams provided are purely schematic.

MOMOYAMA Period	SEVENTEENTH CENTURY First half	SEVENTEENTH CENTURY 1658–73	SEVENTEENTH CENTURY 1673–84

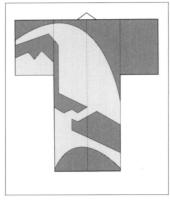

KATASUSO

KEICHŌ-KAN'EI STYLE

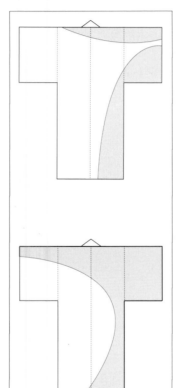

KATAMI-GAWARI

KANBUN STYLE

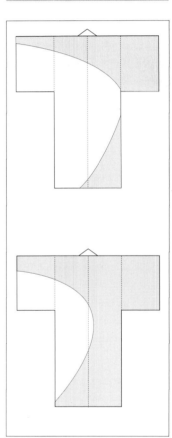

DAN-GAWARI

SEVENTEENTH–EIGHTEENTH CENTURY 1684–1716	EIGHTEENTH CENTURY First half	EIGHTEENTH CENTURY Second half	NINETEENTH CENTURY First half

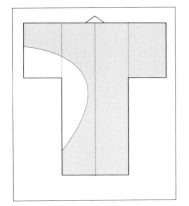

GENROKU STYLE

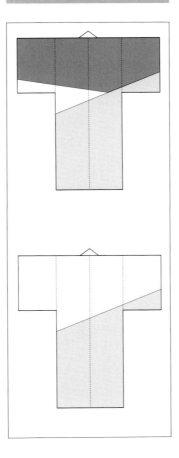

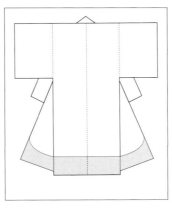

SUSO MOYŌ

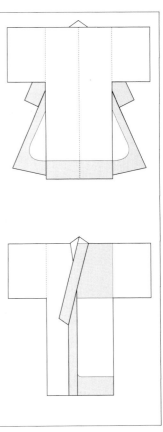

TSUMA MOYŌ
(EDO-ZUMA)

Appendix B

$$\boxed{\text{MARUYAMA NOBUHIKO}}$$

NOTE: These drawings provide measurements (in centimeters only) of kosode fragments on screens. Overall dimensions of the screens can be found in the checklist. (Adapted from National Museum of Japanese History 1990, 185–209.)

 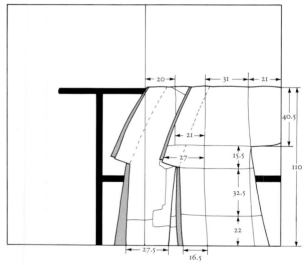

CATALOGUE NO. 1

 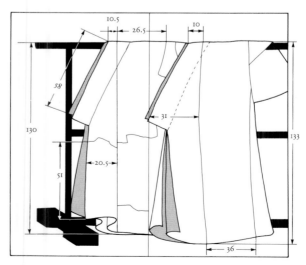

CATALOGUE NO. 2

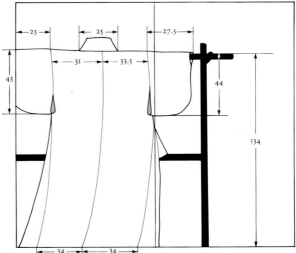

CATALOGUE NO. 3

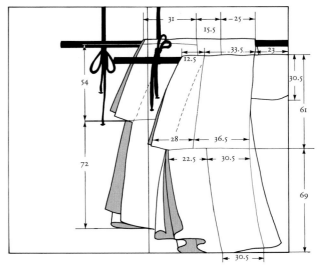

CATALOGUE NO. 4

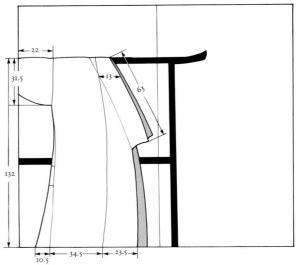

CATALOGUE NO. 6

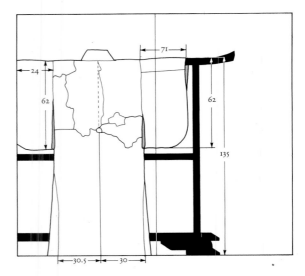

CATALOGUE NO. 36

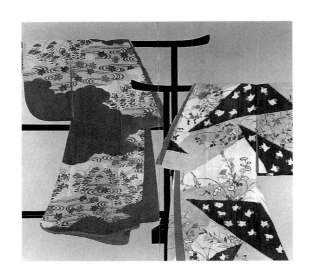
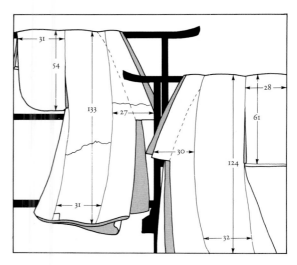

CATALOGUE NO. 71

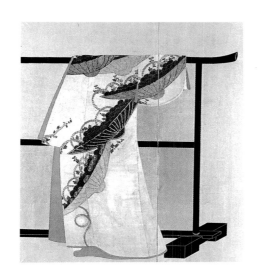
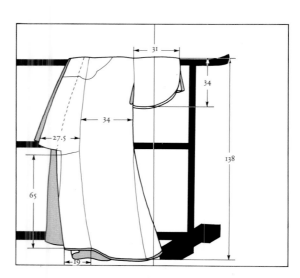

CATALOGUE NO. 92

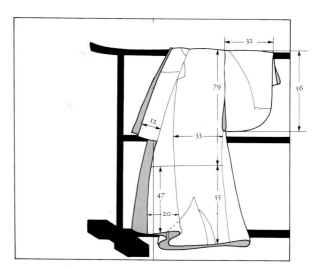

CATALOGUE NO. 93

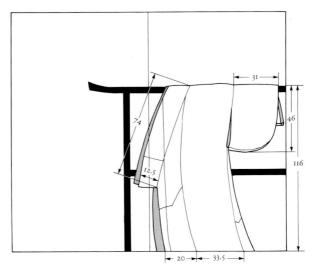

CATALOGUE NO. 100

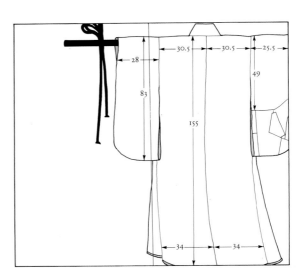

CATALOGUE NO. 108

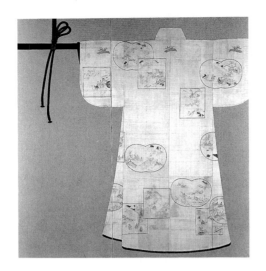
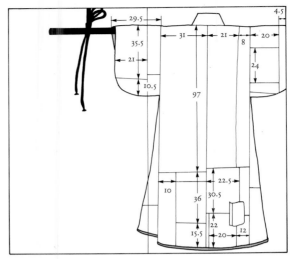

CATALOGUE NO. 115

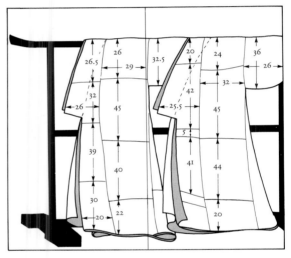

CATALOGUE NO. 127

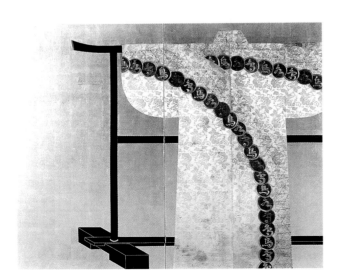
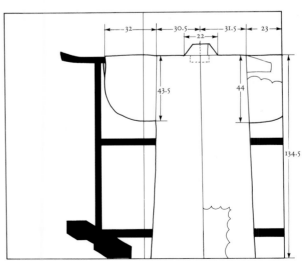

CATALOGUE NO. 128

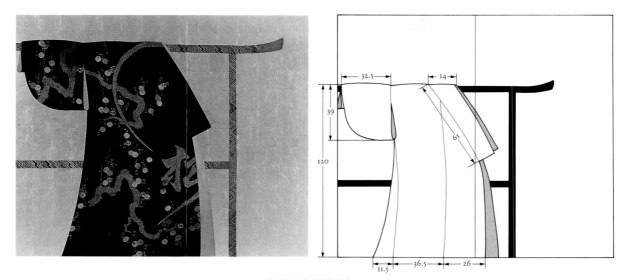

CATALOGUE NO. 132

Glossary

NOTE: The glossary provides expanded definitions of Japanese textile terms used in the essays and/or checklist.

AI
(*Polygonum tinctorium* Lour.)

AI
(*Indigofera tinctoria*)

AI
(*Mercurialis leiocarpa* Sieb. et Zucc.)

AI: The color blue and the dye of the same color obtained from the leaves and stems of more than fifty varieties of herbaceous shrubs containing indican. Known in the West as indigo, the most widely cultivated source is *Indigofera tinctoria*, native to India. Evidence of this dye has been found on textiles from dynastic Egypt (2500 B.C.). In the nineteenth century the plant was introduced into Okinawa and was widely cultivated. Before its introduction the two main sources of indigo in Japan were *yama ai* (mountain indigo; *Mercurialis leiocarpa* Sieb. et Zucc.), which yields a light blue dye, and *tade ai* (buckwheat; *Polygonum tinctorium* Lour.), which was introduced from the mainland before the Nara period and largely replaced yama ai as the main source of blue dye. *See* AI-ZURI. A vat dye, indigo reacts with oxygen to turn a blue color that adheres to fiber without the aid of a mordant (fixative).

AI-ZURI: The rubbing of AI (indigo) onto cloth, usually of silk or cotton. The most direct application is the rubbing of *yama ai* (mountain indigo) leaves or their juice onto fabric. Indigo in stick form (*ai bō*) can also be employed.

ASA: Generic term for a variety of bast fibers, including flax, hemp (*taima*), jute, and ramie (*karamushi* or *chōma*). Before the introduction of cotton to Japan in the sixteenth century, commoners' clothing was made from asa, primarily hemp (*Cannabis sativa* L.). Ramie (*Boehmeria nivea* Gaud.) was used to produce fine, high-quality cloth that was well suited for KATABIRA.

BAN: A ritual banner used as decoration in Buddhist temples. Several types of ban were preserved in the Shōsō-in.

BENI: A red dye extracted from the petals of the safflower plant. *See* BENIBANA.

BENIBANA: The safflower plant (*Carthamus tinctorius*).

BENIBANA

BOKASHI: The gradual shading of ink or color seen in YŪZEN-ZOME. Surviving examples from the Shōsō-in are evidence that the technique was known from at least the eighth century.

BŌSHI SHIBORI: A form of stitch-resist (NUISHIME SHIBORI) used to protect large areas of cloth from dye penetration. The section to be reserved is outlined with running stitches that are drawn tightly together; it is then wrapped in bamboo sheaths (plastic is now used) that were said to resemble the conical hats of Dutch traders, hence the name bōshi (hat) shibori. Also referred to as "capped" shibori.

CHA: The tea plant (*Thea sinensis* L.), the drink, and the color brown it produces when used as a dye. First used as a dye in the Muromachi period, a wide variety of shades were created during the Edo period, several associated with kabuki actors.

CHAYA-ZOME: A paste-resist dyeing technique that resulted in a blue design on a white or pale yellow ground; developed in Kyoto more or less contemporaneously with YŪZEN-ZOME in the latter part of the seventeenth century. Although the exact process is lost today, it generally consisted of the extensive application of a starch-paste resist to both sides of a fabric, leaving only fine lines and small areas of design to receive the blue color upon submersion into a vat of indigo dye. Blues of varying intensity on the same garment, a hallmark of chaya-zome, could be achieved by varying the number of dippings in the dye vat for any given area and protecting lighter areas with paste resist. Obviously a highly skilled, costly, and labor-intensive technique, chaya-zome became the exclusive prerogative of the women of the highest levels of the samurai class. Chaya-zome was primarily used on formal summer robes of unlined silk CHIRIMEN or very fine ASA and frequently depicted an imaginary landscape often accented with touches of embroidery. On KATABIRA the technique is called *chaya-tsuji*, possibly referring to a pre-Edo-period name for dyed katabira (*tsuji*), which could be of either silk or asa. Some authorities state that the Chaya merchant family of Kyoto invented the technique, but there is no firm evidence to substantiate this claim.

CHIJIMI: Generic term for plain-weave crepe. The allover crinkled surface of chijimi is created by the use of highly twisted weft and/or warp threads. Chijimi is typically made of ASA, cotton, or silk. *See also* CHIRIMEN.

CHIRIMEN: Plain-weave silk crepe. The warp is usually composed of untwisted raw silk; the weft of tightly twisted (1,500–4,000 twists per meter) raw silk. After the weft is twisted (in either a right twist [S-twist] or left twist [Z-twist]), it is starched to maintain the twist during the weaving process. Once removed from the loom, the cloth is boiled with soap and ash to remove the starch and sericin from the raw silk. Shrinkage occurs as the twisted weft reacts against the untwisted warp, resulting in a crinkled surface. Variations in the fiber composition of warp and weft, the weave structure, and the direction of the twisted weft produce different varieties of chirimen, each with its own name.

The technique of weaving chirimen was introduced into Japan from China during the Momoyama period. It is thought to have been first produced in Japan at Sakai in the Tenshō era. During the Edo period chirimen was a highly favored silk, its surface an ideal ground for YŪZEN-ZOME.

DAI-KECHI SURI (*dai* [large]; *kechi* [resist dyeing]; *suri* [imprint]): Stenciled imitation tie-dyeing used to create large circular patterns. Known in the Heian period (tenth century) from literary sources, the technique did not survive into the early modern period.

DAN-GAWARI (literally, levels different): A type of whole-garment patterning consisting of alternating blocks of differing materials, color, or patterning. The style was particularly popular on KOSODE from the late Muromachi period through the early seventeenth century. As the Edo period progressed, dan-gawari became almost exclusively used for the patterning of Nō robes. *See* Appendix A.

DATE-MON: A fancy, ornamental design or symbol placed on garments in areas generally reserved for family crests. Popular during the late Genroku era, date-mon were often made up of eclectic designs. These elaborate crests had no heraldic significance.

DŌBUKU (or DŌFUKU): Man's hip-length outergarment. Originally worn by commoners, dōbuku were adopted as part of the samurai wardrobe from the late Muromachi period to the early Edo period. Worn over armor as well as other clothing, dōbuku came in different styles, fabrics, and decoration.

EDO-ZUMA (literally, Edo skirts): A late-Edo-period KOSODE fashion where the pattern was concentrated at the hem and along the front edges; originally known as TSUMA MOYŌ. *See* Appendix A.

FURISODE (literally, swinging sleeves): A form of KOSODE with long, hanging sleeves and a small wrist opening. Worn primarily by young girls (it was considered immodest for those over nineteen) and entertainers, the furisode first appeared in the late seventeenth century. As the eighteenth century progressed, the sleeves gradually extended in length while the garment increased in popularity. Woodblock prints from the late Edo period show young women and courtesans with sleeves almost sweeping the ground.

FŪTSŪ-ORI: A type of double-weave cloth with a compound structure utilizing a plain-weave binding system and two sets of warps and wefts that are woven simultaneously. The resulting fabric has the same pattern, in reversed coloration, on each face. This weaving technique was introduced into Japan from China during the third quarter of the sixteenth century.

GOSHODOKI (literally, imperial court style): Landscape designs with seasonal flowers and grasses and objects alluding to literary subjects (such as cypress-wood fans and oxcarts). Classical literature of the Heian period and Nō plays are the most common sources for these motifs. Wearing goshodoki designs, executed in YŪZEN-ZOME, CHAYA-ZOME, or embroidery, on KOSODE or KATABIRA was the exclusive prerogative of women of the samurai class, particularly female attendants in daimyo and shogunal households.

HABUTAE: A soft, lightweight plain-weave silk similar to taffeta. Usually made of untwisted raw silk with paired warps and tightly packed wefts, its slightly ribbed surface gives a lustrous effect. During the Nara period habutae was dyed red and used as an undergarment or lining; in the Muromachi period it became popular for ceremonial robes. Produced in Nishijin since the sixteenth century, the fabric became popular after the Keichō era. During the Edo period habutae was initially considered by the government to be appropriate for the samurai class only, but by the early nineteenth century it was accepted for the clothing of wealthy chōnin. There are several varieties that are used for garments, OBI, and linings. It is known as habutai in the West.

HAKAMA: A pleated, bifurcated lower garment variously described as full-cut trousers or a divided skirt. Long and trailing, it was worn at the Heian court by men as an overgarment and by women under the KASANE SHŌZOKU. Men continued to wear the garment in the early modern period, but women ceased wearing it in the late Muromachi period, when KOSODE had became general wear.

HAKU: Metallic leaf, usually gold or silver; also metallic leaf imprint. *See also* SURIHAKU.

HAORI: An outer garment of varying lengths worn over the KOSODE and similar to it in cut. The front edges of the haori do not overlap, but hang parallel and are tied together by a pair of braided silk cords.

HIKI-ZOME: The application of dye to cloth by means of a brush; employed in YŪZEN-ZOME to add the ground color.

HIRA-GINU (literally, plain silk): One kind of monochrome plain-weave silk. Hira-ginu, usually thin, is often used as a garment lining.

HITOE: An unlined garment. Two types of garments were called hitoe: the unlined silk KOSODE worn in the summer and the unlined undergarment of twill- or plain-weave silk worn closest to the skin in KASANE SHŌZOKU. *See also* JŪNI-HITOE.

IRO-ZASHI: The application of dye or pigment with a brush to a design area; used in YŪZEN-ZOME and certain stencil-dyeing processes. The technique is similar to HIKI-ZOME but is applied to small areas only rather than the entire background.

ITAJIME: A resist method in which a pair of woodblocks carved with mirror-image patterns are clamped around folded cloth before being vat-dyed. Small holes in the blocks allow the dye to seep between the raised sections of the carved pattern, resulting in a design with attractively blurred edges. Itajime was especially popular in the Nara period, when it was called *kyōkechi*; several examples survived in the Shōsō-in. While the technique fell out of fashion in the Heian period, it must have continued in occasional use: a Muromachi-period itajime-dyed garment (from the Amano Shrine on Mount Koya) is in the Tokyo National Museum (illustrated in Yamanobe 1966, pl. 5).

JINASHI (literally, without ground): A textile term referring to a style of KOSODE decoration in which the ground pattern and the decorative pattern bear equal weight in the total composition. KEICHŌ SOME-WAKE and NUIHAKU kosode are examples of jinashi; in the former, the SOMEWAKE-dyed ground is not negative space but equal in importance to the decorative motif.

JUBAN (or JIBAN): A KOSODElike undergarment worn by men and women. The term is derived from the Portuguese word *gibāo* (a short, sleeveless garment).

JŪNI-HITOE (literally, twelve unlined robes): A sixteenth-century term for the most formal version of the KASANE SHŌZOKU. The actual number of layered robes varied from five to twenty but was established by edict as five in the Kamakura period. Originally called *karaginu-mo*.

KAKI-E: A textile term denoting pictorial imagery created by brush painting on fabric with ink, dye, or pigment. The ink painting in TSUJIGAHANA-style decoration is a good example.

KAN'I (*kan* [official]; *i* [rank]): A system of indicating court rank through the colors of clothing and headdress (*kammuri*). The system, based on a Chinese model, was first instituted by the Empress Suiko in the eleventh year of her reign (A.D. 603).

KANOKO SHIBORI (literally, fawn-spot dyeing): A type of resist dyeing; specifically, a method of tie-dyeing (SHIBORI) whole cloth that involves binding or wrapping small pinches of fabric with string or twine. When the bindings are removed after immersion of the cloth in dye, a white spot (usually circular or square) with a small raised dot of color at the center is formed. The technique can be used to fill space, create lines, delineate shapes, or add texture. Known in the Nara period as *meyui*; also called *hitta*, *hitta kanoko*, or *hitta shibori*. There are many variations of the technique, each with its own name.

KARAORI (literally, Chinese weave): A general term referring to Chinese woven fabrics introduced into Japan during the Muromachi period and to textiles produced domestically to imitate them. Specifically, a heavily brocaded fabric (NISHIKI) often composed of both multicolored silk and metallic thread in which long weft floats on a three-harness twill ground give the impression of being embroidered rather than woven; also a KOSODE made of this cloth.

Karaori kosode, according to one literary source, were restricted to the shogun and those closely associated with him. Later this regulation was relaxed to include daimyo wives and eventually wealthy Edo-period commoners. Karaori kosode were awarded to Nō actors by their samurai-class patrons and thus became a conventional Nō costume worn as an outer robe for women's roles.

KASANE IRO (literally, layered colors): *See* KASANE SHŌZOKU.

KASANE SHŌZOKU (literally, layered clothing): The dress style of the women of the Heian-period aristocracy. The essential element of this style was the layering of garments (particularly of UCHIGI) to display set combinations of colors collectively known as *kasane no irome* (sets of layered colors). These combinations were given poetic names referring to natural phenomena, particularly flowers. *See* JŪNI-HITOE.

KATABIRA: An unlined summer KOSODE originally made of silk; in the Kamakura period versions made of fine bleached ASA came into use. When the word *katabira* appears in Muromachi-period texts it seems to refer to robes of either silk or asa; by the latter part of the period it refers only to unlined summer garments made of asa. In the Edo period women of both the chōnin and samurai classes wore the katabira, but those with particular patterns and/or decorative techniques were restricted to the latter class. *See* GOSHODOKI and CHAYA-ZOME.

KATA KANOKO: An imitation of the SHIBORI technique by means of applying a resist paste through a stencil. The visual effect of kata kanoko is flat, unlike the slightly puckered surface of KANOKO SHIBORI. The centers can be left blank or any one of several techniques can be used to add texture. The central dot can be painted in by hand or the center can be pushed outward from the wrong side of the fabric with a blunt stick tipped with wax or resin, a variant known as *uchidashi kanoko*. The technique is generally thought to have begun in the Genroku era as a result of restrictions on the use of true kanoko shibori. Evidence of stenciled shibori on a garment dating from the mid-seventeenth century belonging to a woman of the samurai elite, however, indicates that kata kanoko may have been neither a temporary substitute nor an inexpensive technique (*see* Stinchecum 1984, 32). Also known as *suri-hitta* or *kata-hitta*.

KATAMI-GAWARI: A type of whole-garment patterning in which the right and left halves of the back and/or front are composed of different fabrics or patterns. Katami-gawari division of a three-quarter-length outer garment (*hitatare*) worn by male commoners may have originated in the Heian period. In the Kamakura period the style was first seen on KOSODE, becoming especially popular from the late Muromachi period to the first half of the seventeenth century. *See* Appendix A.

KATASUSO (literally, shoulders and hem): A form of whole-garment patterning in which the KOSODE is decorated only across the shoulder and upper torso area and from below the knees to the hemline. The areas so decorated may be delineated by straight, undulating (SUHAMA KATASUSO), or sharply angular lines. The style was popular from at least the second half of the twelfth century to the end of the sixteenth century. *See* Appendix A.

KATSUGI (or KAZUKI): A KIMONO-shaped head covering worn by women when out-of-doors. The katsugi probably evolved from an extra KOSODE draped over the head to protect the upper-class wearer from the sun and prying eyes. It eventually became a special garment with the neckband placed two or three inches below the shoulder line to form a kind of pocket for the head. By the Edo period wearing the katsugi was no longer confined to a specific class. The garment could be made of silk, ramie, or cotton and decorated in any technique.

KEICHŌ SOMEWAKE: A decorative style that appeared in the Keichō era on the KOSODE of women of the samurai class and remained in fashion through the Kan'ei era. The parti-colored SOMEWAKE ground was divided by means of NUISHIME SHIBORI into complex interlocking shapes of contrasting color (usually black, brown, red, deep purple, or white) further embellished with KANOKO SHIBORI, minute embroidery, and SURIHAKU.

KESA: A Buddhist cleric's mantle often referred to as a robe or stole. Worn over other garments in Japan, kesa are worn alone by monks in Southeast Asia (as they were originally in India and Nepal). As a symbol of poverty, the kesa began as a patchwork of rags but eventually came to be pieced together from donations of clothing or new, whole cloth (sometimes left uncut, the seams of "piecing" indicated by the application of silk cords).

KIHADA: The dye from the philodendron tree (*Philodendron amurense* Rupr.), believed to be the oldest known Japanese dye. It yields a light yellow color on fabric dipped in a liquor made from boiling the inner bark and woody tissue in water. When top-dyed over SUŌ, a rich red is achieved that was often used as a substitute for BENIBANA by Edo-period dyers.

KIMONO (literally, thing to wear): A general Japanese term for clothing that came into use in the Meiji period to distinguish indigenous dress from Western-style clothing (YŌFUKU). It is a variation of the Edo-period term *kirumono*. In the narrow sense the term is used to refer to the KOSODE and its subtypes but does not include HAORI or JUBAN. The term *kimono* should not be confused with the wrapper of Western fashionable dress that was inspired by the Japanese kimono but is a European creation.

KOMA-NUI: An embroidery technique involving the stitching of thick or twisted thread to the surface of a fabric by means of a different, usually finer, thread. Known as couching in the West, the technique is used with embroidery threads too thick to pass through the fabric, such as various types of metallic threads.

KOMON: A type of paste-resist-dyed patterning in which grouped repeats of minute patterns are often composed in geometric arrangements, although the individual motifs themselves may not be geometric. The process involves painstaking preparation in the making and cutting of the stencils used to apply the resist (traditionally rice paste). The stencils are made of paper mulberry fiber (*Broussonetia papyrifera*) that has been stiffened with fermented persimmon juice and smoked for several days (traditionally, for months). The finest patterns have six to seven hundred holes per three square centimeters (1 1/5 square inches). Until the introduction of synthetic dyes in the Meiji period, komon patterns were white (undyed) on a brushed-on dark ground of a somber color. Komon patterning was used on official samurai dress throughout the early modern period. It is also known as *Edo komon*.

KOSHIMAKI (literally, waist wrap): Refers to both a specific garment and to the style of wearing it. The garment is a type of KOSODE made of NERINUKI silk, dyed dark red, black, or brown, and embroidered with small repeating patterns of auspicious motifs. The style began in the middle of the Muromachi period (fifteenth century), with a Kosode or an UCHIKAKE tied at the waist over the outer kosode with the upper part draping from the waistline; the koshimaki replaced the uchikake in the seventeenth century. In the eighteenth century a special OBI (KOSHIMAKI OBI) was used to support the koshimaki and to extend the sleeves on either side of the body. It was worn by women of the upper echelons of the samurai class over the KATABIRA as formal summer attire. By the latter part of the Edo period the style had become formulaic dress for attendants in daimyo and shogunal households, worn over a katabira decorated with GOSHODOKI motifs in embroidery, CHAYA-ZOME, YŪZEN-ZOME, or SHIRO-AGE.

KOSHIMAKI

KOSHIMAKI OBI: An OBI stiffened with straw to create a tubular shape; used to hold the KOSHIMAKI in place. The obi is wrapped around the waist, securing the koshimaki; the ends are then extended through the sleeves to hold them out to either side of the body. Also called a *tsuke-obi*.

KOSHIMAKI OBI

KOSODE (literally, small sleeves): The predecessor of the modern KIMONO. In contemporary usage a generic term for any full-length garment made prior to the Meiji period, in any fiber, with a "small sleeve." In the Edo period the kosode was a specific variation of that garment, with a wadded silk lining. The "small sleeve" refers not to the length of the sleeve (which can be long or short in its vertical dimension), but to the small wrist opening, which is the kosode's salient characteristic and which distinguishes it from the ŌSODE (literally, large sleeves). The two main pieces of the kosode are joined at the center of the back and hang from the shoulders to the ground both front and back. Two shorter lengths of the same width are sewn together to form rectangular sleeves. Two panels half the width and length of the main pieces are sewn to the front of the garment to add extra width for overlap. An additional half-width of cloth encircles the neck and crosses the front panels on a long diagonal forming a collar and reaching about two-thirds of the way down the front of the garment. The FURISODE, HITOE, KATABIRA, KOSHIMAKI, and UCHIKAKE are generally considered subtypes of the kosode, although technically they only qualify for that designation if they have small wrist openings.

KUCHINASHI: Gardenia (*Gardenia jasminoides* Ellis f. Grandiflora Makino), a low evergreen shrub native to Japan whose seed pods yield a warm yellow dye. When top-dyed over SUŌ, a red color results; this was often used as a substitute for BENIBANA. Kuchinashi seeds have been known as a dyeing agent in Japan since the Nara period.

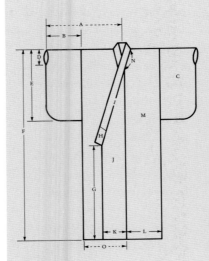

A *yuki*: width between center back to sleeve opening

B *sode-haba*: sleeve width

C *sode*: sleeve

D *sode-guchi*: sleeve opening

E *sode take*: sleeve length

F *mi-take*: height

G *tatezuma*: lower edge of neckband to lower edge of overlap

H *eri-haba*: neckband width

I *eri*: neckband

J *okumi*: overlap

K *okumi-haba*: overlap width at hem

L *mae-haba*: front half-width at hem

M *migoro*: body

N *okumi-sagari*: top of overlap to shoulder

O *ushiro-haba*: back half-width at hem

KUKURIBAKAMA: A type of HAKAMA gathered at the ankle; initially worn by laborers and other commoners in the Nara period. Kukuribakama became popular with low-ranking warriors in the Kamakura period.

KUKUSHI: A resist-dyeing technique in which areas of fabric are kept undyed by stitching or clamping. The uncolored areas are often filled with motifs executed in YŪZEN-ZOME.

MO: An apronlike skirt. Clay figurines from the fourth and fifth centuries show women wearing a pleated wrap skirt, the mo. By the beginning of the Nara period women of the aristocracy were wearing a trailing mo over a long, loose gown; a vestige of that skirt became the mo of the Heian period, worn by female court attendants when on official duty at the palace. In the Heian period the mo was often decorated by various techniques, including ink painting (KAKI-E) depicting landscapes or

other scenes. The Edokoro (Office of painting) of the Heian court employed skilled artists who produced not only paintings but also pictorial designs for mo and formal jackets (*ko-uchigi*). *See* McCullough and McCullough 1980, 92n. 112.

MOBAKAMA: A combination of the MO and HAKAMA that formed a full, deeply-pleated skirtlike garment worn over the KOSODE by women of the upper levels of the samurai class in the Kamakura period. The style began with female court attendants in the late Heian period.

MOKUME SHIBORI (literally, woodgrain tie-dyeing): Rows of parallel running stitches spaced five to ten millimeters apart are tightly drawn up before the cloth is immersed in dye. When untied, the resultant irregular pattern resembles wood grain or tree bark.

MON: Japanese family crests. These heraldic insignias were first used by the aristocracy during the Heian period. Later, military families used mon for purposes of identification on the battlefield. The placement of five mon, at the center of the back at the base of the neck and on the back and front of each sleeve, became a convention during the Edo period. Also known as *monshō*. *See also* DATE-MON.

MŌRU-ORI (literally, Mughal weave): A fabric generally composed of a silk warp and a weft of silk and/or gold or silver threads. Typically it is a plain-weave cloth with vertical or horizontal stripes and floral and arabesque designs although examples with satin or double-weave grounds exist. This kind of textile was produced in India during the Mughal period (1526–1857) and in Iran during the Safavid period (1501–1722). It was imported into Japan by Dutch and Portuguese traders in the late sixteenth and early seventeenth centuries; the term *mōru* is derived from the Portuguese word *Mogol*, which refers to the Mughal dynasty. Popular in Japan, mōru-ori was eventually produced in the country during the Edo period and was used for women's OBI.

MURASAKI

MURASAKI: The perennial flowering plant gromwell (*Lithospermum erythrorhizon* Sieb. et Zucc.) and the highly prized color purple that results from dyeing with its roots. Native to Japan, murasaki was one of the most valued and restricted colors in the Nara and Heian periods. In the Muromachi period commoners were permitted to wear it, but murasaki was again restricted in the Edo period to the highest ranks of society. Purple was a particularly fashionable color for all classes in the Genroku era. To meet a demand for the color from the chōnin, dyers in Edo developed a slightly reddish purple from top-dyeing SUŌ over AI or using an iron mordant with suō.

NAGOYA OBI

NAGOYA OBI: A narrow OBI of twisted silken cords popular with both men and women from the late sixteenth century through the first half of the seventeenth century. It was supposedly introduced by female camp followers of Hideyoshi's troops in Kyushu during his second campaign against Korea in 1598. *See* Cole 1967, 81–82.

NARABI-SAKUME: A type of very fine SHIBORI (probably KANOKO) used in the Heian period for the dress of the empress and other high-ranking women of the imperial court.

NERINUKI: A plain-weave silk composed of warps of unglossed silk (gummed, sericin not removed) and wefts of glossed silk (degummed, sericin removed). Although in use as early as the Heian period, the name was not used until after the Ōnin War. It was popular from the late Muromachi period through the Momoyama period for TSU-JIGAHANA, but demand decreased radically in the Edo period with the introduction of RINZU. The fabric continued in use, however, as a ground fabric for the KOSHIMAKI.

NISHIKI (brocade): A general term for a variety of multicolored, patterned-weave fabrics. Typically the term now suggests silk woven with supplementary weft patterns in glossed silks and metallic threads. The ground structure can be either plain, twill, or satin weave. The earliest record of nishiki in Japan (a gift from a Chinese emperor) dates to the third century. KARAORI is one type of nishiki.

NORIBŌSEN: General term for paste-resist dyeing. In order to keep dye from penetrating a certain design area, a paste is applied as a resist.

NUI (literally, sewing): The term for embroidery in use until the Meiji period, when the word *shishū* came into use; now used to refer to Western-style embroidery. Japanese-style embroidery using traditional techniques and motifs is called *Nihon shishū*.

NUIHAKU (literally, sewing and metallic leaf): A method of decorating KOSODE by combining embroidery and the application of metallic leaf, creating a lustrous surface fully exploiting the contrast between the three-dimensional effect of the floats of untwisted silk floss and the flat sheen of the gold and/or silver leaf. Also the name of a type of NŌ robe decorated with the technique and used primarily as an inner robe for women's roles. Nuihaku may have originated as a substitute for expensive woven textiles imported from China in the late Muromachi period, but its full development came in the Momoyama period. Unlike TSUJIGAHANA (which it paralleled as a decorative style), nuihaku was confined to the kosode of women of the higher levels of society. Nuihaku of the Momoyama period closely followed the symmetry and repetition of the woven textiles for which it was a substitute; Edo-period nuihaku, by contrast, exhibited a greater variety of design elements, the use of asymmetrical composition, the treatment of representational motifs, and an increased use of HAKU.

NUISHIME SHIBORI: Stitch resist; a form of tie-dyeing (SHIBORI). A method of protecting fabric from dye penetration by the use of running stitches that are drawn up tightly and knotted. The cloth within the shirred area is wound with thread or other material for further protection. Areas remaining undyed or protected from additional coloration can thus be achieved. It is a far more precise method than KANOKO SHIBORI and played a significant role in TSUJIGAHANA, KEICHŌ SOMEWAKE, and later KOSODE decoration. The stitching-off process is also preliminary to other types of dyeing such as SOMEWAKE and BŌSHI SHIBORI.

NUME: A thin, unfigured satin-weave cloth. Woven of unglossed (gummed) silk threads, the fabric is degummed (sericin removed) after weaving. The technique was introduced from China during the Tenna era.

OBI: The waist wrapper worn with the KOSODE to keep it closed (the garment has no fastening devices). The obi formed an integral part of the costume. At the beginning of the seventeenth century the obi was a narrow string or twisted cord (NAGOYA OBI) wrapped around the waist. A wider obi of six or seven inches became fashionable in the Genroku era; the obi continued to widen throughout the eighteenth century, changing the pattern distribution on the kosode (see Appendix A). Methods of tying varied with fashion. As increasingly restrictive sumptuary laws limited costs, materials, and colors for the kosode of chōnin, the obi was often of elaborately patterned fabric and represented a considerable expense.

ŌSODE (literally, large sleeves): A general category of garment characterized by having a wrist opening that extends the full width of the sleeve; worn by the aristocracy in the Heian period.

RINZU (literally, thread or string): A soft, monochromatic figured silk satin with a high lustre. Introduced into Japan from China in the late Muromachi period, large quantities were imported in the Momoyama period. Domestic production began in the 1680s at Sakai and not long thereafter in Kyoto at Nishijin (which remained the primary producer throughout the Edo period, followed by Edo and Kanazawa). The warp and weft are raw (unglossed) silk, which is degummed by boiling. The ground and pattern are created by the juxtaposition of warp-faced and weft-faced satin weave areas in a ratio of 4/1 or 7/1 (that is, the warp floats over four or seven wefts before interlacing with the weft to form the pattern and the weft floats over four or seven warps before interlacing with the warp to create the ground). Several authorities state that rinzu is a damasklike fabric; it is not a true damask, because while the pattern is reversible, the structure is not. A key-fret pattern (SAYAGATA) with alternating orchids (ran) and chrysanthemums (kiku) at regular intervals was the most common on rinzu in the Edo period; it is called sayagata rangiku. See also SAYA.

SARASA: Chintz, calico, or batik. Primarily a cotton cloth with printed, painted, or dyed designs of flowering plants, animals, birds, and figures. During the late Muromachi period Spanish, Portuguese, and Dutch traders brought sarasa to Japan from such places as India, Iran, Indonesia, Holland, and China. In the late sixteenth century and seventeenth century sarasa was favored by the military elite and rich merchants. As cotton became more accessible in the mid-Edo period, sarasa was produced in several locations in Japan and its use

spread. The term probably comes from the Hindi word sarasa (superior).

SARASA-ZOME (sarasa dyeing): A paste-resist dyeing technique and style of patterning derived from imported SARASA fabrics.

SAYA: A plain-weave silk with a twill-weave pattern (usually a 3/1 warp-faced twill). Also referred to as saya-ori.

SAYAGATA: A diaper pattern of interlocking swastikas forming a key-fret design, often with the addition of flowers or auspicious motifs at regular intervals. It probably first arrived in Japan on objects (perhaps textiles) brought from Ming China in the sixteenth century. A twill-weave silk in this pattern was first woven in Japan about 1570 in Kyoto.

SHIBORI: A resist-dyeing technique and the fabric produced by it. Often equated with tie-dyeing, shibori actually encompasses a wide variety of resist techniques utilizing folding, stitching (NUISHIME SHIBORI), binding (KANOKO SHIBORI), and sheathing (BŌSHI SHIBORI) in numerous combinations. The basic method involves protecting parts of the fabric by any of the above means from penetration of the dye when the cloth is submerged in a dye vat. It is sometimes combined with other techniques such as YŪZEN-ZOME or embroidery. In the Nara period it was called kōkechi. During the Edo period specialties arose in certain areas such as Kyoto, Narumi, and Arimatsu (near present-day Nagoya) that are still major shibori-producing centers.

SHIRO-AGE: In its strictest sense a form of YŪZEN-ZOME in which the design consists of fine white lines on a monochrome ground resembling ink drawing. The term is also used when white lines predominate in a multicolored yūzen-dyed design. See also SU-NUI.

SHUSU: A smooth, lustrous satin-weave textile with long warp or weft floats; structurally similar to twill, except the floats are intermittently bound to the ground structure. The technique for making shusu was introduced into Japan from China during the late Muromachi period.

SODE (sleeve): The salient feature by which certain Japanese garments (such as the KOSODE, ŌSODE, and FURISODE) are named. Also a poetic metaphor for a woman (e.g., a glimpse of a sleeve) or an emotional state (e.g., tear-soaked sleeves). Long, swinging sleeves were considered seductive and therefore inappropriate for a married woman.

SŌ-KANOKO: Allover KANOKO SHIBORI. The entire surface of the cloth is covered with small reserved areas. Also known as sō-hitta.

SOMEWAKE: Parti-colored dyeing involving the use of NUISHIME SHIBORI to create a background divided into areas of different colors. See also KEICHŌ SOMEWAKE.

SUHAMA KATASUSO: A KATASUSO design format with undulating edges suggesting the irregular shoreline of a sandy beach. The suhama pattern was used in many art forms throughout Japanese history and appears in various contexts and techniques on early modern KOSODE.

Su-nui: An embroidery style used on KOSODE, popular in the late Edo period, in which designs resembling ink painting were achieved through the use of fine lines and a limited color range on a monochrome ground. Su-nui was part of the same fashion aesthetic as SHIRO-AGE, which it paralleled in time.

Suō: Sappanwood (*Caesalpinia sappan* L.), imported into Japan in the Nara period, is native to India and Southeast Asia. The bark of the tree yields a red dye that was popular in the Edo period as an alternative to the restricted and costly BENIBANA.

Surihaku: A technique of textile decoration in which rice paste is applied to the fabric through a stencil; gold and/or silver foil (HAKU) is pressed onto the pattern created by the paste while it is still wet. When the paste has dried, excess foil is brushed away. It can be used alone as the sole decoration of a KOSODE or in combination with other techniques. Also a type of Nō robe decorated in the technique and used as an inner robe for female roles.

Suso moyō (literally, hem design): Patterning concentrated along the hem of a KOSODE. The style became fashionable during the second half of the Edo period. *See* Appendix A.

Tan: A measure of cloth; the amount required to make one KOSODE.

Tatejima (literally, vertical stripes): Tatejima KOSODE became popular during the latter half of the Edo period, when a long, narrow silhouette became fashionable.

Tsujigahana: A decorative style combining several techniques and the resulting textiles and designs that flourished from the late Muromachi period through the first decade of the seventeenth century. The techniques used always included SHIBORI (both NUISHIME and KANOKO) along with painting (KAKI-E), metallic leaf (HAKU), and embroidery (NUI). The origin of the word is uncertain.

Tsuke-zome (literally, dip-dyeing): A basic method of dyeing in which cloth is submerged in a dye bath.

Tsuma moyō (literally, skirt design): Decorative pattern located primarily along the hem and front edges of the KOSODE, ending at the lower end of the neckband. *See also* EDO-ZUMA; Appendix A.

Uchigi: A type of large-sleeved robe (ŌSODE) worn in multiple layers by women of the Heian court on a daily basis. The robe is a lined garment of twill-weave silk. Each successive layer is cut slightly smaller than the previous one so that the colors of all the layers show at the sleeves and neck edge. From the Kamakura period on it became ceremonial attire only, comprising part of the JŪNI-HITOE.

Uchikake: A garment worn unbelted over all other robes on formal or ceremonial occasions. The style originated in the Kamakura period among women of the upper levels of the samurai class; from the end of the Muromachi period it was their formal winter attire. In the eighteenth century padding was added to the hem of the uchikake.

Uchishiki: An altar cloth used in Buddhist temples. Frequently made of donated fabric, sometimes from KOSODE, and often of a patchwork construction.

Ura-nuki: An embroidery style of the Muromachi and Momoyama periods utilizing untwisted silk and worked in long, parallel float stitches over a paper support on the reverse of the fabric. The stitches appear primarily on the face of the fabric, being returned across the face rather than on the reverse, and are held by a tiny stitch at the edge of the area being worked.

Yōfuku: The term used to distinguish Western-style dress from traditional Japanese attire (*wafuku*).

Yogi: Bedding shaped like a KOSODE. Usually made of cotton fabric and thickly padded with cotton wadding.

Yūhata: A type of large, rather crude KANOKO SHIBORI worn by mounted imperial soldiers during the Heian period.

Yukashi: The Heian-period practice of wearing a BENI-red underrobe as the bottom-most layer of the KASANE SHŌZOKU and allowing only a small line of red to show along the sleeve edges and collar.

Yukata: Unlined cotton garment typically worn for the bath or as informal summer wear. The term is an abbreviation of *yu-katabira*, an unlined bath garment. *See* KATABIRA.

Yūzen-zome: A form of paste-resist dyeing. Rice paste is used to outline each shape and prevent bleeding; dyes are applied with a brush, set, and then the resist is washed away. Yūzen-zome is distinguished by the fine white lines left by the paste resist that delineate shapes. The direct application of dyes with a brush permitted by the technique led to the development of sophisticated landscape and pictorial representations on KOSODE. Yūzen-zome was developed around the last quarter of the seventeenth century and reached full technical maturity by the second quarter of the eighteenth century; it was popular with all classes, particularly chōnin, and is still an important decorative technique on the modern KIMONO.

Bibliography

NOTE: Referenced authors' surnames appear in LARGE AND SMALL CAPITALS. A comma separating the surname and given name for Japanese authors indicates that the name was published in accordance with Western convention (surname last) in the reference cited.

AMINO and ISHIDA 1983.
AMINO Yoshihiko, and ISHIDA Hisatoyo, eds. *Shokunin* (Craftsmen). Kinsei fūzoku zufu (Genre painting of the early modern period), vol. 12. Tokyo: Shogakkan, 1983.

BETHE 1984.
BETHE, Monica. "Color: Dyes and Pigments." In *Kosode: Sixteenth–Nineteenth Century Textiles from the Nomura Collection*, by Amanda Mayer Stinchecum, 58–76. Exh. cat. New York: Japan Society and Kodansha International, 1984.

BOLITHO 1974.
BOLITHO, Harold. *Treasures among Men: The Fudai Daimyo in Tokugawa Japan*. New Haven: Yale University Press, 1974.

BOWRING 1963.
BOWRING, Richard. *Murasaki Shikibu: Her Diary and Poetic Memoirs*. Princeton: Princeton University Press, 1963.

BOXER 1930.
BOXER, C. R. "Jan Compagnie in Japan 1672–1674: Anglo-Dutch Rivalry in Japan and Formosa." *Transactions of the Asiatic Society of Japan*, 2d ser., 7 (1930): 138–95.

BOXER 1959.
BOXER, C. R. *The Great Ship from Amacon: Annals of Macao and the Old Japan Trade, 1555–1640*. Lisbon: Centro de Estudos Históricos Ultramarinos, 1959.

CHISOLM 1963.
CHISOLM, Lawrence W. *Fenollosa: The Far East and American Culture*. New Haven: Yale University Press, 1963.

CHIZAWA 1970.
CHIZAWA Teiji, ed. *Kōrin*. Nihon no bijutsu (Arts of Japan), no. 53. Tokyo: Shibundō, 1970.

COLE 1967.
COLE, Wendell. *Kyoto in the Momoyama Period*. Norman: University of Oklahoma Press, 1967.

COOPER 1965.
COOPER, Michael, ed. *They Came to Japan: An Anthology of European Reports on Japan, 1543–1640*. Berkeley and Los Angeles: University of California Press, 1965.

COOPER 1971.
COOPER, Michael, ed. *The Southern Barbarians: The First Europeans in Japan*. Tokyo: Kodansha International, 1971.

DALBY 1988.
DALBY, Liza. "The Cultured Nature of Heian Colors." *Transactions of the Asiatic Society of Japan*, 4th ser., 3 (1988): 1–19.

DE BARY, CHAN, and WATSON 1960.
DE BARY, Theodore, Wing Tsit CHAN, and Burton WATSON, eds. *Sources of Chinese Tradition*. Vol. 1. New York: Columbia University Press, 1960.

DŌMYŌ 1990.
DŌMYŌ Mihoko. "Mitsui-ke denrai no kosode to Maruyama-ha shita-e" (Mitsui Collection kosode and their relationship to Maruyama school sketches). In *Mitsui-ke denrai kosode-ten* (An exhibition of kosode from the Mitsui Collection), 84–87. Exh. cat. Tokyo: Bunka Gakuen Costume Museum, 1990.

DUNN 1987.
DUNN, Charles J. *Everyday Life in Traditional Japan*. Rutland, Vermont: Charles E. Tuttle Co., 1987.

EBATA 1982.
EBATA Jun. *Shikimei no yurai* (Origins of color names). Tokyo: Shoseki, 1982.

ELISON 1973.
ELISON, George. *Deus Destroyed: The Image of Christianity in Early Modern Japan*. Cambridge, Massachusetts: Harvard University Press, 1973.

ENDO 1978.
ENDO Yasuo, ed. *Benibana-zome: Hana no seimei o someta nuno* (Dyeing with safflower: Cloth dyed in the life-force of a flower). Nihon no senshoku (Japanese textiles), no. 18. Tokyo: Tairyūsha, 1978.

GOTŌ S. 1978.
GOTŌ Shirō, ed. *Shōsō-in*. Nihon bijutsu zenshū (Arts of Japan), vol. 5. Tokyo: Gakken, 1978.

GOTŌ Y. 1960.
GOTŌ Yasushi. "Nishijin ori" (Nishijin cloth). In *Kinki chihōhen* (Kinki regional volume), edited by Chihōshi Kenkyū Kyōgikai (Society for the study of regional history), 33–57. Nihon sangyōshi taikei (Outline of Japanese industrial history), vol. 6. Tokyo: Tokyo Daigaku Shuppankai, 1960.

GUNJI 1970.
GUNJI Masakatsu, et al., eds. *Meisaku kabuki zenshū* (Complete works of kabuki masterpieces), vol. 19. Tokyo: Tokyo Sōgensha, 1970.

HAAK 1973.
HAAK, Ronald Otto. "Nishijin Weavers: A Study of the Functions of Tradition in Modern Japanese Society." Ph.D. diss., University of Illinois at Urbana-Champaign, 1973.

HABEIN 1984.
HABEIN, Yaeko Sato. *The History of the Japanese Written Language*. Tokyo: University of Tokyo Press, 1984.

HALL 1968.
HALL, John W. "The Castle Town and Japan's Modern Urbanization." In *Studies in the Institutional History of Early Modern Japan*, edited by John W. Hall and Marius B. Jansen, 169–88. Princeton: Princeton University Press, 1968.

HALL 1974.
HALL, John W. "Rule by Status in Tokugawa Japan." *The Journal of Japanese Studies* 1, no. 1 (Autumn 1974): 39–49.

HANLEY 1991.
HANLEY, Susan B. "Tokugawa Society: Material Culture, Standards of Living, and Life-Styles." In *Early Modern Japan*, edited by John Whitney Hall, 660–705. Cambridge History of Japan, vol. 4. Cambridge, England: Cambridge University Press, 1991.

HANLEY and YAMAMURA 1977.
HANLEY, Susan B., and Kozo YAMAMURA. *Economic and Demographic Change in Pre-Industrial Japan, 1600–1868*. Princeton: Princeton University Press, 1977.

HASHIMOTO 1980a.
HASHIMOTO Sumiko. "Tōkyō Kokuritsu Hakubutsukan hokan no moji-chirashi ishō kosode ni tsuite" (Kosode with designs of scattered characters in the Tokyo National Museum collection). *Museum*, no. 349 (April 1980): 4–20.

HASHIMOTO 1980b.
HASHIMOTO Sumiko. "Tōkyō Kokuritsu Hakubutsukan hokan no moji-chirashi ishō kosode ni tsuite zoku" (Kosode with designs of scattered characters in the Tokyo National Museum collection, part 2). *Museum*, no. 353 (August 1980): 27–34.

HAUSER 1974a.
HAUSER, William B. "The Diffusion of Cotton Processing and Trade in the Kinai Region of Tokugawa Japan." *Journal of Asian Studies* 33, no. 4 (August 1974): 633–49.

HAUSER 1974b.
HAUSER, William B. *Economic Institutional Change in Tokugawa Japan: Ōsaka and the Kinai Cotton Trade*. Cambridge, England: Cambridge University Press, 1974.

HAUSER 1977.
HAUSER, William B. "Ōsaka: A Commercial City in Tokugawa Japan." *Urbanism Past and Present*, no. 5 (Winter 1977–78): 23–36.

HAUSER 1983.
HAUSER, William B. "Some Misconceptions about the Economic History of Tokugawa Japan." *The History Teacher* 16, no. 4 (August 1983): 569–83.

HAUSER 1985.
HAUSER, William B. "Ōsaka Castle and Tokugawa Authority in Western Japan." In *The Bakufu in Japanese History*, edited by Jeffrey P. Mass and William B. Hauser, 153–72. Stanford: Stanford University Press, 1985.

HAYASHIYA 1977.
HAYASHIYA Tatsusaburō. "Kyoto in the Muromachi Age." In *Japan in the Muromachi Age*, edited by John W. Hall and Toyoda Takeshi, 15–36. Berkeley and Los Angeles: University of California Press, 1977.

HAYASHIYA and MURASHIGE 1983.
HAYASHIYA Tatsusaburō, and MURASHIGE Yasushi, eds. *Rakuchū rakugai* (Scenes in and around Kyoto), vol. 1. Kinsei fūzoku zufu (Genre paintings of the early modern period), vol. 3. Tokyo: Shogakkan, 1983.

HAYASHIYA, NAKAMURA, and HAYASHIYA 1974.
HAYASHIYA, Tatsusaburō, Masao NAKAMURA, and Seizō HAYASHIYA. *Japanese Arts and the Tea Ceremony*. Translated and adapted by Joseph P. Macadam. Heibonsha Survey of Japanese Art, vol. 15. New York/Tokyo: Weatherhill/Heibonsha, 1974.

HIBBETT 1960.
HIBBETT, Howard. *The Floating World in Japanese Fiction*. New York: Grove Press, 1960.

HINONISHI 1968.
HINONISHI Sukenori, ed. *Fukushoku* (Costume). Nihon no bijutsu (Arts of Japan), no. 26. Tokyo: Shibundō, 1968.

HUNAN PROVINCIAL MUSEUM 1973.
Hunan Provincial Museum and Institute of Archaeology, Academia Sinica. *The Han Tomb No. 1 at Mawangtui, Changsha*. 2 vols. Peking: Wenwu Press, 1973.

IENAGA 1979.
IENAGA, Saburo. *Japanese Art: A Cultural Appreciation*. Translated by Richard L. Gage. Heibonsha Survey of Japanese Art, vol. 30. New York/Tokyo: Weatherhill/Heibonsha, 1979.

IHARA 1982.
IHARA Aki. *Heian-chō no bungaku to shikisai* (Literature and colors in the Heian court). Tokyo: Chūōkōronsha, 1982.

IMADA 1973.
IMADA Shinichi. "Mogami benibana no rekishi" (History of Mogami benibana). *Senshoku to seikatsu* (Textiles and daily life) 2 (August 1973): 31–36.

IMANAGA 1983a.
IMANAGA Seiji. "Fukushoku no runesansu: Kosode no seiritsu to tenkai" (Renaissance of dress: The formation and development of kosode). In *Kosode*, vol. 1, edited by Imanaga Seiji, 101–25. Nihon no senshoku (Japanese textiles), edited by Yamanobe Tomoyuki, vol. 5. Tokyo: Chūōkōronsha, 1983.

IMANAGA 1983b.
IMANAGA Seiji, ed. *Kosode*, vol. 1. Nihon no senshoku (Japanese textiles), edited by Yamanobe Tomoyuki, vol. 5. Tokyo: Chūōkōronsha, 1983.

INUI 1977.
INUI Hiromi. *Naniwa, Ōsaka Kikuya-chō*. Kyoto: Yanagihara Shōten, 1977.

ISHIMURA and MARUYAMA 1988.
ISHIMURA Hayao, and MARUYAMA Nobuhiko. *Robes of Elegance: Japanese Kimonos of the Sixteenth–Twentieth Centuries*. Exh. cat. Raleigh: North Carolina Museum of Art, 1988.

ITŌ 1985.
ITŌ, Toshiko. *Tsujigahana: The Flower of Japanese Textile Art*. Translated by Monica Bethe. Tokyo: Kodansha International, 1985.

IZUMI 1991.
IZUMI Mari. "Kasuga taisha-zō kurabeuma-zu byōbu o megutte" (The horse race screens in the collection of Kasuga Shrine). *Machikaneyama ronsō* (Machikaneyama research papers), no. 25 (December 1991): 23–44.

KADOKAWA SHOTEN 1983.
Shinhen kokka taikan (Anthology of Japanese poetry, new edition), vol. 1. Tokyo: Kadokawa Shoten, 1983.

KAKUDO 1991.
KAKUDO, Yoshiko. *The Art of Japan: Masterworks in the Asian Art Museum of San Francisco.* San Francisco: Asian Art Museum/Chronicle Books, 1991.

KAMIJŌ 1981.
KAMIJŌ Kōnosuke. *Nihon mon'yō jiten* (Japanese pattern dictionary). Tokyo: Yūzankaku Shuppan Kabushiki Kaisha, 1981.

KAMIYA 1971.
KAMIYA Eiko, ed. *Kosode.* Nihon no bijutsu (Arts of Japan), no. 67. Tokyo: Shibundō, 1971.

KAWAGUCHI and SHIDA 1979.
KAWAGUCHI Hisao, and SHIDA Nobuyoshi, eds. *Wakan rōeishū, Ryōjin hishō* (Collection of Japanese and Chinese poems for recitation; A secret store of marvelous song). Nihon koten bungaku taikei (Anthology of classical Japanese literature), no. 73. Tokyo: Iwanami Shoten, 1979.

KAWAKAMI 1982.
KAWAKAMI Shigeki. "Edo jidai zenki no kosode—Keichō kosode kara Kanbun kosode e" (Early Edo-period kosode: From Keichō kosode to Kanbun kosode). *Bunkazai* (Cultural properties), no. 228 (September 1982): 27–34.

KAWASHIMA and TSUJI 1983.
KAWASHIMA Masao, and TSUJI Nobuo, eds. *Rakuchū rakugai* (Scenes in and around Kyoto), vol. 2. Kinsei fūzoku zufu (Genre paintings of the early modern period), vol. 4. Tokyo: Shogakkan, 1983.

KEYS 1976.
KEYS, John D. *Chinese Herbs: Their Botany, Chemistry, and Pharmacodynamics.* Tokyo: Charles E. Tuttle Co., 1976.

KIRIHATA 1980.
KIRIHATA Ken. "Kinsei senshoku ni okeru bungei ishō" (Literary motifs in textile design of the early modern period). In *Kōgei ni miru koten bungaku ishō* (Classical literary themes in the applied arts), edited by the Kyoto National Museum, 307–24. Kyoto: Shikōsha, 1980.

KIRIHATA 1983a.
KIRIHATA Ken. "Heian, Kamakura, Muromachi no senshoku" (Textiles of the Heian, Kamakura, and Muromachi periods). *Senshoku no bi* (Textile arts), no. 23 (early Summer 1983): 9–80.

KIRIHATA 1983b.
KIRIHATA Ken. *Iro no bunkashi* (A cultural history of color). Osaka: Asahi Shimbunsha, 1983.

KIRIHATA 1988a.
KIRIHATA Ken. "Fūkei moyō no senshoku" (Textiles with landscape designs). *Gakusō* (Kyoto National Museum bulletin), no. 10 (March 1988): 49–63.

KIRIHATA 1988b.
KIRIHATA Ken, ed. *Senshoku: Kinsei hen* (Dyed and woven textiles: Modern era). Nihon no bijutsu (Arts of Japan), no. 265. Tokyo: Shibundō, 1988.

KIRIHATA and MARUYAMA 1988.
KIRIHATA Ken, and MARUYAMA Nobuhiko. *Kosode: Kanebō korekushon* (Kosode: Kanebo Collection), vol. 2. Tokyo: Mainichi Shimbunsha, 1988.

KITAGAWA and TSUCHIDA 1975.
KITAGAWA Hiroshi, and Bruce TSUCHIDA, trans. *The Tale of the Heike.* Tokyo: University of Tokyo Press, 1975.

KODANSHA 1983.
Kodansha Encyclopedia of Japan. 9 vols. Tokyo: Kodansha International, 1983.

KOJIMA, KINOSHITA, and SATAKE 1971–75.
KOJIMA Noriyuki, KINOSHITA Masatochi, and SATAKE Akihiro, eds. *Man'yōshū.* 4 vols. Nihon koten bungakushū (Anthology of classical Japanese literature), vols. 2–5. Tokyo: Shogakkan, 1971–75.

KOYAMA, SATŌ, and SATŌ 1973–75.
KOYAMA Hiroshi, SATŌ Kikuo, and SATŌ Kenichirō. *Yōkyokushū* (Nō drama). 2 vols. Nihon koten bungakushū (Anthology of classical Japanese literature), vols. 33–34. Tokyo: Shogakkan, 1973–75.

KUBO 1972.
KUBO, Fusako. "Japanese Court Ladies' Formal Costume—Jūnihitoe." *Costume,* no. 6 (1972): 5–9.

KUKI 1930.
KUKI Shūzo. *Iki no kōzō* (The structure of iki). Tokyo: Iwanami Shoten, 1930.

KYOTO NATIONAL MUSEUM 1980.
Kōgei ni miru koten bungaku ishō (Classical literary themes in the applied arts), edited by the Kyoto National Museum. Kyoto: Shikōsha, 1980.

KYOTO SHOIN 1985.
Nihon no ishō (Japanese design). 16 vols. Kyoto: Kyoto Shoin, 1985.

LEE 1963.
LEE, Sherman E. *Tea Taste in Japanese Art.* Exh. cat. New York: Asia Society, 1963.

LEE 1983.
LEE, Sherman E. *Reflections of Reality in Japanese Art.* Exh. cat. Cleveland: Cleveland Museum of Art, 1983.

LEITER 1979.
LEITER, Samuel L., trans. and adapter. *Kabuki Encyclopedia: An English-Language Adaption of "Kabuki Jiten."* Westport, Connecticut: Greenwood Press, 1979.

MAEDA U. 1975.
MAEDA Ujō. *Nihon kodai no saishiki to some* (Japanese colors and dyes of ancient times). Tokyo: Kawade Shobōshinsha, 1975.

MAEDA Y. 1960.
MAEDA Yukichika. *Nihon shikisai bunkashi* (A cultural history of Japanese colors). Tokyo: Iwanami Shoten, 1960.

MARUYAMA 1986.
MARUYAMA Nobuhiko. "Kinsei zenki kosode ishō no keifu—Kanbun kosode ni itaru futatsu no keitō" (Genealogy of early modern kosode: Two lines leading to the Kanbun style). *Kokuritsu rekishi minzoku hakubutsukan kenkyū hōkoku* (Bulletin of the National Museum of Japanese History) 11 (March 1986): 195–246.

MARUYAMA 1988.
MARUYAMA Nobuhiko. "Kosode no keitai henka ni tsuite no ichi kōsatsu" (A study of the changes in the shape of the kosode). *Bijutsushi* (Art history) 123 (May 1988): 21–33.

MARUYAMA 1989.
MARUYAMA Nobuhiko. "Edo fuasshon jijō—ryūkō to egakareta yosōi" (Edo fashion: Popular trends as seen in dress). In *Edo no fuasshon—nikuhitsu ukiyo-e ni miru onna tachi no yosōi* ("Fashion of Edo": Women's dress in ukiyo-e paintings), 4–7. Exh. cat. Tokyo: Azabu Museum of Arts and Crafts, 1989.

Matsumoto 1984.
Matsumoto, Kaneo. *Jōdai-gire: Seventh and Eighth Century Textiles in Japan from the Shōsō-in and Hōryū-ji.* Kyoto: Shikōsha Publishing Co., 1984.

McCullough 1968.
McCullough, Helen Craig, trans. *Tales of Ise: Lyrical Episodes from Tenth-Century Japan.* Stanford: Stanford University Press, 1968.

McCullough 1985.
McCullough, Helen Craig. *Brocade by Night: "Kokin Wakashū" and the Court Style in Japanese Classical Poetry.* Stanford: Stanford University Press, 1985.

McCullough and McCullough 1980.
McCullough, William H., and Helen Craig McCullough, trans. *A Tale of Flowering Fortunes.* 2 vols. Stanford: Stanford University Press, 1980.

Meech-Pekarik 1975.
Meech-Pekarik, Julia. Introduction to *Momoyama: Japanese Art in the Age of Grandeur.* Exh. cat. New York: Metropolitan Museum of Art, 1975.

Minnich 1963.
Minnich, Helen Benton, in collaboration with Shōjirō Nomura. *Japanese Costume and the Makers of Its Elegant Tradition.* Rutland, Vermont: Charles E. Tuttle Co., 1963.

Miura 1975.
Miura Saburō. "Murasaki no bunka: Kankei nenpyō" (The culture of purple: A time chart). *Senshoku to seikatsu* (Textiles and daily life) 11 (Winter 1975): 45.

Miyajima 1988.
Miyajima Shin'ichi, et al. *Ōmi hakkei* (Eight views of Ōmi). Shiga: Museum of Modern Art, 1988.

Moeran 1987.
Moeran, Brian. "The Art World of Contemporary Japanese Ceramics." *The Journal of Japanese Studies* 13, no. 1 (Winter 1987): 27–50.

Moriya 1990.
Moriya, Katsuhisa. "Urban Networks and Information Networks." In *Tokugawa Japan: The Social and Economic Antecedents of Modern Japan,* edited by Chie Nakane and Shinzaburō Ōishi, translation edited by Conrad Totman, 97–123. Tokyo: University of Tokyo Press, 1990.

Morris 1971.
Morris, Ivan, trans. and ed. *The Pillow Book of Sei Shōnagon.* New York: Penguin Books, 1971.

Morris 1986.
Morris, Ivan. *The World of the Shining Prince: Court Life in Ancient Japan.* Middlesex: Penguin Books, Ltd., 1986.

Mostow 1988.
Mostow, Joshua Scott. "*Uta-e* and Interrelations between Poetry and Painting in the Heian Era." Ph.D. diss., University of Pennsylvania, 1988.

Munakata 1991.
Munakata, Kiyohiko. *Sacred Mountains in Chinese Art.* Exh. cat. Urbana-Champaign: Krannert Art Museum, University of Illinois, 1991.

Murakami 1987.
Murakami Tetsurō. *Iro no kataru Nihon no rekishi* (Japanese history as related by colors). Tokyo: Soshiete, 1987.

Murasaki 1979.
Murasaki Shikibu. *The Tale of Genji.* Translated by Edward G. Seidensticker. New York: Alfred A. Knopf, 1979.

Museum of Fine Arts 1990.
Courtly Splendor: Twelve Centuries of Treasures from Japan. Exh. cat. Boston: Museum of Fine Arts, 1990.

Nagasaki I. 1987.
Nagasaki Iwao. "Edo jidai zenki no kosode—Kanbun kosode no seiritsu o chūshin ni" (Kosode of the first half of the Edo period: Focusing on the development of Kanbun-era kosode). In *Kosode: Kanebō korekushon* (Kosode: Kanebo Collection), by Kawakami Shigeki and Nagasaki Iwao, vol. 1, 141–55. Tokyo: Mainichi Shimbunsha, 1987.

Nagasaki I. 1989.
Nagasaki Iwao. "Amerika no bijutsukan ni miru Nihon senshoku no hihō" (Secret treasures of Japanese textiles in American museums). *Utsukushii kimono* (Beautiful kimono), no. 149 (Fall 1989): 163–81.

Nagasaki I. 1991.
Nagasaki Iwao. "Baiju ni onagadori-zu kakefuku" (A hanging scroll of a long-tailed bird on a plum branch). *Kokka,* no. 1149 (August 1991): 27–32.

Nagasaki S. 1977.
Nagasaki Seiki. *Iro no Nihonshi* (History of Japanese colors). Tokyo: Tankōsha, 1977.

Nagasaki S. 1987.
Nagasaki Seiki. *Kasane no irome* (The combination of colors in layers). Kyoto: Kyoto Shoin, 1987.

Nagasaki S. 1990.
Nagasaki Seiki. *Iro, saishiki no Nihonshi: Nihonjin wa ikani iro ni ikite kita ka* (Japanese history of colors and pigments: How colors have been brought to life by the Japanese). Tokyo: Tankōsha, 1990.

Nakane, Ōishi, and Totman 1990.
Nakane Chie, and Ōishi Shinzaburō, eds., translation edited by Conrad Totman. *Tokugawa Japan: The Social and Economic Antecedents of Modern Japan.* Tokyo: University of Tokyo Press, 1990.

Nara National Museum 1978.
Shōsō-in-ten mokuroku (Shōsō-in exhibition catalogue). Exh. cat. Nara: Nara National Museum, 1978).

National Museum of Japanese History 1990.
Nomura korekushon kosode byōbu (Nomura Collection: Kosode screens). Sakura, Chiba Prefecture: National Museum of Japanese History, 1990.

Nippon Gakujutsu Shinkōkai 1955.
Nippon Gakujutsu Shinkōkai (Japan classics translation committee). *The Noh Drama: Ten Plays from the Japanese.* Tokyo: Charles E. Tuttle Co., 1955.

Nishimoto 1982.
Nishimoto Shūko. "Kariganeya ishō zuanchō ni tsuite" (Kariganeya's clothing pattern books). *Bijutsushi* (Art history) 113 (November 1982): 40–51.

Noguchi 1982.
Noguchi Takehiko. "Engi suru shikisai: Shiro, aka, ao no shikisai zushiki" (Dramatic color: White, red, blue color schema). In *Iro* (Color), edited by Shichiji Eiwa, 45–54. Tokyo: Pōra Bunka Kenkyūjo, 1982.

NOMA K. 1960.
NOMA Kōshin, ed. *Saikaku-shū* (Collection of Saikaku's works), vol. 2. Nihon koten bungaku taikei (Anthology of classical Japanese literature), vol. 48. Tokyo: Iwanami Shoten, 1960.

NOMA S. 1974.
NOMA, Seiroku. *Japanese Costume and Textile Arts*. Translated by Armins Nikovskis. Heibonsha Survey of Japanese Art, vol. 16. New York/Tokyo: Weatherhill/Heibonsha, 1974.

NOSCO 1990.
Nosco, Peter. *Remembering Paradise: Nativism and Nostalgia in Eighteenth-Century Japan.* Cambridge, Massachusetts: Council on East Asian Studies, Harvard University, 1990.

OGASAWARA 1988.
OGASAWARA Sae, ed. *Senshoku— Chūsei hen* (Dyed and woven textiles of the medieval era). Nihon no bijutsu (Arts of Japan), no. 264. Tokyo: Shibundō, 1988.

OKADA 1958.
OKADA, Yuzuru. "The Textile Craft." In *Pageant of Japanese Art: Textiles and Lacquer*, edited by Masao Ishizawa, et al., 3–32. Tokyo: Tōto Shuppan Company, 1958.

OOMS 1985.
OOMS, Harold. *Tokugawa Ideology: Early Constructs, 1570–1680.* Princeton: Princeton University Press, 1985.

ŌSONE 1989.
ŌSONE Sanae. "Tsujigahana ni kansuru kōsatsu—Sono shiryō bunrui o chūshin to shite" (Tsujigahana: Focus on data classification). *Museum*, no. 456 (March 1989): 19–30.

PAUL 1984.
PAUL, Margot. "A Creative Connoisseur: Nomura Shōjirō." In *Kosode: Sixteenth–Nineteenth Century Textiles from the Nomura Collection*, by Amanda Mayer Stinchecum, 12–21. Exh. cat. New York: Japan Society and Kodansha International, 1984.

RAZ 1983.
RAZ, Jacob. *Audience and Actors: A Study of Their Interaction in the Japanese Traditional Theatre.* Leiden: E. J. Brill, 1983.

RODRIGUES 1973.
RODRIGUES, João. *This Island of Japon: João Rodrigues' Account of Sixteenth-Century Japan*. Translated and edited by Michael Cooper. Tokyo: Kodansha International, 1973.

ROSENFIELD, CRANSTON, and CRANSTON 1973.
ROSENFIELD, John M., Fumiko E. CRANSTON, and Edwin A. CRANSTON. *The Courtly Tradition in Japanese Art and Literature: Selections from the Hofer and Hyde Collections*. Exh. cat. Cambridge, Massachusetts: Fogg Art Museum, Harvard University, 1973.

ROZMAN 1989.
ROZMAN, Gilbert. "Social Change." In *The Nineteenth Century*, edited by Marius B. Jansen, 499–568. Cambridge History of Japan, vol. 5. Cambridge, England: Cambridge University Press, 1989.

SAIKAKU 1956.
IHARA Saikaku. *Five Women Who Loved Love*. Translated by William Theodore de Bary. Rutland, Vermont: Charles E. Tuttle Co., 1956.

SAIKAKU 1964.
IHARA Saikaku. *The Life of an Amorous Man*. Translated by Hamada Kengi. Rutland, Vermont: Charles E. Tuttle Co., 1964.

SAIKAKU 1965.
IHARA Saikaku. *This Scheming World*. Translated by Masanori Takatsuka and David C. Stubbs. Rutland, Vermont: Charles E. Tuttle Co., 1965.

SAIKAKU 1990.
IHARA Saikaku. *The Great Mirror of Male Love*. Translated by Paul Gordon Schalow. Stanford: Stanford University Press, 1990.

SAITŌ 1987.
SAITŌ Osamu. *Shōka no sekai, uramise no sekai: Edo to Ōsaka no hikaku toshi-shi* (The world of merchant houses, the world of back street shops: A comparative urban history of Edo and Osaka). Tokyo: Riburopotto, 1987.

SANSEIDŌ 1987.
Edo Tōkyō gaku jiten (Edo and Tokyo dictionary). Tokyo: Sanseidō, 1987.

SANSOM 1978.
SANSOM, George B. *Japan: A Short Cultural History*. Stanford: Stanford University Press, 1978.

SANTŌ 1975.
SANTŌ Kyōzan. *Rekisei josō kō* (History of women's fashions). Reprint. *Nihon zuihitsu taisei* (Anthology of Japanese essays), no. 6, 145–337. Tokyo: Tanchōsha, 1975.

SATŌ 1990.
SATŌ Tsuneo. "Tokugawa Villages and Agriculture." In *Tokugawa Japan: The Social and Economic Antecedents of Modern Japan*, edited by Nakane Chie, Ōishi Shinzaburō, translation edited by Conrad Totman, 37–80. Tokyo: University of Tokyo Press, 1990.

SAWADA 1967.
SAWADA Akira. *Edo jidai ni okeru kabunakama kumiai seidō, tokuni Nishijin oriya nakama no kenkyū* (The Edo-period craft guild system: A study of the Nishijin weavers guild). Kyoto: Daigaku Shōten, 1967.

SENSHOKU NO BI 1983.
"Benibana." *Senshoku no bi* (Textile art) 21 (early Spring 1983): 93–104.

SHAVER 1990.
SHAVER, Ruth M. *Kabuki Costume*. 2d ed. Tokyo: Charles E. Tuttle Co., 1990.

SHIMIZU 1988.
SHIMIZU, Yoshiaki, ed. *Japan: The Shaping of Daimyo Culture 1185– 1868*. Exh. cat. Washington, D.C.: National Gallery of Art, 1988.

SHIMIZU and ROSENFIELD 1984.
SHIMIZU, Yoshiaki, and John M. ROSENFIELD. *Masters of Japanese Calligraphy: Eighth–Nineteenth Century*. Exh. cat. New York: Asia Society Galleries and Japan House Gallery, 1984.

SHIVELY 1955.
SHIVELY, Donald H. "*Bakufu* versus *Kabuki*." *Harvard Journal of Asiatic Studies* 18 (1955): 326–56.

SHIVELY 1965.
SHIVELY, Donald H. "Sumptuary Regulation and Status in Early Tokugawa Japan." *Harvard Journal of Asiatic Studies* 25 (1964–65): 123–64.

SINGER 1984.
SINGER, Robert T. "Kasuga Wakamiya onmatsuri-zu" (A pair of screen paintings of the Wakamiya festival of Kasuga Shrine). In *Kinsei Nihon kaiga shūsei* (A collection of Japanese paintings of the early modern period [The Shin'enkan Collection]), by Yamane Yūzō, et al., 331. Kyoto: Kyoto Shoin, 1984.

SMITH 1988.
SMITH, Thomas C. *Native Sources of Japanese Industrialization, 1750–1920* Berkeley and Los Angeles: University of California Press, 1988.

SMITH and HARRIS 1982.
SMITH, Lawrence, and Victor HARRIS. *Japanese Decorative Arts from the Seventeenth to the Nineteenth Centuries.* London: British Museum Publications Limited, 1982.

STINCHECUM 1984.
STINCHECUM, Amanda Mayer. *Kosode: Sixteenth–Nineteenth Century Textiles from the Nomura Collection.* Exh. cat. New York: Japan Society and Kodansha International, 1984.

SUGIMOTO 1934.
SUGIMOTO, Etsu Inagaki. *A Daughter of the Samurai.* Garden City, New York: Doubleday, Doran & Company, 1934.

TAKUBO 1976.
TAKUBO Hideo. "Beni: Kin no naka no bi no seiren" (Beni: Refinement of the beauty produced within restriction). In *Nihon no iro* (Japanese colors), edited by Ōoka Makoto, 153–60. Tokyo: Asahi Shimbunsha, 1976.

TANAKA 1973.
TANAKA Naoichi. "Kōkahō taikenki" (Diary of my experience using safflower medicine). *Senshoku to seikatsu* (Textiles and daily life) 2 (August 1973): 81.

TOBY 1984.
TOBY, Ronald P. *State and Diplomacy in Early Modern Japan.* Princeton: Princeton University Press, 1984.

TOYODA and SUGIYAMA 1977.
TOYODA Takeshi, and SUGIYAMA Hiroshi, with V. Dixon Morris. "The Growth of Commerce and the Trades." In *Japan in the Muromachi Age*, edited by John W. Hall and Toyoda Takeshi, 129–44. Berkeley and Los Angeles: University of California Press, 1977.

TSUJI 1986.
TSUJI Nobuo. *Playfulness in Japanese Art.* Translated by Joseph Seubert. Franklin D. Murphy Lectures, no. 7. Lawrence: Spencer Museum of Art, University of Kansas, 1986.

TSUKAHIRA 1966.
TSUKAHIRA, Toshio G. *Feudal Control in Tokugawa Japan: The Sankin Kōtai System.* Cambridge, Massachusetts: East Asian Research Center, Harvard University, 1966.

TSUKAMOTO 1982.
TSUKAMOTO Mizuyo. "Momoyama kara kanbun no kosode moyō—Kariganeya hinagata-chō o chūshin toshite" (Kosode design from the Momoyama period to the Kanbun era: Focusing on the Kariganeya order books). In *Kariganeya hinagata-chō no senshokushi-teki kaigashi-teki kenkyū—Konishi-ke denrai Kōrin kankei shiryō o chūshin ni* (Textile-historical and art-historical studies of the Kariganeya order books: Focusing on Kōrin documents preserved by the Konishi family), 3–7. Gunmaken: Gunma Kenritsu Jōshi Daigaku, 1982.

UEDA 1977.
UEDA Mannen, et al., eds. *Daijiten* (Unabridged dictionary of Chinese characters). Tokyo: Kodansha International, 1977.

UENO 1974.
UENO Saeko. "Kosode moyō hinagata-bon shūsei kaidai" (Collection of printed kosode pattern books: Explanatory notes). In *Kosode moyō hinagata-bon shūsei* (Collection of printed kosode pattern books), 4 vols., edited by Ueno Saeko. Tokyo: Gakushū Kenkyūsha, 1974.

VARLEY 1977.
VARLEY, H. Paul. "Ashikaga Yoshimitsu and the World of Kitayama: Social Change and Shogunal Patronage in Early Muromachi Japan." In *Japan in the Muromachi Age*, edited by John W. Hall and Toyoda Takeshi, 183–204. Berkeley and Los Angeles: University of California Press, 1977.

WADA, RICE, and BARTON 1983.
WADA, Yoshiko, Mary Kellogg RICE, and Jane BARTON. *Shibori: The Inventive Art of Japanese Shaped Resist Dyeing.* Tokyo: Kodansha International, 1983.

WAKIMOTO 1933.
WAKIMOTO Sokurō, ed. "Eiroku ninen koshahon 'Kundaikan sayūchōki'" (1559 version of *Kundaikan sayūchōki*). *Bijutsu kenkyū* (Art research), no. 20 (August 1933): 27–40.

WILSON 1990.
WILSON, Richard L. "Aspects of Rimpa Design." *Orientations* 21, no. 12 (December 1990): 28–35.

WILSON 1991.
WILSON, Richard L. *The Art of Ogata Kenzan: Persona and Production in Japanese Ceramics.* New York: Weatherhill, 1991.

YAMAMURA 1974.
YAMAMURA, Kozo. *A Study of Samurai Income and Entrepreneurship.* Cambridge, Massachusetts: Harvard University Press, 1974.

YAMAMURA 1990.
YAMAMURA, Kozo. "The Growth of Commerce in Medieval Japan." In *Medieval Japan*, edited by Kozo Yamamura, 344–95. Cambridge History of Japan, vol. 3. Cambridge, England: Cambridge University Press, 1990.

YAMANAKA 1982.
YAMANAKA, Norio. *The Book of Kimono.* Tokyo: Kodansha International, 1982.

YAMANOBE 1966.
YAMANOBE Tomoyuki, ed. *Some* (Dyed textiles). Nihon no bijutsu (Arts of Japan), no. 7. Tokyo: Shibundō, 1966.

YAMAZAKI 1974.
YAMAZAKI Seiju. *Kusaki-zome: Iro to shuhō* (Vegetable dyeing: Colors and methods). Tokyo: Bijutsu Shuppansha, 1974.

YASUKURO and OZEKI 1782.
YASUKURO Hahan, and OZEKI Masunari. *Saishoku ruijū* (Classification of colors). 1782. Reprint of chapter on beni. *Senshoku to seikatsu* (Textiles and daily life) 2 (August 1973): 46–49.

YOSHIOKA 1973.
YOSHIOKA Tsuneo. "Kyō no beni itajime-zome" (Kyoto beni block-resist dyeing). *Senshoku to seikatsu* (Textiles and daily life) 2 (August 1973): 43–45.

YOSHIOKA 1974.
YOSHIOKA Tsuneo. *Tennen senryō no kenkyū* (A study of natural dyes). Kyoto: Mitsumura Shiko Shoin, 1974.

YOUNG and SMITH 1966.
YOUNG, Martie W., and Robert J. SMITH. *Japanese Painters of the Floating World.* Exh. cat. Ithaca, New York: Andrew Dickson White Museum of Art, Cornell University, 1966.

Index

Lenders to the Exhibition

Azabu Museum of Arts and Crafts, Tokyo

Bunka Gakuen Costume Museum, Tokyo

Frank Lloyd Wright Foundation, Scottsdale, Arizona

Kanebo, Ltd., Osaka

Kawashima Textile Museum, Kyoto

Kuriyama Kōbō Co., Ltd., Kyoto

Kyoto National Museum

Kyoto Senshoku Kaikan

Los Angeles County Museum of Art

Marubeni Corporation, Tokyo

Matsuzakaya Co., Ltd., Tokyo

Metropolitan Museum of Art, New York

Nara Prefectural Museum of Art

National Museum of Japanese History, Chiba Prefecture

Newark Museum

Okajima Collection, Kyoto

Sendai City Museum, Miyagi Prefecture

Suntory Museum of Art, Tokyo

Tabata Collection, Kyoto

Tokyo National Museum

Tokyo National University of Fine Art and Music

Tōyama Memorial Museum, Saitama Prefecture